Building the Sea Eagles

D1027122

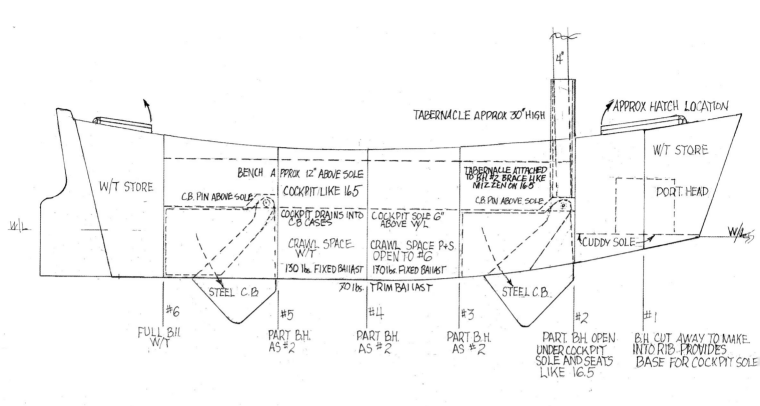

TABERNACLE APPROX 30" HIGH

APPROX HATCH LOCATION

W/T STORE

W/T STORE

PORT. HEAD

BENCH APPROX 12" ABOVE SOLE

C.B. PIN ABOVE SOLE

COCKPIT/ LIKE 16.5

TABERNACLE ATTACHED TO BH #2 BRACE LIKE MIZZEN ON 16.5

C.B. PIN ABOVE SOLE

COCKPIT DRAINS INTO C.B. CASES

COCKPIT SOLE 6" ABOVE V.L

CUDDY SOLE

W/L   W/L

CRAWL SPACE W/T

CRAWL SPACE P+S. OPEN TO #6

130 lbs. FIXED BALLAST

170 lbs. FIXED BALLAST

70 lbs. TRIM BALLAST

STEEL C.B.

STEEL C.B.

#6   #5   #4   #3   #2   #1

FULL B.H. W/T

PART. B.H. AS #2

PART B.H. AS #2

PART. B.H. AS #2

PART. BH. OPEN UNDER COCKPIT SOLE AND SEATS LIKE 16.5

B.H. CUT AWAY TO MAKE INTO RIB. PROVIDES BASE FOR COCKPIT SOLE

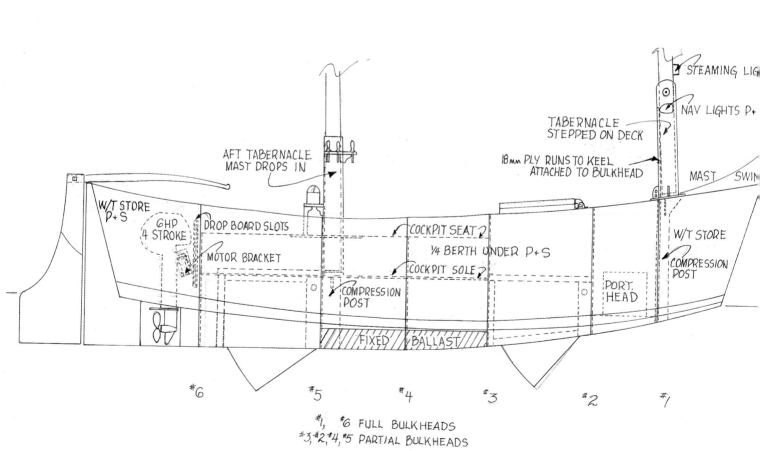

STEAMING LIG

NAV LIGHTS P+

TABERNACLE STEPPED ON DECK

AFT TABERNACLE MAST DROPS IN

18 mm PLY RUNS TO KEEL ATTACHED TO BULKHEAD

MAST   SWIN

W/T STORE P+S

6 HP 4 STROKE

DROP BOARD SLOTS

COCKPIT SEAT

1/4 BERTH UNDER P+S

W/T STORE

MOTOR BRACKET

COCKPIT SOLE

COMPRESSION POST

PORT. HEAD

COMPRESSION POST

COMPRESSION POST

FIXED   BALLAST

#6   #5   #4   #3   #2   #1

#1, #6 FULL BULKHEADS
#3, #2, #4, #5 PARTIAL BULKHEADS

Building
the
Sea Eagles

A Pair of Safe and Seaworthy
Beach and Coastal Cruisers

David L. Nichols

BREAKAWAY BOOKS
HALCOTTSVILLE, NEW YORK
2010

Building the Sea Eagles
Copyright 2010 by David L. Nichols

ISBN: 978-1-891369-87-2
Library of Congress Control Number:
2009940012
PRINTED IN CHINA

Published by Breakaway Books
P.O. Box 24
Halcottsville, NY 12438
www.breakawaybooks.com

FIRST EDITION

ACKNOWLEDGEMENTS

This book and these boats were large complex projects and there are two people that I particularly need to need to thank.

The unwavering support of my wife was very important. Without it this book wouldn't have happened.

I worked very closely with my son, Harlan, on these boats and I came to appreciate what a fine craftsman he's become. His workmanship always made me proud. Also the time we spent working together on this project was time spent with a good friend and I don't believe it gets any better than that.

Contents

Introduction

I'm in love with boats and I'm in love with sailboats in particular. There is something very satisfying about a sailboat gliding through the water, sails full of wind. They come alive as the wind pushes them forward. For me, the sound of the water on the bow, the wind moving through the rigging, and the feel of the tiller in my hand all contribute to the pulse of the boat. And it's the pulse of the boat that speaks to my heart. I feel it every time I step on board a sailboat and I yearn for it when I'm ashore.

This feeling has shaped the way I interact with sailboats—the way I choose and design sailboats. And while I may love all sailboats, I pick my personal boats the way I pick a friend, or to be more accurate, the way I would choose a mate—with care and thought.

I see selecting a sailboat and more specifically, selecting a sailboat to build, as a long term commitment. Most sailboats, unless they are incredibly simple and boxlike, require a substantial period of time to build.

Given that kind of time commitment, I have devoted some careful thought to what I want in a boat. I spent some time thinking about where I realistically want to sail, not only today, but say ten years from now. Most of us dream about sailing off into the sunset to wander the oceans of the world, but for me that just isn't practical. For that matter, it isn't practical for most of us. What I do find practical is a small, simple beach cruiser that I can sail in a variety of waters both big and small. A boat large enough to provide some creature comforts but not so big that her size limits where I can take the boat. The boats in this book fill that bill.

Both Sea Eagles do have some creature comforts. In the cockpits, the seats are wide for pleasant sleeping and both are easily rigged for a cozy cockpit tent or sun shade. The 16.5 has a small cuddy with comfortable quarter berths for sleeping when the weather is frosty and both boats have plenty of storage space below decks. It's possible to carry enough gear below decks for lavish beach living and still have the cockpit clean and uncluttered. And both boats carry a portable head, an important consideration for many.

Also, I want boats that are forgiving and I designed the Sea Eagles to be forgiving. You'll find both boats stable to at least 90 degrees of heel and the cockpits are self bailing. The heavy bottom and generous fixed ballast in the keel help to bring them back up in case of a knock down. Her tandem centerboards keep her balanced on all points of sail and well mannered in a following sea.

Good manners and a forgiving nature are crucial, but I think a sailboat that is easily launched from a trailer is important as well. Boat slips are expensive and are becoming increasingly hard to find. A boat that lives on a trailer doesn't need a slip and has a virtually unlimited cruising ground. Sea Eagles' free-standing masts and simple traditional sails mean the time spent getting ready to launch is short and their shallow draft makes them as easy to launch as a power boat.

In addition, I want a sailboat that is relatively simple to build. And because these boats go together with a modified stitch-and-glue building technique using epoxy, they are less complex and less labor intensive to build than more traditional methods.

So that is what you'll find with the boats in this book. Both Sea Eagles are boats that are simple and easily handled, boats that you can take on big adventures or small adventures, and boats that you will not easily outgrow.

You will also find that this book is written as if you had little or no boatbuilding experience. My goal was to make the book turn-key. That is, show you not only how to build the boat but make the sails and most everything you need to get the boat on the water.

If you are an experienced builder then take what information you need and use the methods that work best for you. I have always said there is no right or wrong way to build a boat. If this is your first boat then you should find enough information here to do a fine job of building.

Whatever your level of building experience, you will find these boats worth building. They are everything I look for in a small boat and will serve you well for many years to come. Enjoy!

1

What You Will Need

Space

Building a boat requires space, tools, materials, and time. I've listed space first as this is one of the most difficult commodities for the boatbuilder to find. Most of us live in subdivisions where there are covenants against building a boat in the front or back yard. I have always found this type of covenant to be very narrow minded but they exist, so the front and back yards are out of the question. Realistically this just leaves the garage, and fortunately both the boats in this book can be built in a two-car garage.

Building in the garage has one very obvious advantage—it's enclosed. It can be heated in the winter and if necessary cooled in the summer. Building can go on year round and rain or shine you can continue to work. Also, because it's close at hand, you can work a few hours a night if the opportunity presents itself.

Building in the garage has an added benefit of muffling the noise that comes with boat construction. Not many neighbors will tolerate the sound of a saber saw or random orbital sander at 9:00 P.M., and having all the noise contained by the garage means building can start earlier and go later.

So if the only space available to you is a two-car garage in the middle of a residential subdivision, you have the first commodity you need for building a nice cruiser.

Tools

Building these boats doesn't require a full blown woodworking shop either. Simple hand and power tools will do the job nicely. Most people are surprised by how few tools it really takes to build a boat. I like to remind them that for several thousand years large complex ships were built with nothing but axes, hand saws, and various other hand-operated tools. In fact, the ancient Greeks could not only build large ships with hand-operated tools, they could build a 60-foot bireme in about 30 days. It was built in a long narrow shed on an assembly line with the boat moving from station to station during the process and emerging a complete boat at the end of the shed. So, if the ancient Greeks could build a 60-foot boat using nothing more than hand tools, just think what you can accomplish with the list below.

The first list is the minimum needed to do the job in a timely manner and the second list is comprised of tools that will make the building process even easier.

Primary list
saber saw
hand saw (Japanese pull saw is best)
drill and drill bits (3/8-inch cordless drill will be
    best)
small hammer
block plane
¾-inch chisel
orbital sander (5-inch is best)
tape measure (25 foot)
spring clamps
bar clamps
mat knife or razor blades
safety glasses
dust mask
square
string snap line or string

Helpful tools

6-inch circular saw
router (table mounted option)
table saw
Makita 1900B 3¼-inch power planer (my choice
    for scarfing)
belt sander and frame (for scarfing)
8-inch jack plane
6, 8, 10 countersinks and bits
set of chisels

Sticky Stuff epoxy pump
6-inch random orbital sander

You will notice that there is only one stationary tool listed, the table saw, and that's number three on the helpful list. If you have other stationary tools like a band saw or drill press you'll find them useful but not necessary. Actually, simply turning over a hand-power tool like a saber saw or circular saw and mounting it in a table allows it to do the job of a stationary tool.

There is one tool I would like to mention because I find it indispensable. I'm not sure when I discovered the Japanese pull saw, but this tool has become so important that I don't have another type of saw in my shop. In fact, I consider them so important that I'm always surprised when people aren't familiar with them.

Western saws cut on the push stroke, and the pull saw, as the name suggests, cuts on the pull stroke. This allows the blade to be very thin and very sharp, and for some reason cutting on the pull makes this saw very easy for me to use. When students who aren't familiar with the pull saw come to my classes, they always go home swearing they will never use a push saw again. So, if you don't already own a pull saw, invest in one or more. Most of the big chain building supply stores now carry them and I suggest having two. The cutting edge is very thin and can be damaged if you hit a nail or some hard epoxy. I use the slightly damaged saw when I have to cut around hard epoxy or nails and save the good saw for clean wood.

The Japanese pull saw is great for all sorts of jobs but I feel I must add a caveat. As I mentioned, the blade is sharp and therefore capable of inflicting a nasty cut. I know this from personal experience and I have learned to be aware of where my hands are in relation to the blade's stroke.

Actually, I have recently just started using one more saw and I now find it one of the saws I pick most often. A year or so ago I purchased a 6-inch circular saw. (Actually it came with a cordless tool kit I bought). I don't think I would have bought it, but I found it so useful I bought a corded 6-inch

saw as well. I like to use the corded 6-inch saw for long involved jobs that would quickly run down a battery, like cutting out planks. If you can only buy one then buy the corded version. You'll find it a good investment.

Materials

Good tools are an investment, so buy the best you can afford and the same applies to the materials you put into the boat. These boats are built with plywood, solid wood, epoxy, and fiberglass cloth.

The boats are mostly plywood and you should use marine grade plywood. Not too many years ago there was American marine grade fir and marine plywood manufactured to British Standard 1088. Both had to meet very strict standards and if they didn't meet those standards the plywood wasn't marine grade.

That has changed. Marine grade fir is still manufactured but not widely available, and there now seems to be different grades of plywood made to BS 1088. At the upper end of the scale there is Lloyd's of London certified. This means that Lloyd's of London certifies that the plywood meets 100% of BS 1088. Because it meets all of the requirements of BS 1088, it is at the upper end of the price scale as well.

This group is followed a general category just stamped BS 1088. This group meets all or most of BS 1088. I occasionally find small voids in this group of plywood and BS 1088 doesn't allow for voids. It has been my experience that quality in this group can range from good to moderately good.

Generally, the species are Okoume and Meranti. Both are good but Meranti is rather brittle and is heavier than Okoume. Meranti is a dark reddish color with lighter streaks of grain pattern while the Okoume tends to be light tan with darker grain pattern. If weight is a consideration or you are going to finish the surface of the plywood bright, that is varnish it, then use Okoume. If weight isn't an issue and you're going to paint the surface, then use Meranti.

Under this middle group is BS 6566 plywood.

In the 1980s BS 6566 was classified as exterior plywood, not marine, but that it seems to have changed. Now I regularly see BS 6566 plywood stamped as marine plywood. Does this mean you shouldn't use BS 6566 plywood? No, I use 6566 when I want to keep costs down. In fact, I used it on the boat in this book. And if you use BS 6566 just be aware that it will have voids and it is of lesser quality than BS 1088.

I've really just scratched the surface about marine plywood, and if you really want to be an informed consumer *WoodenBoat* magazine has a number of articles on the subject. In issues #56 Jan/Feb 1984 and #57 March/April 1984, Richard Jagels discusses marine fir plywood, issue #106 May/June 1992 David Platt discusses BS 1088 plywood, and in issue #174 Oct 2003 Chris Kulczycki writes about BS 1088 plywood.

While there can be a wide quality difference in marine grade plywood, that is not the case with epoxy. There are three major brands of epoxy (System Three, Mas, and West System) and you can't go wrong with any of the three. I have used all three brands and have had no problems with any. There are some subtle differences between them, like mixing ratios, but any of the three will do a good job.

Of the three major brands, I use and recommend System Three. I have used System Three for more than fifteen years and every boat I've built in my shop has been built with System Three. It's an excellent product and I see no reason to change. . . . "If it ain't broke don't fix it."

There are many reasons I like System Three, but the two main reasons are the mixing ratio and it is very resistant to amine blush. The mixing ratio is two parts resin to one part hardener. This is very straightforward and somewhat forgiving if the measuring is a little off. That doesn't mean you can be careless with the ratios but a two-to-one ratio is, I suspect, somewhat tolerant of small errors. **99.9 percent of all epoxy failures are either errors in the mixing ratios or insufficient mixing time . . . so measure carefully and mix each batch for at least 90 seconds.**

Also, the two-to-one ratio makes it very easy to mix small batches of epoxy. This is important because all the epoxy left in the bottom of the cup is money thrown in the garbage and not put on the boat. I like small batches for that reason and many of the jobs on these boats are done with two- or three-ounce batches of epoxy.

There are several ways to measure out a batch of epoxy, with "mustard pumps" and graduated cups being the least expensive. Both are good simple methods and both have their drawbacks. "Mustard pumps" can lose their prime over time and the first pump or so can be incorrect. Also it's easy to lose count with the graduated cups. I've learned the hard way to throw away a questionable batch of epoxy. Dealing with a batch that didn't harden can cost you far more than the small amount of money you might have saved. I know that from personal experience.

I have used both the pumps and cups but now I use a measuring pump from Michael Engineering. The pump is calibrated to squirt the proper ratio of resin and hardener into your cup with each stroke of the lever. It would be difficult to justify the expense of this type of pump on a small canoe or kayak, but on a project as large as either of these two boats, it will pay for itself with less waste and more reliability.

Other than the ease of mixing small amounts of epoxy, I find that System Three is very resistant to developing amine blush. Amine blush is a greasy-feeling chemical that can collect on the surface of the epoxy. If it's there, it will keep another layer of epoxy or paint from bonding, and then you have a problem.

Amine blush was always a problem until recently. Now all of the three of the epoxies advertise that their epoxy is blush-free. My experience is that System Three's Silver Tip Epoxy is blush-free and I like that.

Lack of amine blush is one of the best reasons for using System Three or the other two major brands. It can be tempting to try and save money by ordering a less expensive brand of epoxy, but epoxy is what holds your boat together, so stick with the three major brands.

Any epoxy, regardless of the brand, has about the same consistency as honey and that means it will run down a vertical surface. But there are times you will want it to be a thick paste and not sag out of a vertical joint. An example of this is a fillet (pronounced fill-it) between a bulkhead and the hull.

But how thick is thick? In this book I refer to thickened epoxy in food terms like heavy cream or peanut butter. The descriptive terms go from unthickened epoxy to heavy cream, catsup, mayonnaise, peanut butter, to crunchy peanut butter. It's a really simple and easy way to describe something very subjective and everyone who works with epoxy uses food terms.

To achieve this spectrum it is necessary to add some kind of filler that doesn't interfere with the adhesive qualities of the epoxy. I use three fillers—silica thickener (also known by the brand name Cab-o-sil), wood flour, and milled glass fibers. Of the three, I use silica thickener the most.

Wood flour and milled glass fibers are added to the silica thickener for different reasons. Small amounts of wood flour change the color. Milled fibers are added to increase strength. Wood flour, by the way, has the consistency of flour and it is not saw dust. I only made that mistake once.

There are other fillers. West System has a large number, each with a specific job, and System Three has premixed fillet in a tub and tube. All those products work well, but I find I can get everything done with silica thickener, wood flour and milled glass fibers.

I think it's very important to add a warning about all three—**Do not breathe them.** Always, and I mean, always wear a good tight-fitting dust mast when you are mixing them. Once they are captured in the epoxy you can take off the mask.

But even though the mask is off, you still need to exercise care with the epoxy and keep it off your skin. It is possible, over time, to develop sensitivity to it. Once you are allergic to it you are done; even if you are only half finished with the boat. So keep the epoxy off your skin and don't breathe the fillers. It's important!

While I'm discussing stuff you shouldn't breathe I should mention sawdust and sanding dust from plywood and wood. The glues used in plywood are full of chemicals that are toxic, not to mention the wood itself is full of chemicals that make it unattractive to insects.

All this makes a comfortable, well fitting dust mask critical. If it is uncomfortable you won't wear it, and it can't protect your lungs sitting on the work bench. So don't try and save money on a cheap disposable one. Buy a very good dust mask. Your lungs are worth it.

There are ways to save money or at least spread the cost out over a time line. I found that dividing the construction process into blocks and ordering the materials and supplies for that block helped spread out the cost for the entire boat.

The strongback and molds are a major block and that will take 4 sheets of 6mm BS1088, 3 sheets 9mm BS1088, two 4X8 sheets cheap plywood minimum 5/8-inch thickness, one 4X8 sheet cheap plywood ¼ thick, and four 8-foot long 2X4s.

When the molds and strongback are assembled, then you are ready to purchase the plywood for the first layer of the hull and then the plywood for the following layers and so on. Combining several blocks can save on shipping if you don't have local suppliers.

Another way to save on material costs is to use the drop or scrap from cut sheets. Careful storage and labeling of the scrap will make it easier to utilize the drop for small parts. It's frustrating to cut into a full sheet only to discover a piece of scrap that would have worked. Don't be afraid to laminate thinner pieces to make the needed thickness or glue up two shorts to make the needed length. This can become a point of pride and satisfaction in the building process. It has with me.

It would be the unusual builder who didn't approach a project this size without giving any thought to containing costs. But more importantly I feel we owe it to our planet to use the materials with as little waste as possible. This also has a positive effect on our wallets and that's always nice.

Time

It is also the unusual builder who can work 40 to 50 hours a week on the boat. After all, most of us have regular jobs that we must go to 40 to 50 hours a week and mates as well as families that require our attention. And while the hermit boatbuilder might be an occasionally tempting and appealing scenario, the truth is we wouldn't be happy. I don't speak from personal experience in this matter, never having tried the hermit boatbuilder scenario but the reality is we must juggle our time.

There are many ways that allow us to juggle our time. A number of the jobs on these boats are small and can be done in an hour or so. Gluing up or coating parts have to be done for the overall project to move forward. Being able to do these small jobs in the evening during the week allows the builder makes giant strides on the weekend.

Making sure that the materials and parts are ready when you have a large block of time to work on the boat will help keep the satisfaction level high. Scheduling the work flow so all the epoxy work is done at the end of the day means you won't waste the last three hours waiting for epoxy to kick off. Let the epoxy go off while you sleep.

For me, working on the boat is relaxing and therapy, and because it's relaxing and therapy I spend every moment I can working on the boat. If you can take your satisfaction and gratification from small jobs rather than the whole then you'll find yourself drawn to spending time working on the boat.

There is no silver bullet—even the hermit boatbuilder isn't a solution.

Because I know that these boats are worth the time and effort they require, I just complete one small job after another and enjoy the process until launch.

2

The Process

Building a boat, particularly a boat the size of the Sea Eagle, can seem overwhelming at first glance, but there is nothing complicated about the process. It just looks complex or complicated when you look at the entire project. Actually it's very linear, nothing but a long string of individual jobs or steps that are combined together to make a boat.

This book is laid out in a series of individual steps—one following the other. For the most part each step can be looked on as a separate job. I find this is important because I find a sense of completion in the small steps or jobs. I learned very early on to treat each step as a separate job, because if I waited until the boat was completed to get a sense of gratification I would become discouraged and give up.

I like to organize the building process into large steps that are broken down into smaller ones. For example in **Figure 2-1** and **2-2** the foundation of the boat is being assembled. The strongback is built and the bulkheads are being cut out.

Figure 2-2

Figure 2-3

In **Figure 2-3** all the bulkheads are on the strongback and the boat is ready to plank. As I proceed from step to step I like to stop and focus on what I've accomplished. I like to take pride in the job I've done so far. In this case the skeleton of the boat is ready for the skin or planks. I can begin to see the shape of the boat and I'm watching it grow.

Figure 2-4

Figure 2-1

Figure 2-4 shows the boat planked and painted. Now the boat is ready to leave the shop for the first time and be turned right side up in photo 2-5. At this point I had a party to celebrate turning the boat over, which is a major point in

Figure 2-5

the construction process. More importantly, the party was to entice friends to help me turn the boat over. I learned long ago to have the party after the boat has been turned over and safely back in the shop.

Figure 2-6

Once the boat was back in the shop I could start putting in the interior of the boat (**Figure 2-6**). I enjoyed this part of the process a great deal. I found myself sitting inside the hull at the end of the work session planning voyages.

Figure 2-7

In **Figure** 2-7 the boat has been loaded on the trailer, the masts are being fitted and all the small parts that comprise the finished boat are being added. This maybe the most difficult time for the builder, I know it is for me. You think you are very close to the launch but all those small jobs take longer than you think. I always feel like I'm running in slow motion and I'm tempted to jump ahead or cut corners. I've learned to resist this temptation. You'll be sorry in the long run if you give in and cut corners or rush. I always have been. Just continue to work to high standards and before you know it you'll be sitting in the cockpit on the boat's maiden voyage (**Figure 2-8**).

I did learn a very important lesson while I was building this boat. I had planned to have to the boat completed by the end of May. I wanted to take the boat to Michigan's Upper Peninsula where I was teaching for the summer. As the end of May approached, I worked longer and longer hours to try to meet the deadline. Every time I thought I would make the deadline more small projects cropped up. When I found myself cutting corners and quality, I stopped and made the decision to leave the boat behind. I'll always be glad that I made that decision. That wasn't the lesson. The lesson was waiting for me when I returned.

When I returned to my shop at the end of September I had a terrible time picking up where I had left off at the end of May. What I was going to do next, and the method I was going to use, was completely forgotten. It had been pushed from my mind by a summer of teaching how to build other boats. I spent a couple of months trying to gather all the small projects into a construction plan.

It occurred to me that most builders, who work part time constructing the boat, would also find it difficult to pick back up where they had left off after a lengthy period of down time. Had I made careful notes and drawings about the projects, I would have been able to pick up where I left off with a minimum of lost time.

So now at the end of each work session, I take the time to make detailed notes about how I plan to complete the project and where I plan to go next. This way, if I must set the construction of the boat aside for a few days, it's easy to pick up the thread and start right back where I left off. Even if I was able to jump right back the next day, it helped me organize my thoughts and waste less time.

Learning this lesson has saved me from wasting a great deal of time, and if you will make careful notes at the end of each work session it will save you time and frustration as well.

3

Scarfing

Building both Sea Eagles requires that you scarf sections of plywood together, and I've found that scarfing seems to intimidate some builders. If the truth be told, I found it scary at first, as well. But after cutting a great many scarfs, it's difficult to see what was so intimidating.

Briefly, scarfing is nothing more than joining two pieces of wood or plywood together to form a longer continuous plank or bigger piece of plywood. This generally involves cutting a matching slope on both pieces and then gluing them together with an adhesive, like epoxy (**Figure 3-1**).

8:1 Scarf

The slope itself is expressed as a ratio like 8 to 1 (8:1) or 12 to 1 (12:1). For example an 8:1 scarf in ¼-inch material would be 2 inches long or an 8:1 scarf in 4mm (5/32) material would be 1¼ inches long. It should be pointed out that an 8:1 scarf is the bare minimum and will require careful handling to keep the plank from breaking before it is attached to the boat. Actually, any scarfed plank should be handled with care, turning it so the scarf gets little or no stress, but an 8:1 scarf will require having extra support on each side of the scarf as the plank is put on or taken off the molds. This kind of special care will lessen the chance of a snapped plank.

I prefer to use a 12:1 scarf as the minimum length, but will often use a scarf that is about 20:1 in thinner material. This means a 12:1 scarf in ¼-inch or 6mm thick material will be about 3 inches long. A 20:1 scarf in 4mm (5/32) is 3 1/8 inches long. I've found that a 20:1 slope is much less likely to have hard spots—spots that are stiffer than the rest of the plank after glue-up.

And for glue-up it would be hard to find a better adhesive than epoxy because the thickened epoxy can fill the small gaps where the slope doesn't match perfectly. This doesn't mean you can be careless and sloppy, but it does give a bit of latitude with the match. The closer the better, of course, and the perfectly cut slope is always the goal.

The quest for the perfect slope has lead to quite a few methods for scarfing plywood and many involve some kind of shop-made jig. There is a jig for a router, a circular saw, and one jig I have heard about, but not seen, that involves turning a 4 X 8 sheet of plywood on edge and cutting the scarf on a table saw. Many of these shop-made jigs are detailed in various issues of *WoodenBoat Magazine* and can be found there by those interested.

However, shop-made jigs can be too time consuming for the one-time builder and most don't have a high enough ceiling in their shop to upend a sheet of plywood. But all is not lost. There are several jigs you can buy, one of which involves a tool you already have, and the other doesn't use any tools.

The first jig you can buy requires a slight modification but otherwise is an out-of-the-box jig. **Figure 3-2** shows the two parts for this jig—a Bosh 1276 belt sander with its sanding frame and a base made from plywood.

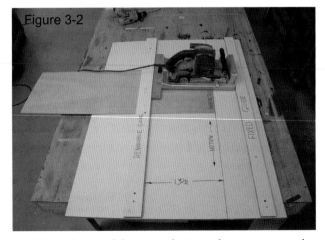

Figure 3-2

The plywood base is designed to capture the sander as it moves across the edge of the plywood being scarfed, and the aluminum sanding framing raises the sander at an angle to cut the scarf. Notice that the plywood base has two plywood guides in front and back of the sanding frame. The front guide is permanent, but the back guide is removable to allow the marine plywood to be secured in the scarfing unit. To make reassembly easy, I've drawn a line where the removable guide is refastened each time, and the other line is for the forward edge of the plywood. This line is 13½ inches from the face of the back/removable guide as indicated in the photo.

It will take a 60 X 48 inch base to scarf plywood 48 inches wide. The 60-inch width will allow enough space on each side of the 48-inch wide plywood for the sander frame. The base in **Figure 3-2** is 48 X 30 inches and I find this works very well as I seldom scarf a 48-inch wide piece of plywood. Also, I only have about 1/8-inch play between the sanding frame and the two parallel guides. This seems to be about right for the frame to move easily back and forth without jamming.

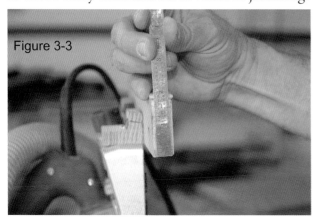

Figure 3-3

Figure 3-3 shows the only modification necessary to the frame. I've used two wooden L's to attach a ¾ X 2 X 15½-inch block to the back of the sanding frame. Another option is the small 90-degree corner braces, available at any building supply store, shown in **Figure 3-4**. Making the block about 15½ inches long seems to give

Figure 3-4

enough bearing to control any twist in the scarfing unit as it moves back and forth across the edge of the plywood.

A smooth back-and-forth motion is necessary because if the sander stops even for a moment, it will cut a gouge. I use a 40 grit belt on the sander and it will cut a scarf in 4mm plywood in very short order.

Figure 3-5 shows a scarf cut in 4mm plywood. Notice that the ply lines are fairly straight and parallel. This indicates that the slope is relatively even and that's something you will want to look for with any method you use. When I first started

Figure 3-5

using this method I would take a scarf like this and epoxy it together with its mate. It worked well, but I did find it was difficult to keep each board straight.

Because of this, I included a couple of more steps before glue-up. In **Figure 3-6** the sander has been removed and a guide screwed down 3 1/8 inches back from, and parallel to, the front edge of the plywood (a 20:1 scarf). Now, put a block plane against the guide and plane down about 1/32-inch, maybe a little less. This creates a slight indention that the edge of the other sheet will rest in and because the edge of both sheets is about

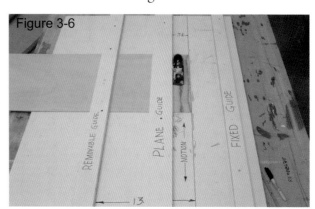

Figure 3-6

1/32-inch thick, it will be flush with the surface. This line is also a visual reference for aligning and keeping both sheets square during the glue-up process (**Figure 3**-7).

Figure 3-7

I've used this system for a number of years and it has always worked very well. I keep the jig in a corner of my shop and bring it out when needed. However, in the beginning, with the addition of another accessory, I used the sander as an upright stationary sander. This way I didn't have an expensive tool sitting idle a good deal of the time.

One off-the-shelf scarfing unit may be the least expensive; particularly if you already have a 7½-inch circular saw. The 875 Scarfer, made and sold by West System Epoxies, bolts directly on most circular saws. It requires that holes be drilled in the base so the two pieces of aluminum can be bolted on and removed easily. If you decide to purchase this unit, you will want to check with West System to be sure your circular saw is compatible with the unit.

I've used this scarfing attachment and it does the job. Certainly for the builder that already has a circular saw it is a good option. The attachment will allow plywood up to 3/8-inch thick to be scarfed with an 8:1 scarf. I find that the saw blade leaves a somewhat rough surface, but this is a minor issue. This is a small jig that can store in a drawer when off the circular saw, and that's a real plus in a very small space.

If you want to build the shop-made version of this jig get *WoodenBoat* issue 175. Bill Thomas wrote a great article on how to construct both the

jig and its integral hold-down system.

While the 875 Scarfer and the shop-made jig by Bill Thomas use a circular saw, the John Henry scarfer-planer uses a power plane. This unit has a rigid frame that screws to the bottom of a Makita 1900B 3¼-inch power planer or the larger unit that screws to a Makita 1911B 4 3/8-inch power planer. The 1900B will scarf material up to 3/8-inch thick and is more than adequate for any of the boats in this book.

I should point out that the John Henry scarfer/ planer frame will *only* work with a Makita 1900B or 1911B planers. If you don't already own a power planer this would be a good option, as the Makita planer is a good unit. The frame detaches easily from the planer so the Makita can be used for other planing jobs on the boat.

In addition to the rigid frame, this system also uses a base sheet much like the sander scarfing uses. In **Figure 3–8** the base sheet has been temporarily fastened to the table and a piece of 4mm plywood tacked to the base sheet. **Figure 3-9** shows the planer with the guide runner (left side)

Figure 3-8

Figure 3-9

pushed against the base sheet and positioned at the edge of the plywood to be scarfed. I've added a spacer to the guide runner and removed all the spaces from free side (right side) runner.

The purpose of the spacers is to fine tune the angle of the cut and the depth of the cut. The base sheet needs to just touch the attachment plate for the depth of the cut to be correct (**Figure 3-10**). If the cut is too deep you'll get an edge that looks like **Figure 3-11**.

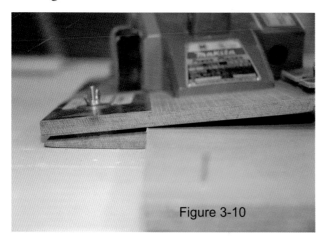

Figure 3-10

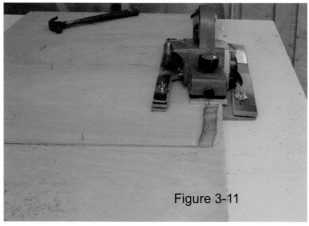

Figure 3-11

I had to add an additional thin cardboard shim to get the depth of cut just right. The runner guide comes set for a 9mm base sheet but I was using a 12mm base sheet. Because of that, I added a spacer to the guide runner but I still needed to add two more thin shims. Also I pulled the spacer from the free side (right side) runner because I wanted a scarf with a ratio greater than the 8:1 factory setting.

For the first few tests I was getting a snipe at the end of the run (**Figure 3-12**). I corrected this

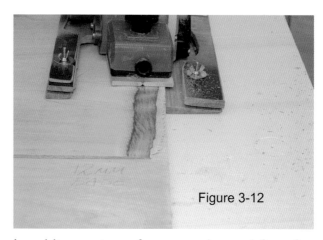

Figure 3-12

by adding a piece of scrap on that end for a few practice scarfs. In short order I was able to get consistent 18:1 scarfs like **Figure 3-13** without using the scrap at the end of the planer run. The snipe seemed to be caused by how the planer was held and how pressure was applied rather than something out of adjustment.

Figure 3-13

I did add one last step before glue-up, however. In **Figure 3-14**, I added a guide for a block plane 2¾ inches back from the edge of the scarf. This gave a nice clean line and recess for the edge

Figure 3-14

of the opposite scarf. The drill and driver point to the line (**Figure 3-15**). It also served as a reference line to keep the two pieces square and straight.

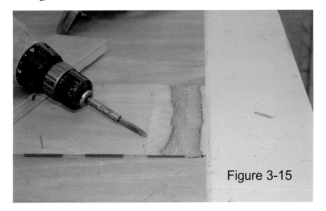

Figure 3-15

The addition of the last step is purely a personal preference and is not necessary for the planer to cut good scarfs. In fact, any of the three over-the-counter scarfing units do a good job. Are they worth the money to buy them? Absolutely, and considering the length of the scarfs you need to cut for both these boats, you find they save a great deal of time. Also, both the power planer and the belt sander can do double duty on other jobs. But there will be some builders that find the expense is not justified.

So, if all of the over-the-counter scarfing jigs seem like too much money and the shop-made jigs too much trouble, turn to your tool box and pick up your ready-to-go scarfing unit—the plane. That's right, either a block plane, which I like best, or a 9 to 10-inch bench plane. I use a Bailey #3 and a Record #4 that both belonged to my father and either a Stanley low angle or Buck block plane.

Before you start to think how impossible it would be to cut a sloping scarf by hand, let me say that a good many boatbuilders cut scarfs just that way and by choice. I had a conversation with a British boatbuilder a number of years back, and he felt it was so easy and fast there was no reason for him to go to the trouble of building a scarfing jig. He explained that he could cut the scarfs in the time it took to set up the jigs.

I'm not sure that I really believed him until I

cut a few with a block plane. And sure enough, it was fast and easy. However, your plane must be sharp, very sharp, or it will not go smoothly or quickly. A few strokes on a stone between scarfs will do wonders for the quality of the scarfs. Also I find it much easier to scarf Okoume with a plane than Meranti. Meranti is harder and more brittle and takes the edge off the plane blade much faster.

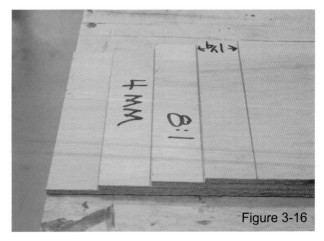

Figure 3-16

Most builders seem to prefer stacking the plywood and cutting several scarfs at a time. One, it's faster, and two, because the stack forms a ramp that helps cut the angle. In **Figure 3-16** the 4mm plywood has been staggered back 1¼ inches from the edge of the sheet below and the scarf is then cut. A pencil line at 1¼ inches will help keep the slope matching its mates. Notice the bottom sheet is flush with the table underneath. This is important—otherwise the plane can't stay at the correct angle. It takes a little practice but acceptable scarfs can be achieved in either 4mm or 6mm after just a few practice runs (**Figure 3-17**).

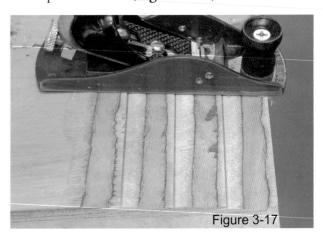

Figure 3-17

The stacking technique seems to work best if the ratio is 8:1. I haven't had a great deal of success cutting a 12:1 scarf by stacking and I cut these one at a time. Place a piece of plywood, in this case 4mm, flush with edge of the table and strike a line 2 inches back from the edge for 12:1 scarf (**Figure 3-18**). Then plane the forward edge

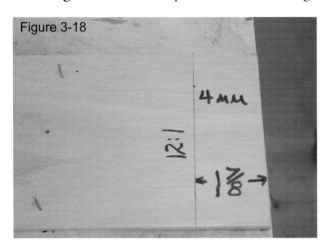

Figure 3-18

down and work the slope back to the pencil line (**Figure 3-19**). At this point, I screw a guide down 1/8-inch behind the pencil line and place the plane against the guide to clean up the slope (**Figure 3-20**). The finished scarf should look like **Figure 3-21.**

Figure 3-19

I'm always pleasantly surprised by how easy it is to cut scarfs this way, but allow yourself some time to practice on scrap plywood. Don't expect to get a perfect scarf with the first try; it always takes a while to learn a new skill. Be patient and after a bit you will be able to use the plane to cut scarfs. As you work, just think about the money

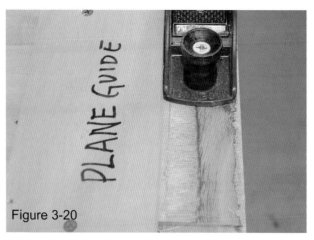

Figure 3-20

Figure 3-21

you will save by learning this skill.

However, the rewards go way beyond the money you save by cutting the scarfs by hand. There is a satisfaction that comes from mastering a task that has no monetary value, and this is one of the great joys of building a boat.

There is one other way to join plywood together to make a long plank out of two shorter pieces and it doesn't require any monetary outlay either. I first read about this method in an article written by Dynamite Payson for the out-of-print *Small Boat Journal.* Payson just butted the ends of two pieces of plywood together and put fiberglass cloth or tape across both sides for support. Unlike Payson, who suggests using polyester resin, I recommend that you saturate the fiberglass cloth in epoxy. Also, you'll want to use a small amount of peanut butter thick epoxy between the edges.

Figure 3-22 shows a butt splice with peanut butter epoxy between the two edges and a layer of fiberglass cloth before being saturated with epoxy. If you choose this method use as light a

Figure 3-22

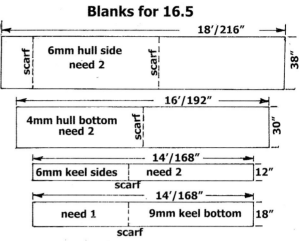

Blanks for 16.5

18'/216"

scarf | 6mm hull side need 2 | scarf | 38"

16'/192"

4mm hull bottom need 2 | scarf | 30"

14'/168"

6mm keel sides | need 2 | 12"
scarf

14'/168"

need 1 | 9mm keel bottom | 18"
scarf

Location of scarfs is approximate
use drop from hull bottom for keel sides
Figure 3-23

cloth as you can, like 4 ounce or 6 ounce cloth, and sand the edges of the cloth smooth once the epoxy has cured. Be sure to put freezer paper under the butt joint so the epoxy and the plywood don't become a permanent part of the table.

You will have to put the cloth on one side, and then when the epoxy cures, apply the cloth to the opposite side. Be careful as you turn the splice over because the unsupported side will allow the splice to break.

There are those who swear by this method, but I'm not one of them. Given how easy it is to cut a scarf by hand and the excellent jigs available over-the-counter, it's hard to justify using this method and I would counsel against it. I put it in as a fall-back plan, a disaster plan to be used in case all else fails, nothing more.

Once you settle on the scarfing method you will use—hopefully a method other than the disaster plan—the next step will be to cut the 4X8 sheets of plywood into smaller pieces or blanks. Ripping the sheets into smaller pieces or blanks allows the long pieces to be easily handled while the plank, or more accurately the plate, is lofted and cut out. This also helps cut down on waste because the drop from the 4X8 sheet can be scarfed to form another plate or blank.

Each boat has a different set of blanks, and **Figure 3-23** shows how to rip the sheets of 4mm or 6mm used for the bottom and side planks as well as the keel bottom and keel side for the Sea Eagle 16.5. You will find the blank size for the Sea

Eagle 14.5 in the appendix.

When the 4mm or the 6mm blanks are ripped and the scarfs cut it will be time to glue up the short pieces to make the full length blanks. In **Figure 3-24**, the individual pieces have been placed on freezer paper to keep the plywood from becoming permanently bonded to the table or surface underneath. Also, clear packing tape has been

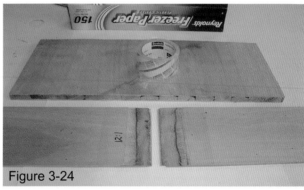

Figure 3-24

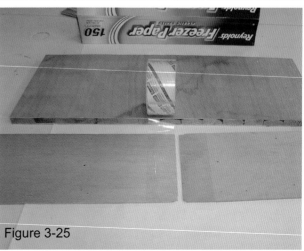

Figure 3-25

applied to each piece where the scarf starts and in **Figure** 3-25 clear tape has been applied to the opposite sides. This is an important step because the tape helps protect the plywood from the epoxy squeeze out. The epoxy is much harder than the plywood when it cures and having it peel off with the tape is much better that trying to sand it off.

The next step is to mix up a small batch of epoxy, about two or three ounces of resin should do it, stir the recommended 90 seconds, and brush on the epoxy with a disposable brush (**Figure 3-26**). Next, add a small amount of silica and wood flour until a heavy cream/runny catsup consistency is reached and brush a light coat on each side (**Figure 3-27**).

I like to use a heavy cream epoxy rather than a thicker mixture when scarfing because I found the

Figure 3-26

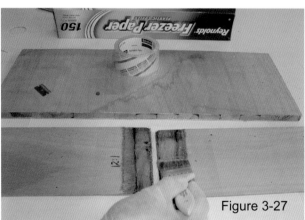

Figure 3-27

thicker epoxy created a hard spot in the plank. The heavy cream mixture comes closer to matching the stiffness of the glue between the plies.

Also, it wouldn't hurt to take some of the practice scarfs you cut and glue them up before you

start on the blanks. This will give you a good idea of how much epoxy to put on and be a good test of your clamping technique.

Once both sides have a light coat of heavy cream epoxy just flip one piece over on top of the other. I like to move the top piece around a bit to spread the epoxy. Then use the line created by the plane (see **Figure 3-7**) as a reference to square both pieces.

Be sure to wipe up the excess squeeze-out with paper towels (**Figure 3-28**), check to be sure the pieces are square to each other and then screw down a 1 X 8 or scrap plywood as a clamp (**Figure 3-29**). However, don't forget to put a nonstick barrier between the plywood clamp and the scarf.

I think you'll find that 6 X 1 5/8-inch coarse-thread drywall screws can apply an amazing

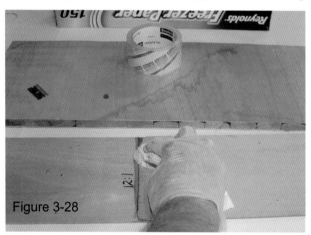

Figure 3-28

Figure 3-29

amount of clamping pressure. On wide pieces, like the bottom or side, I'll put several drywall screws spread across the center to distribute the clamping pressure. It's better to have a few holes in the center of the plank and get good even clamping pressure across the entire plank because any holes created by these drywalls can be filled later with thickened epoxy.

You'll want to allow a minimum of twenty-four hours (in colder weather allow more time) before you remove the clamp and work on the plank. The first job will be to remove the clear tape and as much squeeze-out as possible. **Figure 3-30** shows just how much squeeze-out can be pulled up with the tape.

Once you've removed the majority of squeeze-out, take a random orbital sander with 100 grit

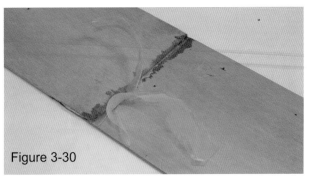
Figure 3-30

paper and finish cleaning up the scarf (**Figure 3-31**). Exercise a bit of care with this task because the sander can cut through the top ply fairly quickly. Should this happen don't worry because it won't be a problem unless you plan to varnish the entire boat and I do not recommend that anyway.

Just be sure to support the scarf on each side by spreading your hands out a good twelve inches on

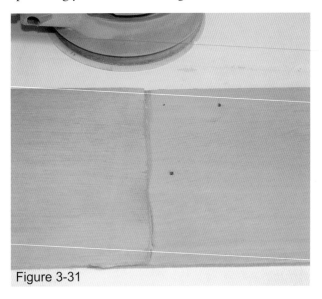
Figure 3-31

either side of the scarf when picking up the blank. Turning the blank on edge will help lessen the stress on the scarf. Use another person, if possible, to help handle what now resembles a big limber noodle.

This will be a good time to coat the side of the blank that faces the inside of the hull with unthickened epoxy and sand it smooth. It may seem unnecessary at this point, but it will save time later. It is much easier to coat and sand the blanks while they are flat on a table or floor than when they are on the boat. It is not necessary to coat and sand both side because more layers will be laminated on the side facing out.

Actually, I've found that the hour or so spent coating and sanding a blank smooth at this point will save hours of labor when finishing out the interior. You'll really be glad you did the work in advance because you'll be in a hurry to launch the boat.

So take the time and coat each blank with a layer of epoxy, let it cure, sand it smooth, apply another coat and sand smooth. As each blank is finished and sanded, store them in a safe out of the way place until you're ready for them.

4

Lofting the Developed Plates and Bulkheads

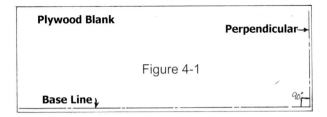

Figure 4-1

When you have all the blanks scarfed together you'll want to cut those blanks into developed plates or planks. Let me define these terms now and I think it will save a great deal of confusion down the road.

The "blanks" are the rough plywood rectangles that you have scarfed together. The "developed plates" (what the computer generated from the program) will be lofted or, more correctly, drawn on the plywood blanks and this drawing will be cut out to create the planks that go on the boat. Really, the plate and the plank are the same thing but one is a computer-generated shape and the plank is the plywood piece that goes on the boat.

Basically, you are taking the same information the CNC router uses and cutting out the planks. You will plot the points by hand, connect them with a batten (I like a ½" X ¾" X 16' clear fir batten), strike a line, and then cut the shape.

In the beginning, it all seemed very alien to me but then I realized it's just an X/Y axis graph. I was just going down or over so much and then up so much. The main thing is to do one step at a time.

The first step is to get the blank on a level flat surface. A table is going to be easier on your back but the floor will do as well. If you have to work on the floor a pair of good knee pads is a must and it will also be a good idea to put the blank on a piece of hard foam insulation. The hard foam makes working on large pieces of plywood much easier.

In **Figure 4-1** a baseline has been put down and a perpendicular line has been drawn on the blank. You will want to use a snap line rather than trying to draw a straight line for the base.

Nylon kite string can be finer than the string

in a commercial snap line and the finer string will mean more accurate measurements.

An accurate perpendicular is just as important as a dead straight baseline. It needs to be as close to a perfect 90 degrees as you can make it. Jump ahead to **Figure 5-2** in chapter 5 for an excellent way to insure you have a good 90 degree line.

Don't even think about using the edges of the blank for your baseline and perpendicular. It may look straight enough and perpendicular enough, but it isn't. I know this from unhappy personal experience, so put the baseline about ½ to ¾-inch in from the bottom and perpendicular about ½ to ¾-inch from the upright edge.

At this point, you are ready to lay out the plates/planks. Normally I'm fairly relaxed about being extremely accurate with measurements, but in this case I'm not. You are trying to duplicate the accuracy of a CNC router so extreme care is the order of the day.

Figure 4-2 is a detail of the hull bottom plate for the Sea Eagle 16.5. There is a huge amount of information just in this small detail, but if you start by locating the baseline and the perpendicular you can see how the information is organized.

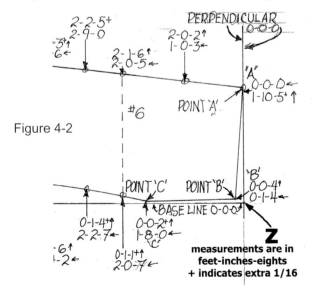

Figure 4-2

25

The intersection of the baseline and the perpendicular is at the end of the Z arrow. The baseline is the X axis and the perpendicular is the Y axis and the intersection is (0-0-0, 0-0-0).

Now find point "A." Notice that the coordinates for point "A" are 0-0-0 to the left (X axis) and 1-10-5+ up (Y axis). That means the Y point is 1 foot 10 inches and 5/8 inches + (the + sign indicates an extra 1/16-inch added so 5/8 becomes 11/16). You put a dot at those coordinates.

Next find point "B". The coordinates for "B" are 0-0-4 up (Y axis) and 0-1-4 left (X axis). That's 0 feet-0 inches-4/8 inches up (fractions are not reduced and always given as eights) and 0 feet-1 inch-4/8 inches to the left. You put a dot at those coordinates and then draw a line between point "A" and point "B." It's just connecting the dots.

I have tried to always place the Y coordinate on top and you will always find a small arrow by each to indicate if it's up or out. Occasionally I put the out on top but the arrows are always correct and tell if it's X or Y.

Figure 4-3 shows the coordinates for the whole plate/plank. It's a lot of numbers, but I found by locating all the lettered points (in this case A, B, C, and D) and then doing the top curve first, I'm less scattered and make fewer mistakes.

I don't move on to the bottom curve until I've connected all the dots with a batten and drawn the line. It should be a fair curve and resemble the plate/plank in the book. Points that stand out and don't fall on the line should be rechecked.

When you are satisfied that your curve is an accurate duplication of the curve in the book then you can move on to the next curve. Check and

recheck your figures. There is an enormous amount of measuring involved in this process and mistakes are going to creep in, but with care you can catch them all.

Figure 4-4 is a bird's eye view of what the hull bottom should look like as you lay it out on the blank. The snap line is at the bottom. A square and metal measuring stick help assure the points are as accurate as possible. Use the tape for the X axis and the metal ruler for the Y axis.

I can't stress enough the need to be accurate. This is tedious work at best and the temptation is to rush on to the important building part. But this *is* the important building part. This is the foundation of the boat and sloppy work here will reverberate through the whole process.

So set up your baseline and perpendicular with extreme accuracy, locate the lettered points, and then do one curve at a time. Put one foot in front of the other and before you know it all the parts of the boat will be cut out and waiting to be assembled.

The appendix has all the numbers for both boats.

Figure 4-4

Figure 4-3

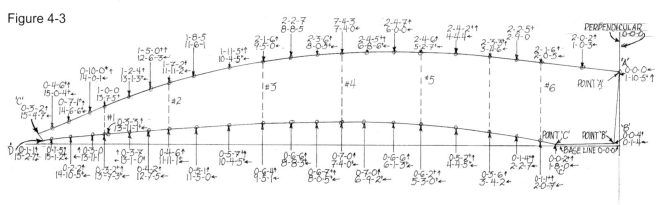

5

Setting up the Strongback and Bulkheads

With the bulkheads and planks, or more accurately the hull plates, lofted, cut out, and set aside, it's time to put the bracing on the bulkheads, build the strongback and set the bulkheads on the strongback. This is a fast and simple job, but it will go faster if you do the layout on the bulkheads first and then build the strongback.

Figure 5-1 shows the layout for a ¼" 4X8 sheet of cheap plywood. Great care should be exercised here to get the layout square and accurate. Having the layout out-of-square or the measurements off will create problems that magnify themselves as boat construction progresses.

16.5 Sea Eagle

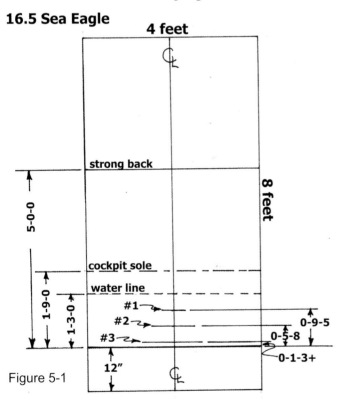

Figure 5-1

A close look at **Figure 5-1** indicates that bulkheads number 3, 2, and 1 are all **above** the baseline. Number 3 for example is 0-1-3+ above the

baseline. Bulkheads numbers 4, 5, and 6 all sit **directly on** the baseline.

The plus sign next to the 3 indicates an additional 1/16-inch. So instead of 0 feet, 1 inch, and 3/8-inch you will want to measure up from the baseline 0 feet, 1 inch, and 7/16-inch. You find the plus sign is used in offsets when it's considered important to measure to a 1/16-inch rather than the normal 1/8-inch.

Figure 5-2 demonstrates how to check the square of the layout, and re-checking the measurements several times will insure no mistakes have slipped by. Remember the old adage— "measure once cut twice, measure twice cut once."

I seldom encourage builders to be super accurate, but this one of the cases that I do recommend measuring as accurately as possible. Just like with the hull plates, you want to be as accurate and careful as you can. It will pay dividends down the road.

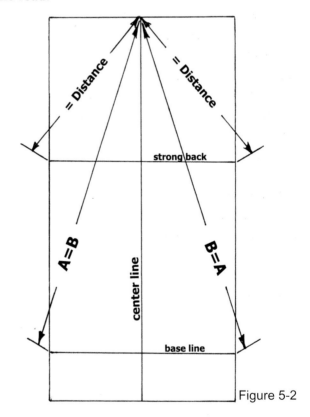

Figure 5-2

In **Figure 5-3** the number 3 bulkhead has been placed on the template at the number 3 hash mark and the centerlines matched up.

Notice that bracing has been added to num-

Figure 5-3

ber 3 in **Figure 5-4a** and the cross piece is **directly on** the strongback line (**Figure 5-4b**). You'll want to place the outside edge of each upright brace approximately 12 inches on either side of the centerline. More than that will place the brace over the edge of the strongback and much less than that will not give enough support to the brace. I used cheap 5/8 plywood for the bracing and found that about the right thickness. ¾-inch ply will work as well but it does add extra weight on the strongback.

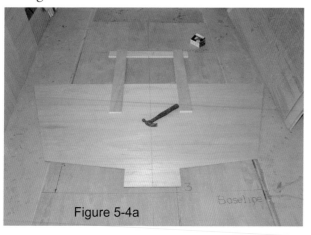

Figure 5-4a

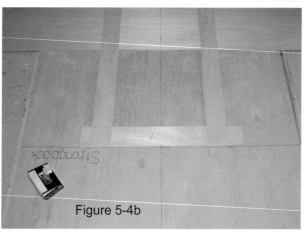

Figure 5-4b

I placed the strongback line five feet above the baseline to allow relatively easy access under the hull during the building process. Five feet was arbitrary on my part but I found that less than five feet and it's too hard to crawl under the hull for clean-up as well as construction, and more than five feet places the keel bottom and hull bottom too high to work on easily.

Figure 5-5

Once the bracing is carefully attached to each bulkhead you'll want to transfer the waterline and the line for the cockpit sole to each bulkhead. In **Figure 5-5** the bulkhead covers in the information on the template so just measure up from the baseline 15 inches for the waterline and 21 inches for the cockpit sole on each side of the centerline. Then draw a line straight across as in **Figure 5-6**.

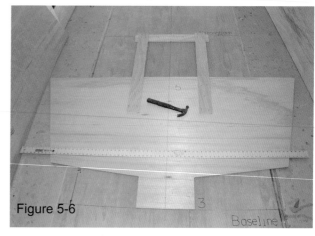

Figure 5-6

Bulkhead number 1 allows the direct transfer from the template (**Figure 5-7**). Note that bulkhead 1 as well as 2 and 3 sit above the baseline. It's also important to remember to mark the centerline on the cross piece as in **Figure 5-8**. In **Figure**

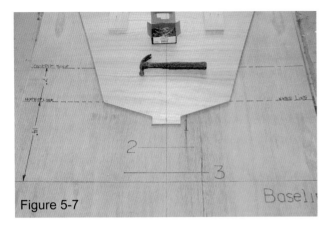
Figure 5-7

Figure 5-8

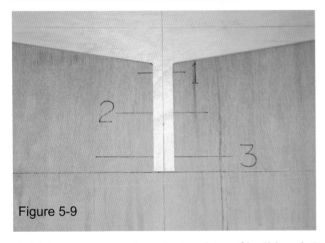
Figure 5-9

In Figure **5-10** I've ripped 3½-inch X 8 foot long strips, butted them end to end (**Figure 5-11**) and clamped them to a straight edge made from a scrap piece of plywood. If you're not sure how straight the scrap piece is, use a tight string as a backup straight edge. Once you're certain that the two pieces are straight and true, add a splice or cleat over the joint (**Figure 5-12**). This gives you one side of the strongback 3½ X 16 foot long.

Figure 5-10

Figure 5-11

5-9 it's easy to see the relationship of bulkhead 6 to the baseline and bulkheads 1, 2, and 3.

Once all the bulkheads have the braces on and all the information is clearly marked, it will be time to construct the strongback. You'll want use ¾-inch plywood for this. My first temptation was to use ¾-inch CD fir but there are too many voids in this grade plywood and that creates weak points. The strongback will have to support a great deal of weight before the hull is turned over so ¾-inch BC exterior will be better.

Figure 5-13 shows both sides of the strongback and some cross braces for additional support sitting on top of two 24 inch X 8 foot pieces of ¾-inch plywood. This was the way I built my strongback, but I found it too weak. The single

29

Figure 5-12

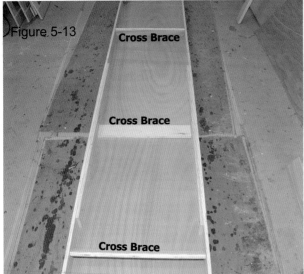

Figure 5-13

Cross Brace

Cross Brace

Cross Brace

Figure 5-14

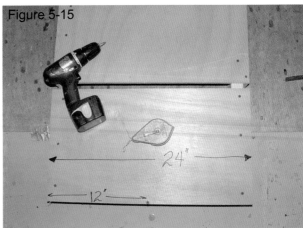

Figure 5-15

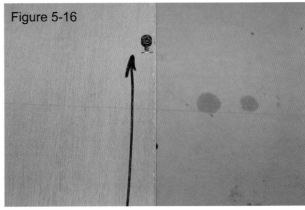

Figure 5-16

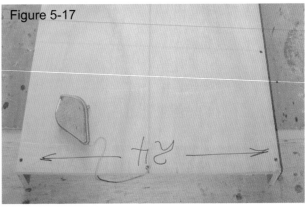

Figure 5-17

¾-inch side just isn't strong enough to take all the weight when you're moving the boat out of the garage to turn the hull over. A 2X4 will need to be added on the inside of both sides of the strongback. Be sure to screw the 2X4 securely into the plywood strip and the 24 inch X 8 foot long pieces that are the top of the strongback.

At this point you have a 16 foot long strongback but the boat is 16 feet 9 inches long so an extension needs to be added (**Figure 5-14**). After that job is done turn the strongback back over and add a small section of plywood, mark a 12-inch center (**Figure 5-15**) and set a drywall screw to one side of the centerline (**Figure 5-16**). It doesn't make any difference which side of the line you put the screw on it just needs to be the same at both ends of the strongback. This is so the string or chalk line will be on the exact centerline

(**Figure 5-17**) when you pull it end to end and give it a snap.

Once the centerline is marked you'll want to take the information in **Figure 5-18** and mark each station on the strongback (station placement for the 14.5 is in the appendix). I find it's better to lay out each station and then put the ¾-inch plywood cleats on the strongback. This way you can double check the station measurements.

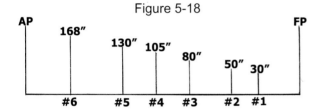

Figure 5-18

As you place the cleats, be sure the cleat is square to the centerline. If the measurement of each side is the same then it's perpendicular to the centerline (**Figures 5-19A** and **5-19B**). It will be important that the tape is on the centerline. If it is just a bit off of center your measurements will be off.

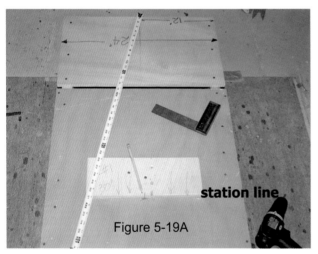

station line

Figure 5-19A

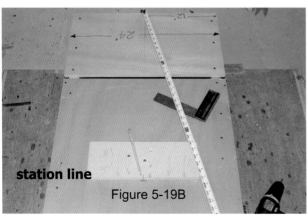

station line

Figure 5-19B

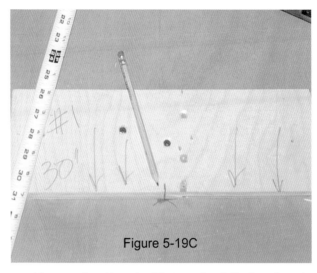

Figure 5-19C

Also notice that in **Figure 5-19C** the cleat is on the bow side of the station line. In **Figure 5-20** all the cleats are in place and the bulkheads are ready to put on the strongback.

Figure 5-20

Having the cleat on the bow side will allow the bulkhead to be placed right on the station line. Stations 1,2,3, and 4 all have the cleat on the bow side of the station line and 5 and 6 have the cleat on the stern side of the station line. This allows the thickness of the bulkhead to be **inside** the curve of the hull (**Figure 5-21**). When the brace was added to the bulkheads **A surface** and **B surface** were on the same plane (**Figure 5-22A**) so when the brace is screwed to the cleat both the **A surface** and **B surface** fall directly on the station line (**Figures 5-22B** and **5-22C**). For this system to work it will be important that the cleats fit inside the brace uprights. You'll also want to make the cleats an inch less than the width of the brace uprights. This will allow for some movement to each side as the bulkheads are centered up.

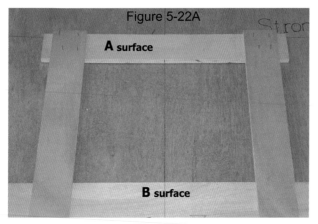

Figure 5-21

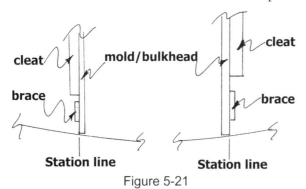

Figure 5-23A shows a bulkhead in place with its centerline matching the centerline of the strongback. As each bulkhead goes on the strongback, match the centerlines (**Figures 5-23B** and **5-23C**).

In addition to lining up the centerline it will be important to have the bulkhead perpendicular to the strongback as well. A level or a framing square will get the bulkhead plumb and then braces can be added as in **Figure 5-24**.

Figure 5-25 shows all the bulkheads on centerline and plumb. The next step is to add the planking.

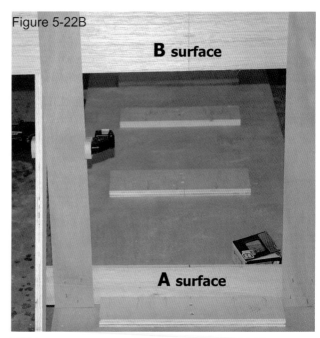

Figure 5-22B

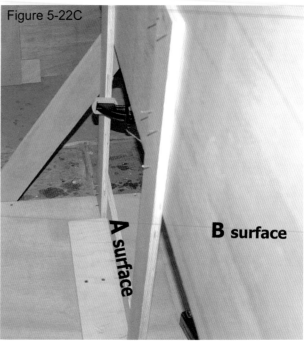

Figure 5-22C

I think it's important to mention a discrepancy in the photos. **Figure 5-18** shows six bulkheads but a count of the bulkheads in the photos shows seven bulkheads. Number 6 bulkhead in the photos is a temporary mold that comes out. I added it because I thought it would be necessary for good hull shape. As it turns out it was completely unnecessary and just got in the way so I no longer include that bulkhead in the construction process. This is good news because it's one less part to loft out and put on the strongback.

Figure 5-23A

Figure 5-23C

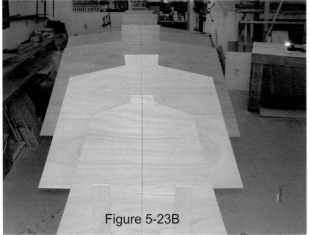

Figure 5-23B

The other good news is you've reached an important point in the construction process. You're ready to start planking the boat and you have a better idea of the size and volume of the boat. It's just a little easier to imagine yourself at the helm loafing along in gentle breeze on broad reach.

6

Planking the Hull

At this point you should have made the templates of each plank from ¼-inch cheap plywood. If you skipped that step or just haven't gotten around to it yet then drop everything and make the templates. It's important because if you plank up the boat without those templates you will have to spile (make a pattern from the plank while it is on the boat) each plank or plate in order to laminate the next layer. While not impossible or particularly difficult, it is time-consuming, and if you have made the templates, completely unnecessary.

After you have rechecked that all the bulkhead centerlines match up (**Figure 6-1**) put the keel bottom on the bulkheads and line up the station numbers and the centerline (**Figure 6-2**). If you are very lucky everything will match perfectly but

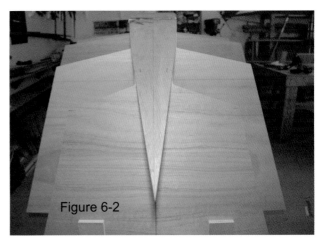

Figure 6-2

in all the boats I have built this has never happened. Generally there will be one or two that are slightly off.

In my case bulkheads 7 through 3 all lined perfectly and 1 and 2 were slightly off (**Figure 6-3**). So I anchored the keel bottom to those bulkheads that lined up and then adjusted 1 and 2 so their centerlines matched the centerline of the keel bottom. **Figure 6-4A** shows the number 2 bulkhead before I shifted it over and **6-4B** shows the bulkhead centered up on the keel bottom.

Figure 6-3

I only had to move Number 2 about 1/8-inch. If you need to move several bulkheads more than about ¼-inch, then it will be a good idea to back up and double check all the measurements and the strongback alignment.

Once you have all the bulkheads aligned on the keel bottom centerline and the bulkheads are all even with the edge of the keel bottom (**Figure 6-5**), you can wire the keel bottom to each bulk-

Figure 6-1

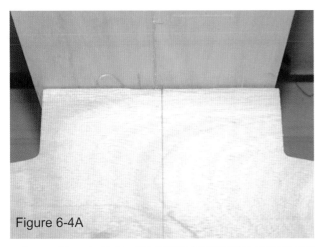

Figure 6-4A

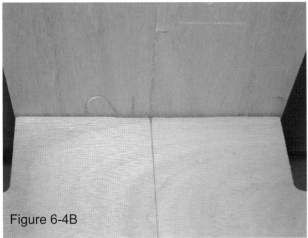

Figure 6-4B

Figure 6-5

Figure 6-6

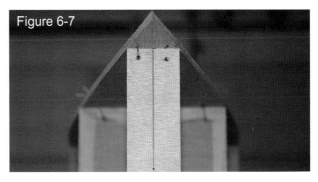

Figure 6-7

head (**Figures 6-6 and 6-7**).

Now will be a good time to double check that all the bulkheads are plumb (vertical) and they match the station lines marked on the keel bottom. Once you are satisfied that all is plumb and in alignment take one side of the hull bottom and place it on the bulkheads (**Figure 6-8**).

Figure 6-8

Figure 6-9

Line up station 4 on the hull bottom with bulkhead 4 and wire it in place with a single 16 gauge copper or brass wire. Then move to bulkhead 6 and line up the bulkhead and station line and wire the bottom to number 6 using 16 gauge wire as well. Now move to bulkhead 1 and repeat the process until all the bulkheads are lined up and wired on the station lines. I used two wires at most of the bulkheads. I placed each wire about 1 to 2 inches in from the edge of the plank. I used 16 gauge wire thoughout the wiring process because the heavier gauge didn't break as much as the lighter wire and could pull the planks together.

When the hull bottom is securely wired down to the bulkheads put the keel side on the boat (**Figure 6-9**). Again start at bulkhead 4 and wire up the keel side the same way you wired the hull bottom. Once you have the keel side secured to the bulkheads you'll want to wire the edges of the

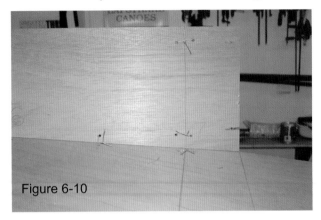

Figure 6-10

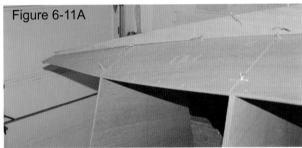

Figure 6-11A

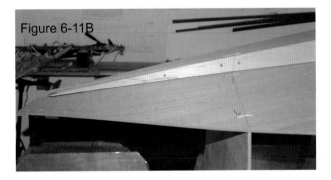

Figure 6-11B

hull bottom, the keel side and the keel bottom together as well. (**Figure 6-10** and **6-11**).

The next step is wiring the other hull bottom in place using the same process as before (**Figure 6-12**). Notice in **Figure 6-12**, the two bottom planks/plates match up very well at the stern. It's important to keep all the planks/plates well matched as this is what gives the boat its shape.

You'll find that this side of the boat will go faster because you have already done the job once. And putting on this keel side is just like the other

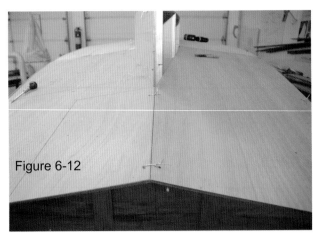

Figure 6-12

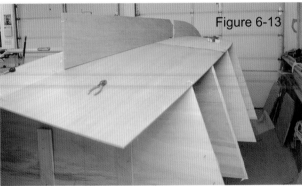

Figure 6-13

side (**Figure 6-13**). All the edges should fit tightly against the joining edge. Now is the time to check and add wire where a little extra squeeze is needed. All the planks should fit snuggly against the bulkheads and each other.

And with all the planks so far, gravity has worked with you, helping to hold each piece in place while you wire it up. However, gravity will work against you when dealing with the sides of the hull. Don't despair; there is a solution to make life easier. In **Figure 6-14A** and **6-14B**, I have temporarily attached an arm to several bulkheads to hold the hull side while it's wired in place. Even if you have an extra pair of hands these "handy helpers" will make life much easier.

There is one more step you can take to simplify the wiring process and that is to pre-drill a few holes in the hull bottom (**Figure 6-14C**). This will be particularly important toward the bow, and they should be spaced closer together as you move in that direction.

In **Figures 6-15** and **6-16** the hull side has been hung and the wiring is almost complete. I found there were several areas where the hull bot-

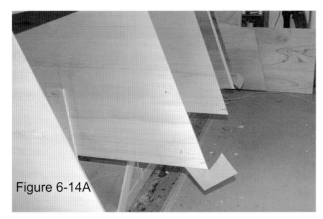

Figure 6-14A

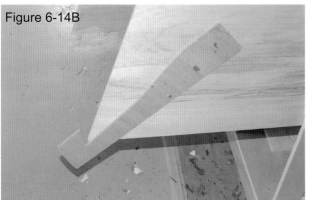

Figure 6-14B

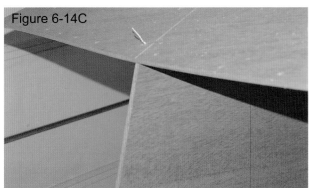

Figure 6-14C

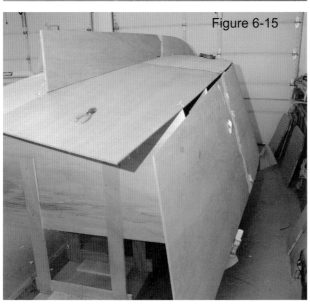

Figure 6-15

Figure 6-16

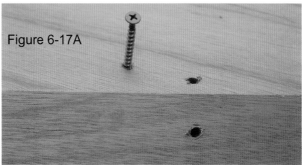

Figure 6-17A

Figure 6-17B

tom would slip below the edge of the hull side making it difficult to get the two in alignment. I solved this problem by setting a drywall screw in the center of the problem area, pulling up with a pair of pliers and then wiring it tight (**Figures 6-17A** and **B**). Of course, you could always push up from the bottom, but I found this method much easier and faster than crawling under the boat.

With the sides in place it's time to wire up the transom. An extra pair of hands will be welcome

37

with this task but not necessary. You'll find if you pre-drill the bottom and the transom so the holes match it isn't so difficult. Set a fairly long piece of wire in the bottom, lift the transom and thread the wire through the hole in the transom and twist it so it holds. A box at the right height will expedite the process. Now tighten the wires to snug up the transom to the hull bottom (the transom fits **inside** the planks and is **flush** with the end of the planks) and wire the sides by alternating sides. When you are satisfied with the fit just tighten everything down.

There was nothing difficult about putting in the transom but I did encounter another minor problem at the bow. **Figure 6-18A** shows the bow with the wiring in place and one side of the hull bottom stuck under the other. I found that the 6mm plywood was too proud (didn't want to bend easily) for the brass wire to pull all the pieces together and no amount of coaxing would get the bottom in its proper place.

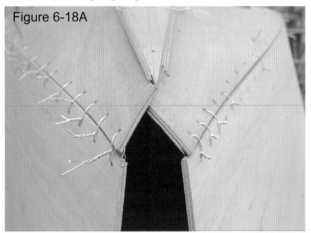

Figure 6-18A

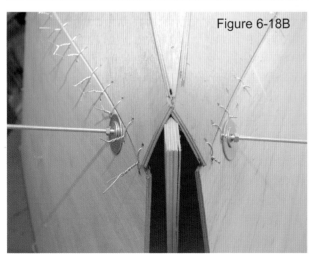

Figure 6-18B

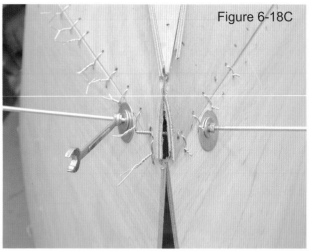

Figure 6-18C

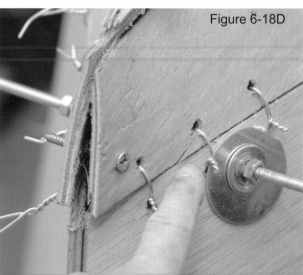

Figure 6-18D

I was able to align and tighten everything using a short piece of 5/16 all-thread, some big fender washers, a plywood jam and a couple of nuts. In **Figure 6-18B** the jam has forced the one side up and even with the other and I tightened the nuts to draw it all together (**Figure 6-18C**). I used a stainless steel screw to draw the two bottom plates together instead of a drywall screw. You'll want to use stainless steel screws in case a screw has to be left in. The drywall might rust and bleed through then nothing short of a screwectomy will solve the problem.

Even though I tightened the stainless screw slowly I had to stop short of drawing the two sides completely together. **Figure 6-18D** shows a small crack that developed as I tightened the screw. Had the hole for the wire been back from the edge a ¼-inch more I don't believe that crack would have happened.

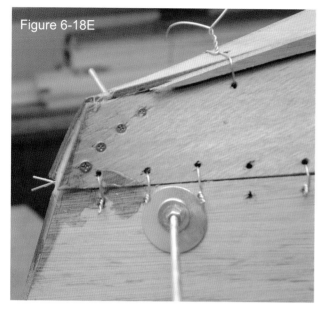

Figure 6-18E

If this sort of problem develops, it's always better to stop and take a good look at what has happened before moving ahead. Leaving a small gap didn't create a problem and having the tip break clean would have been. As a backup, I added a few small stainless screws (**Figure 6-18E**) and then wired the rest of the hull sides together at the bow.

Having to use a bolt to draw the bow sections together may seem a bit extreme but a good many boats need a bit of finesse to pull things up. Builders have a large bag of tricks to convince a difficult plank to drop in place. Using 4mm plywood for the hull bottom would be another solution but that would make for several more layers and more time. I found the bolt to be a fast, easy way to bring the sections together.

At this point I took a break and sat down to look at the boat. She was planked in completely, and while there were more layers of plywood to be added, this was the shape of the hull. I think you'll find that the boat starts to have a personality at this point—this boat certainly did.

When the transom was cut the inked stamp from the manufacturer ended up, by chance, in the upper right hand corner. It looked somewhat like a tattoo. So I decided that with a bolt in her nose and a tattoo on her bum, this was one very pretty and very tough lady.

And with that thought in mind I ended my break, mixed up some peanut butter epoxy and

started tabbing the plates/planks and bulkheads together. My son, who is far more flexible than I am, crawled up under the boat and tabbed the bulkheads in place using epoxy in a baggy (**Figure 6-19**). He used small amounts of epoxy between the wires and smoothed the small bead of epoxy with his gloved finger, and you will want to do the same. He was very careful to clean up the excess and any globs of epoxy, and you should be as well. The goal with this step is to just hold the boat together while you add all the laminations of plywood.

In **Figure 6-20** peanut butter epoxy has been added to the space between the plates/planks but

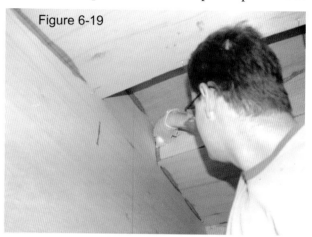

Figure 6-19

Figure 6-20

it doesn't cover the wires. You want to take care to not cover the wires because you will pull the wires out and this is difficult if they are covered with epoxy. Also, notice that **all** the excess epoxy has been wiped up. This is very important!

I only failed to clean up the excess epoxy once and after that I was very meticulous about cleanup. Once epoxy is hard it is time-consuming to sand off. So you should live by the three rules of epoxy—**Clean up**, **Clean up**, and **Clean up**.

Once the epoxy has hardened (at least 24 hours. or more if it's cold), pull all the wires. In **Figure 6-21** all the wires and the bolt have been pulled and the hull is ready for a quick sanding with 80 grit paper. All you want to do is smooth out the epoxy and any rough edges on the outside of the hull. You don't have to worry about the inside of the hull until you turn the boat over.

Figure 6-22 shows the bow area after the wires have been pulled and the bolt taken out. Notice there are two wires that have not been pulled be-

Figure 6-21

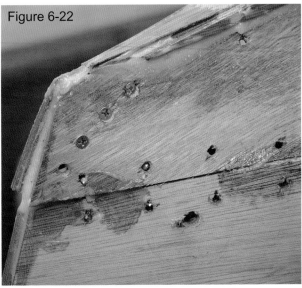

Figure 6-22

cause we added peanut butter epoxy to the inside of the hull in that area. I just cut these off flush and pushed them down with a nail set so they wouldn't interfere with the next layer of plywood. I pulled the small screws right before I sanded the area and the next layer went on the boat.

There is one last check you need to do, and that's to step back and be sure the line of the bow is on centerline and has not been pulled off somehow. In **Figure 6-21** the bow falls right on centerline.

So what do you do if the bow is slightly off? Well, first thing: DON'T PANIC, because you can fix it. Actually, DON'T PANIC is sound advice throughout the building process because there is always a fix for the problem. Remember that when there is a problem.

To fix the bow pick up your Japanese saw (the not-so-good one will be best for sawing through epoxy) and saw right down between both sides (hopefully you have removed all the wires and any screws). Sawing through the epoxy will free up the two sides and you can bring the bow back on the centerline. Wire it tight and apply some peanut butter epoxy and you're ready to move on.

If it sounds to you like that solution was learned through personal experience . . . you are absolutely correct!

7

Let the Laminations Begin

At this point you have the hull sanded and cleaned up; particularly the bow area (**Figure 7-1**) and you're ready to start the laminations. I put the layers on in a specific order so the laminations at the joints were staggered and overlapped by the next. I think this makes for a very strong joint because there is no direct seam and when you add fillets and fiberglass tape and several layers of fiberglass cloth, the joint becomes, shall we say, "bombproof."

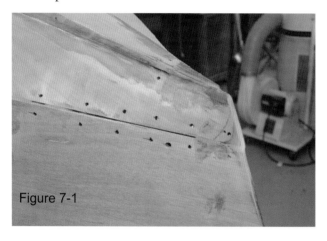

Figure 7-1

The thought "bombproof" and the strength of the hulls on these boats will be of great comfort should you find yourself and the boat in scary place. The scantlings (the thickness of the materials and hull) of the hull are adequate for a boat more than twice her size . . . so why such heavy scantlings?

Both Sea Eagles were designed to live on trailers and to be pulled long distances across rough highways, so every time you hit a pothole that jars your teeth, the boat will do very well, thank you. And the heavy, thick bottom and keel also act as ballast that helps keep them on their feet.

The first step to achieve all this strength will be to laminate the hull bottom in place. If you haven't already, trace the lines of the template of the **hull bottom** on some **4mm** plywood and be

Figure 7-2

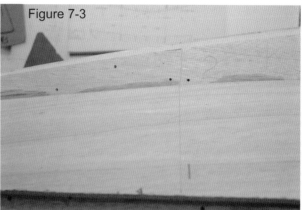

Figure 7-3

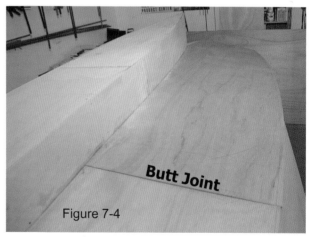

Butt Joint

Figure 7-4

sure to transfer the station lines to the lamination (it is possible to use 3mm for the hull bottom laminations but it will mean four laminations instead of three). Cut out the keel line (**Figure 7-2**) and temporarily tack the **hull bottom** to the boat to check the fit (**Figure 7-3**). In **Figure 7-4** I've just butted the two pieces together and tacked each in place while I checked the fit. **Note: When the next layer goes on be sure to extend the next butt joint at least 12 inches beyond the first butt joint.**

The goal is a snug fit against the side of the keel and it may be necessary to scribe the plate using a spacer and pencil as in **Figure 7-5**. Also there should be about an inch or so overhang at the bottom/side chine (the point where the bottom and side meet). Once marked, pull off the pieces and trim to the keel side line. It would probably be a good idea to put the pieces back on the boat one more time to recheck the fit.

Figure 7-5

Figure 7-6

When you're satisfied with the fit of the plate/plank, drill a series of 3/16" to ¼" holes in the plate/plank on a four- or five-inch grid (**Figure 7-6**). These breather holes allow excess epoxy and air to escape and helps eliminate voids as well.

I think it's easier and faster to lay out a rough grid with pencil and drill the holes. This keeps you from getting carried away and drilling too many holes or not having enough. You're going for what I like to call "The Goldilocks Principle" here; not too many, not too few, but an amount that's just right.

Once the "Goldilocks Principle" has been achieved, coat the underside of the plate/plank and the hull with unthickened epoxy (**Figures 7-7 and 7-8**) and then trowel peanut butter thick

Figure 7-7

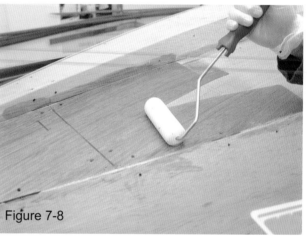

Figure 7-8

Figure 7-9

epoxy on the hull (**Figure 7-9**). A thin even layer of epoxy is the goal (once again the "Goldilocks Principle"), and notice, a tile setter's trowel is used to spread the epoxy.

I think you might find it best to start with the aft section first and if it is warm (warm will equal a shorter pot life for the epoxy) only trowel the peanut butter on the back half. Another pair of hands will be very welcome with this but it is easily manageable solo. If you are working solo then a dry run or two will build confidence and help

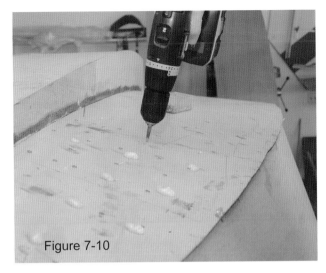

Figure 7-10

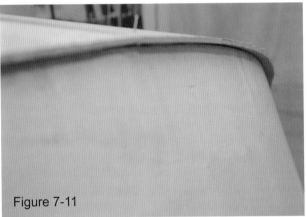

Figure 7-11

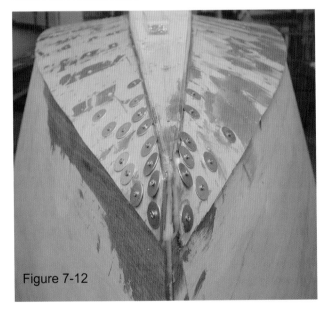

Figure 7-12

rooms. If there is a hole with no squeeze-out, set more screws around it until you get some squeeze-out. This will help insure there are no voids.

When you're setting the screws take care to adjust the clutch on the driver so it doesn't over drive the screw. These screws will all come out or at least they are supposed to come out. If one or two should be left in, it's no big deal because they're stainless and that's why you're using stainless steel instead of cheaper zinc plated screws.

You are using stainless, of course, and of course, you left about a ½- to ¾-inch overhang as shown in **Figure 7-11**.

And of course, you did the back half first and now you can turn your attention to the front half or more correctly the bow of the boat.

In **Figure 7-12** I used a number of stainless screws and large fender washers right at the bow. The fender washers spread the load and help the plywood to pull up tight. You'll need #6 X 1¼-inch screws for this section because the short screws just don't have enough bite to pull the plywood down.

Pay particular attention to the bottom/keel joint. Notice I have spaced the washers and screws fairly close together. You want to make sure everything pulls up tight with no voids. It also helps to have the breather holes in the plywood a bit closer together in this area as well. Just remember the plywood is taking a serious bend at this point and too many holes too close together will create a tear or break line.

With the lamination completed on one side, I just repeated the process on the other side but you will want to clean up any drips that have fallen on the hull. If you wipe these up **before** the epoxy hardens it will mean less sanding. Remember the three rules of epoxy work: Clean Up, Clean Up, and Clean Up.

I found that letting the epoxy mushrooms harden and then popping them off with a cheap chisel was faster than trying to clean them up while they were still soft. **Don't use a good (sharp) chisel for this. Buy a cheap chisel at the chain building supply store and use it for these types of**

you spot potential problems.

In **Figure 7-10** a large number of #6 X ½" stainless screws are being set in a grid around the pre-drilled holes. You'll find that the epoxy squeezes out of the holes to form little mush-

Figure 7-13

Figure 7-14

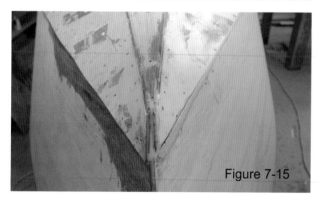

Figure 7-15

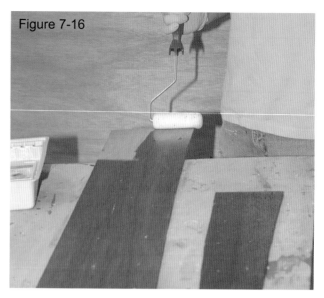

Figure 7-16

Figure 7-17

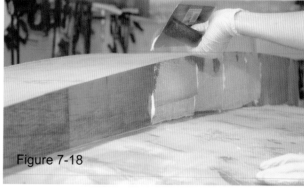

Figure 7-18

jobs. Save the good (sharp) chisels for jobs that won't destroy the edge.

After the epoxy has hardened (generally 24 hours) pull all the stainless screws. In **Figure** 7-13 the mushrooms have been popped off and the screws are being pulled. You can reuse most of the screws but you'll want to discard those screws that have the head stripped. I always use Phillips head screws rather than slot heads. Phillips head screws just lend themselves better to the cordless drivers.

In **Figure** 7-14 the bottom has been trimmed

flush with the side and the chine line has been carried forward from station #2. I used a power planer and then an orbital sander with 80 grit paper to take the bottom down flush with the sides. **Figure** 7-15 shows one side finished and the other waiting to be trimmed flush.

When both sides are trimmed and sanded, coat the sides of the keel and the keel plank with un-thickened epoxy and then trowel on the peanut butter thick epoxy (**Figures** 7-16, 7-17, **and** 7-18). Then screw on the planks/plates. Be sure the planks have the same breather holes grid as the bottom. I let the planks run wild above the keel by several inches, but you may want the bleed to be much less, particularly if you don't have a power planer (**Figure 7-19**).

With the **keel sides** on you'll want to add **another** lamination to the **hull bottom**. Again, a good snug fit against the keel side is the goal. Use the spacer and a pencil to scribe the line and be sure to overlap the previous butt joint by a minimum of 12 inches. Use the washers and #6 1¼-inch screws around the bow area and overlap the chine line by an inch or so. In **Figure 7-20A** both sides have laminations on the **keel sides** and **hull bottom**.

Now wait 24 hours (more if it's below 60 degrees) and then get ready to laminate the sides of hull on the boat. This will involve pulling all the screws once again, popping off the epoxy mushrooms, sanding, and trimming the planks flush.

Figure 7-19

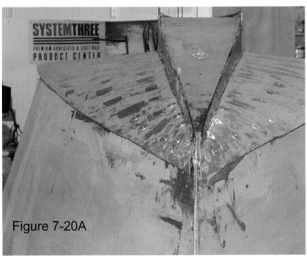

Figure 7-20A

As you trimmed the **hull bottom** planks/plates flush with the side of the hull you probably noticed that something happens between the side of the hull and the bottom of the hull about station #2. The **hull bottom** stops lying on top of the **hull side** and rides out to overlap the hull side (**Figure 7-20B**). If you just laminated the hull over the top it would create an unfair lump in the hull. As with all boatbuilding there are several ways to deal with this issue. This is the method I used.

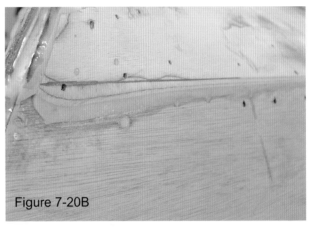

Figure 7-20B

Figure 7-21

I trimmed the **hull bottom** along the chine line so when I laminated the layer on the **side** of the boat the **hull bottom** would lay on top of the **hull side** from station #2 to the bow. That sounds tricky but it's not. In **Figure 7-21** I've nailed a guide for my Japanese saw that follows the chine line from #2 to the bow. Then, using the guide, I cut down though both laminations **but not into the hull side (Figure 7-22)**. I found it best to cut a small amount, look, and then cut again. Once I got to a point where I thought I was close, I

Figure 7-22

Figure 7-23

Figure 7-24A

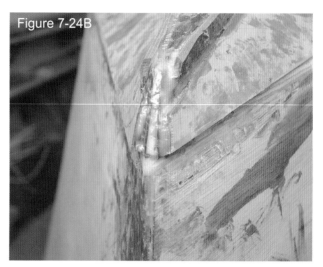

Figure 7-24B

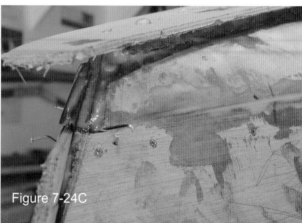

Figure 7-24C

Figure 7-24D

cleaned the cut with a rabbet plane (**Figure 7-23**). A chisel works for this task as well. I kept working until I got a nice straight taper like **Figure 7-24A**. **Figure 24B** shows the cut cleaned down to

the **hull side.** Now the next layer on the **hull side** will fit under the **hull bottom. Figures 7-24C** and **7-24D** jump ahead in time to show how the hull side actually does fit under the hull bottom. Those of you familiar with lapstrake construction will recognize the similarity to cutting a gain.

Once I finished the other side of the bow, I

turned my attention to prepping the hull for the next lamination. As I was trimming the **hull bottom** flush with the side of the hull, I came across a void or two (**Figure 7-25**. The backward 5 is the way the CNC numbered the plank and is a result of flipping the plate for the scarf). This small gap was the result of not putting a screw where one was indicated on the grid. In the rush to get the lamination down it was overlooked. You may find similar gaps. If you do, just put some peanut butter thick epoxy in a baggie, squirt it into the gap, and that will solve the little issue of gaps. Of course you will be more careful than I was and you won't have

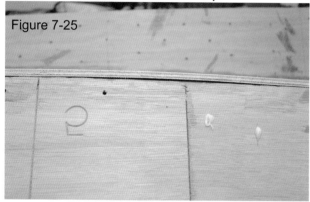

Figure 7-25

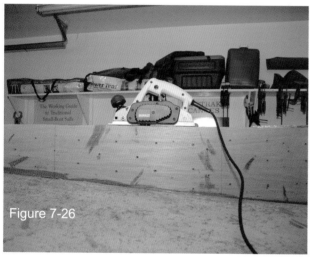

Figure 7-26

Figure 7-27

any gaps. And, unlike the CNC, you will number the station with the 5 turned the correct way.

Once I got the small gap filled, I planed down the **keel sides** flush with the **keel bottom** (**Figure 7-26**). The power planer will make very quick work of this but it throws dust everywhere. This is not a job you want to do if there is wet epoxy anywhere on the boat. In **Figure 7-27** the **keel sides** have been trimmed and I just need to pop the epoxy mushrooms off and fill the bottom/ keel joint with some peanut butter epoxy (**Figure 7-28**). If this joint is a very snug fit then this step will be unnecessary. I found a few areas that were not a perfect fit so I filled them with thickened epoxy. I

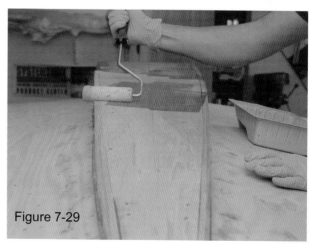

Figure 7-28

Figure 7-29

did make sure to clean up any excess epoxy that might interfere with the next lamination.

When all the clean-up was completed I laminated the **keel bottom** on the boat. In **Figure 7-29** the hull is coated and then I coated the next layer with un-thickened epoxy (never forget to coat with unthickened epoxy first). Next a thin

Figure 7-30

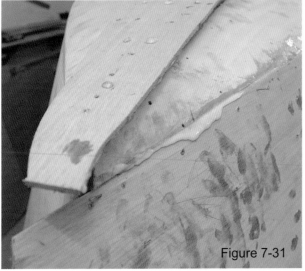

Figure 7-31

layer of peanut butter epoxy was spread out and the layer screwed down (**Figure 7-30**).

As you can see I was fairly generous with the overhang—a little too generous. I think you'll be better served by trimming more carefully. I should have put on each section of the **keel bottom**, marked it, and then cut just proud of the line leaving only ½ to ¾-inch of overhang. A dry fit would have saved me time and energy with the trim work.

I did trim the overhang with a laminate trimmer and a flush trim bit but the power planer will make fast work of the job as well. And with the **keel bottom** trimmed, another layer was lami-

nated on the **keel side,** which was trimmed flushed and then one more layer laminated on the **keel bottom**. Take your time with these steps and get a nice snug fit at the joints. I did tend to get too generous with the keel bottom overhangs. Both on the first layer and with second layer as well. Just remember to dry fit and leave no more than ¾-inch overhang.

Also, a dry fit when you start planking the **hull side** will be very important. The plywood must fit **under** the section of the **hull bottom** that you cut at the bow (**Figure 7-31**). I started with a short section, did my dry fit, and epoxied it in place and then worked my way back toward the transom (**Figures 7-32, 7-33** and **7-34**).

Figure 7-32

Figure 7-33

Figure 7-34

I used smaller pieces for these sections too. Large sections of drop work really well here. Most of what I used was about 48 inch by 48 inch. I found these very fast and easy to handle by myself. Sections that go up fast and easy will be important if you are working with a short pot life on the epoxy.

When I started the first section there was a great deal of overhang at the bow (**Figure 7-35**) and this had to be trimmed in order to laminate the other side of the hull. The Japanese saw works great for this kind of job—just make several cuts in (**Figure 7-36**) and then a cut down.

Figure 7-37

Figure 7-35

Figure 7-38

Figure 7-36

Figure 7-39

With the overhang trimmed out of the way I did the other side, starting at the bow again (**Figure 7-37**) and working my way back to the transom. Small sections were used on this side also and I made sure to overlap the scarf by at least 12 inches.

The gap right at the bow in **Figure 7-37** is less than 1/8-inch but I probably should have done a bit of hand fitting to get a tighter fit. This is always a dilemma for the builder. How much of a gap do you allow, if any. Generally, if the gap is less than an 1/8-inch I'll let it go but more than an 1/8 and I'll do some hand fitting. How much time do you spend hand fitting? Not too little and not too much but just the right amount. . . . The Goldilocks Principle once again.

In **Figure 7-38** both sides have been laminated in place and I've started trimming the side flush with the bottom. First with the power planer (**Figure 7-39**) and then I used an 8-inch jack plane to bring the side down flush with the bottom (**Figure 7-40A**).

Figure 7-40B shows the right side cleaned up and the bow section from station 2 forward sanded fair and on the left side the section from station #2 to the bow needs to be sanded. The goal, of course, is to have the two sides match.

Figure 7-40A

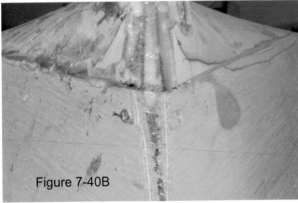
Figure 7-40B

Figure 7-41

Figure 7-41 shows the side trimmed so the surface of the bottom is carried to the outside edge of the hull. In this section of the hull it's easy to trim too much off the side, which will round it

over slightly and create a low spot. So care should be taken with the trimming process because you want the next **hull bottom** lamination to lay directly on the edge of the side. This staggers the seam and helps create that "bomb-proof" hull seam we want.

When you are satisfied that everything is properly trimmed and sanded it's time to put on the last **hull bottom** layer. You will want to make sure that this layer or plank/plate has a good fit against the side of the keel. I did several dry fits; marking and trimming until I was satisfied with the joint (**Figure 7-42**).

Figure 7-42

Figure 7-43

Then I coated the hull and the next lamination with unthickened epoxy and put down a heavy bead of peanut butter thick epoxy (**Figure 7-43**). The bead of epoxy just adds a bit more strength and helps seal that joint. But be sure to stop the bead where the section ends. It will create a problem if the bead hardens before you get the next section down.

I started with the bow section and you can see

that the bead of epoxy doesn't extend beyond the end (**Figure 7-44**). I made sure to clean up any squeeze out at the bottom/keel joint (**Figure 7-45**) and then put down the aft section. In **Figure 7-46** you can see the amount of overhang I had, but again, I think I was too generous.

Figure 7-47A

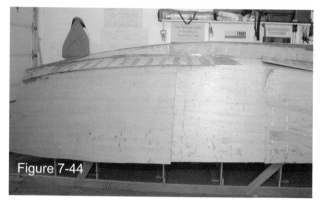

Figure 7-44

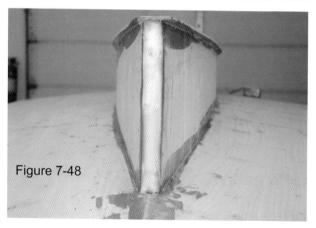

Figure 7-47B

Figure 7-45

Figure 7-48

Figure 7-49

Figure 7-46

Also **Figures 7-47A** and **7-47B** show the amount of overlap I used on the side and bottom joint or chine. Use **Figure 7-40B** to compare how far down the **hull bottom** overlaps the underlying chine. I had the bottom overlap the chine by about 1½ inches but slightly less will work just fine. The idea is to cover that joint with a layer of plywood as well as all the tape and cloth that will be added later.

Once the last **hull bottom** layer is epoxied in place you can start the final clean-up. I added thickened epoxy to the back of the keel and trimmed the bottom and sides flush with the transom (**Figures 7-48 and 7-49**). Now will be a good time to take a baggie of peanut butter epoxy and fill any small gaps you can find.

Now is also a good time to step back and assess what you have accomplished. The hull is at its final thickness. No more wood will be laminated on the boat. It is completely planked, in and in spite of a great many rough edges, it is watertight and a far cry from the flimsy shell you wired together not too long ago.

Even the sound of tapping the hull is different. It's solid, very solid and the order you laminated everything together has a great deal to do with that. **Figure 7-50** gives a quick look at the planking order and shows how the staggered planking makes for an exceptionally strong joint.

Figure 7-50

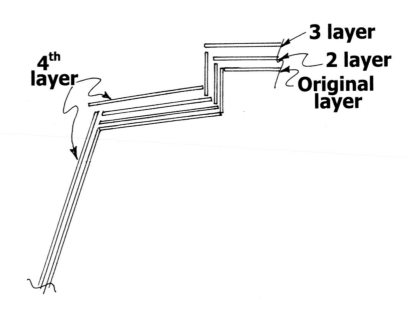

8

Fairing the Hull and Some Boat Rhinoplasty

After an appropriate amount of time spent in self-congratulation and a couple of carbonated beverages of your choice, it will be time to start fairing the hull and cleaning up the bow area. I came to think of working on the bow section as giving the boat a nose job because I was doing what any good plastic surgeon does to an otherwise beautiful woman—giving her nose a lovely shape.

Actually there was more behind what I did than cosmetics. I could have just carried the chine line forward and kept a sharp line from the entry at the bow to the stern, and a good many boats have been built just like that. But a fairly large number of designers and builders, me included, feel that a chine that is very soft or nonexistent at the bow and gradually sharpens about mid-ship will improve performance.

The first step toward that end is to get rid of all the mushrooms and sand the hull smooth. Your cheap chisel and some 80 grit sandpaper will make fast work of that job. I like to vacuum the hull once all the sanding is done. This helps keep airborne dust down, and we all know that airborne dust is a health hazard.

Vacuuming the hull is important because the next job will stir up any dust left in the hull. As it sits, all the laminations are held in place only by epoxy and you will want to mechanically fasten those laminations together as well. On the **hull bottom** and **keel bottom** I used ¾-inch bronze boat nails (**Figure 8-1**). Here the hull was thick enough that the nails didn't break through. In **Figure 8-1** the epoxy filled breather holes are visible and I used these to set the boat nails in a grid around them. Generally I set a boat nail between the two epoxied-filled holes and just applied the

Figure 8-1

"Goldilocks Principle" for the number of nails set.

The same system was used on the **hull side**, but the fasteners were #6 X 5/8 stainless steel screws with the head run down just below the plywood surface. The ¾-inch long boat nails would have broken through the ½-inch thick **hull side**. I did use fewer screws than boat nails just because the screws took longer and weren't as much fun to put in as the boat nails.

It was fun putting in the boat nails but honestly, I had more fun with the boat's rhinoplasty. Taking a sharp plane and an orbital sander (I used a 6-inch sander here because it cuts much faster than the 5-inch) and shaping the chine and bow was very satisfying work.

I found it best to start at station 3 and work back to the stern. In this section of the boat the shape shown by the stick gauge in **Figure 8-2** is carried from #3 to the transom. **Figure 8-3** shows the chine from the other side of the stick gauge and gives you a better idea of how much to cut

Figure 8-2

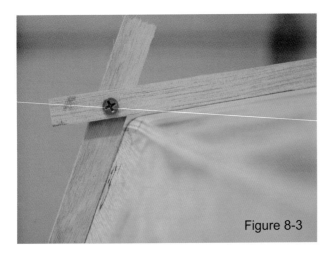

Figure 8-3

Figure 8-4

off. That's a #6 bronze screw in the photo.

What I was going for, and what you should as well, is a slight rounding over of the chine. Fiberglass cloth **does not** like a sharp edge and that was the purpose; just a slight radius to the chine. Does it have to match the radius in **Figure 8-2** exactly? No, it just has to get rid of the sharp edge on the chine. However, better to be slightly too round than too sharp, but you know, the "Goldilocks Principle."

Once the aft part of the chine was done I turned my attention to the forward section. **Figure 8-4** shows the amount of round-over at station 2. Use your eye and your fingers to ensure a gradual increase from station 3 to station 2. You can feel small humps or hollows with your fingers that you can't see with your eye. Take your time

and enjoy the process.

A close look at **Figure 8-4** would suggest that I've taken the chine down slightly more than ¼-inch at station 2. This is just a rough guess. Remember this was done completely by eye rather than with a measuring tape. Here is something to guide you in this process- **It is much easier to take a little more off than try to put it back on.** Go slowly.

I think you'll find that the sander with 80 grit paper moves at about the right pace. The stick gauge (shown in the photos) will help keep you from removing too much of the chine and keep the transition between stations smooth. Remember you are cutting most of the material from the bottom, which is quite thick.

The closer you get to the bow the more severe the transition will become. In **Figure 8-5** (taken at station 1) I have cut the chine down by about half an inch. **Figures 8-6** and **8-7** indicate the chine line has almost disappeared. Those lines at ¼ and ½ stations will help your eye judge how much to grind away. This does get somewhat tricky right at the bow because it is possible to grind away too much material. So let me remind you again to go slowly here.

You might find that lines every 6 inches will

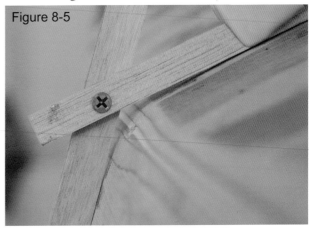

Figure 8-5

give a better picture of how to fair this area because the stick gauge won't be much use from #1 to the bow. Also, in **Figures 8-6** and **8-7** you can see how much I overlapped the original chine with the last layer of plywood.

Once I was satisfied with the right hand side of

Figure 8-6

Figure 8-7

Figure 8-8

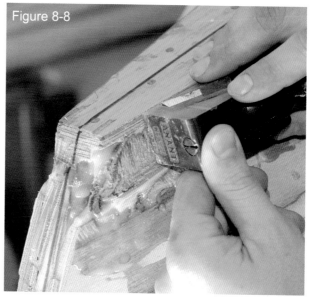

Figure 8-9

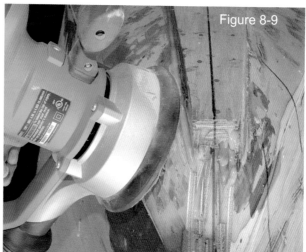

Figure 8-10

the boat (**Figure 8-7** once again), I cleaned up the **keel side** right at the bow (**Figure 8-8**) and started to fair the other side. 80 grit sand paper and the 6-inch orbital sander made fast work fairing the left side to match the right side (**Figure 8-9**). You'll want to put matching lines on the left side as you work. This will be a big help in getting both sides identical. Measure from station #1 to get the ½ section and ¼ section and put a line every 6 inches if that helps. I started with a set of lines, sanded and then re-drew the lines on the left side, checked my work and sanded more. I redrew the left lines each time until the lines matched (**Figure 8-10**).

Then I rounded and faired the rest of the bow. I started with the area where the keel and bow join (**Figure 8-11**) and then finished out the rest of the bow (**Figure 8-12**).

With the boat's rhinoplasty complete I rounded the edges on the aft part of the hull and the keel (**Figures 8-13** and **8-14**).

It will be a good idea to go over the hull and fill any and all holes and gaps that might have appeared as you sanded everything round. I used silica thickener and epoxy for any large gaps, like the areas at the very bow and the aft end of the keel. For small holes and gaps I used System Three's Quickfair. I like Quickfair because it dries fast and sands like the wood.

Take your time with this because you are really prepping the boat for the fiber glass tape and cloth. When all the holes and gaps are filled, re-sand the boat and vacuum the hull.

Figure 8-12

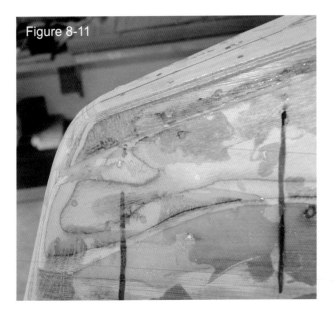

Figure 8-11

Figure 8-13

Figure 8-14

9

Taping and Glassing the Hull

After I had filled all the holes, both large and small, I gave the hull a very close onceover to be sure I hadn't overlooked any small holes or gaps that would create an air space behind the tape and cloth (**Figure 9-1**). Then I stepped to the bow and double checked everything was centered and true (**Figure 9-2**). If I had overlooked something off-center in the bow, now was the time to find it. It's always much simpler to fix a small problem before you really lock everything in place with tape and cloth.

Figure 9-1

Figure 9-2

I put the tape and cloth on in a specific order (**Figure 9-3**) but I don't think it matters too much. There will be much less sanding if you put the tape on first and then put on the cloth, because the cloth helps hide the edges of the tape. Also, I found that doing the hull in sections made the process doable with just one person. It will be easier with another pair of hands but the job is very manageable with only one person. I think what really matters are the number of layers and not so much the order the layers go on the boat.

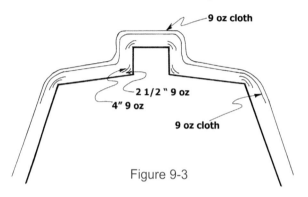

9 oz cloth

2 1/2 " 9 oz

4" 9 oz

9 oz cloth

Figure 9-3

I started with the **hull bottom** and **keel side** joint (**Figure 9-4A**). I coated the area with un-thickened epoxy then, using a filled baggie, I laid down a heavy bead of peanut butter thick epoxy (**Figure 9-4B**). I think you'll get a much better fillet if you take a fillet tool and smooth out the epoxy before you put down the tape. It's just less work to get a nice smooth fillet.

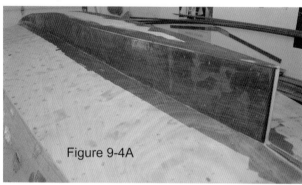
Figure 9-4A

Figure 9-4B

Figure 9-4C

Next 3-inch-wide, 9-ounce tape was put down (**Figure 9-4C**) and then wetted out with un-thickened epoxy (**Figure 9-4D**). I use scrap plywood for a fillet tool. A rough 90 degree section with the corner cut off enough to produce a heavy smooth fillet. I think you'll find a disposable brush is best for wetting out the tape.

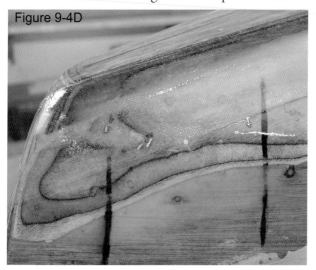

Figure 9-4D

Figure 9-4E

Note that in **Figure 9-4D**, the top edge of the tape is flush with the top of the **keel bottom** and wraps around the bow (**Figure 9-4E**). At the aft

Figure 9-4F

end of the keel you can cut the tape right before the round (**Figure 9-F**) or try to wrap it around the end section.

Next, **Figures 9-5 A, B,** and **C** show tape on the **keel bottom** and **keel side**. Notice that the tape overlaps about station #3. **Figure 9-6** shows how the tape was wrapped around the bow section. After I wet out the tape, I pulled it tight and smooth to eliminate wrinkles and air trapped under the tape. The smoother you can get the tape to lie, the less sanding you'll have to do so make sure to work out all the wrinkles and bubbles.

Figure 9-5A

Figure 9-5B

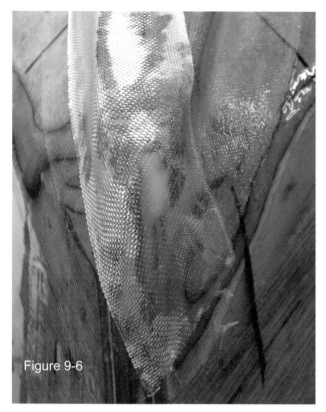

Figure 9-6

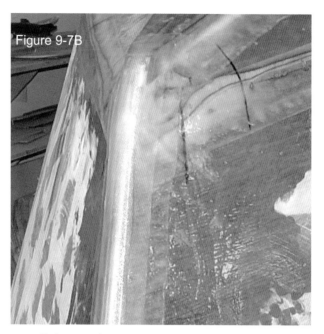

Figure 9-7B

When I taped the **hull side/hull bottom**, I stopped the tape right at the bow and didn't do a wrap. That would have created a lumpy area and there was more tape to go. I just kept the chine centered on the tape and wet it all out.

Once I was satisfied that I had all the wrinkles worked out, I added tape to the bow. I put on three layers of 4-inch 9 ounce tape. The first layer was centered and the following layers were offset by about an inch (**Figures 9-7A** and **9-7B**). If you look closely at **Figure 9-7B** you can see that the bow tape starts about 3 or 4 inches back on the **keel bottom**.

All the overlapping and wrapped tape gave that area of the bow about 8 layers of tape at this point so when I added the next layer of 4-inch tape on the **keel bottom/keel side**, **hull bottom/keel side**, and **hull bottom/ hull side** I stopped the tape short of wrapping around. Again, I didn't want to create a lumpy area and the there was glass cloth yet to come.

I let the epoxy harden and then sanded the tape with 80 grit sand paper. At this point you want to grind down the rough edges of the tape and any lumps and bumpy areas. The tape should look like **Figure 9-7C**. There maybe a few areas where you cut through the top layer of tape, but that's not a problem because there is more going over the top of the tape.

Figure 9-7A

Figure 9-7C

Figure 9-8A shows the boat ready for the first layer of 9 ounce fiberglass cloth. The blue line in the photo is masking tape that marks where I wanted the first layer of cloth to stop.

Figure 9-8A

Figure 9-8B

I felt the hull needed two layers of 9 ounce cloth on the bottom and just one layer on the hull sides. Stopping the first layer at the tape puts the extra cloth and weight where I want it—on the bottom. Having 18 ounces (two layers) of cloth on the hull sides is not necessary and would put extra weight up high where I don't want it.

I've found that weight adds up fast a few pounds at a time. Remember this as you build. Builders have a tendency to overbuild by adding a little here and a little there, but let me remind you that this boat is already overbuilt. So stop the first layer of cloth about 4 inches above the chine. Higher than that is a waste of cloth and money.

Because the fiberglass cloth comes 50 inches at the widest, you will have to lay the cloth on athwart ship. In **Figure 9-8B** and **9-8C** I've cut a dart in the cloth to accommodate the keel and laid a scrap piece over the dart on the bottom. I let the extra at the end of the keel just run wild and trimmed it after the epoxy had hardened. Notice I let the extra at the transom just run wild as well. You'll want to smooth out most if not all the wrinkles in the cloth at this point. I never worry about getting all the wrinkles until later, because as you work a wrinkle or two will get bumped in.

When I had smoothed the cloth down I moved to the bow and draped a section of cloth so I had about 12 to 16 inches of overhang (**Figure 9-8D**). Also, **Figures 9-8 D, E, F,** and **G** show how I cut a dart in the cloth and wrapped the bow. You could just trim it like the aft end of the

Figure 9-8C

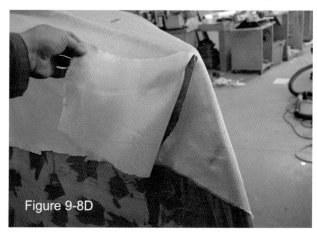
Figure 9-8D

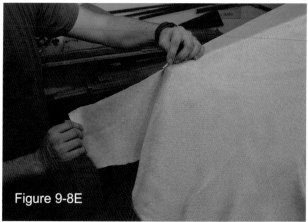
Figure 9-8E

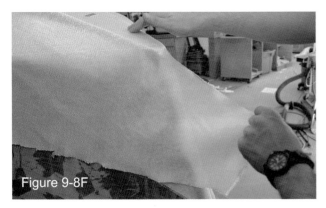
Figure 9-8F

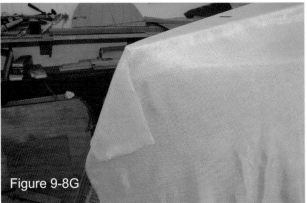
Figure 9-8G

Figure 9-8H

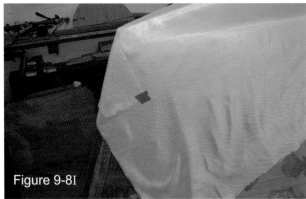
Figure 9-8I

Figure 9-8J

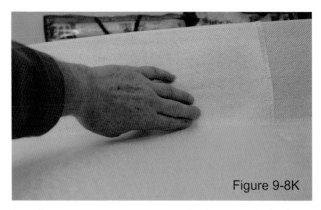
Figure 9-8K

keel but wrapping the extra cloth around the bow just adds strength where you want it. Again, smooth out most of the wrinkles before you drape the next section of cloth.

Then I moved aft to the first section of cloth I put down and overlapped the forward edge by about 1 inch (**Figure 9-8H**). Just make sure the cloth under the overlapping layer is very smooth.

After this layer is in place it will be time to smooth out **all** the wrinkles. Your hand works well for this (**Figure 9-8I**) but a wallpaper brush or 4 or 5-inch paint brush will be better. As you work, tape down the edges of the cloth (**Figure 9-8J**) and tape the wrap at the bow (**Figure 9-8K**). Note that the tape at the bow and the other tape are all below the line of blue tape.

Taping the edges down will be very important, particularly if you are working outside. It just takes a very gentle breeze to undo all your hard work smoothing everything out. I have learned this the hard way and I also learned if the cloth under the overlap is wrinkle free the job is much easier and better.

With all the cloth wrinkle free above the blue tape, I put on the last section of cloth. Another look at **Figure 9-8H** shows a small section about 16 inches wide without cloth. I could have cut a strip about 20 inches by 50 inches and laid that down but I decided to center a 50-inch-wide strip and have about 16 inches of overlap on the forward side and the aft side (**Figure 9-9**). When this layer is wrinkle free you're ready to wet out the cloth.

Wetting out the cloth with un-thickened epoxy isn't difficult but it does require some coordination.

61

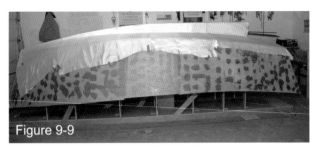
Figure 9-9

Someone to mix the epoxy will be helpful but this can certainly be done without another pair of hands. If it's warm or worse yet, very warm (mid to high 80s) the process will need to be a very co-ordinated ballet.

When I have to do the ballet, and it can look like a strange ballet, I do several dry runs. I figure how long it will take me to me a batch of epoxy (un-thickened of course) and about how long to get that batch spread out. **Remember the bigger the batch the shorter the pot life tends to be**, so really big batches can be counterproductive.

I found that about 15 ounces of resin (plus the appropriate amount of hardener) well mixed (a minimum of 90 seconds) and poured in a paint tray works best. The paint tray helps stretch the pot life because the epoxy spreads out and that helps dissipate the heat. That's the key, keeping the heat from building up. As the epoxy cures, it generates heat and the more heat the faster it cures, which generates heat, which speeds up cur-ing, which . . . you get the picture. I've had epoxy boil and melt the plastic cups holding it. If the re-action is violent enough it can burst into flame. I have never had that happen but I've had the epoxy get so hot it burned my hand. So give some thought to batch size and ambient temperature

What do I do if it's very warm and I can't find a helper? I'll start right at first light when I have just enough light to work and I'll only wet out half the boat (right half or the left half) at a time. You can work at night but the lights always draw bugs and with the wet epoxy. . . . Well, it's not a pretty picture.

One thing you **DO NOT** want is direct sun on the boat as you work or while the epoxy is cur-ing. The heat of the direct sun will cause **out-gassing**, which is the air trapped beneath the cloth and epoxy expanding. As it expands it creates bubbles and like lots of bugs stuck in the epoxy it's not pretty either.

Besides outgassing another potential problem is mixing errors. I am always concerned about mixing errors because epoxy that won't cure is a serious issue. Dry runs and a great deal of thought will help eliminate mixing problems. In the rush to get the epoxy on the boat mistakes can happen, so find a good system for measuring the epoxy and stick to it religiously. You will not be sorry you did but you can be very sorry that you didn't.

At some point you'll be finished with dry runs, trial mixing, and trying to find potential problems so take a deep breath and pour the first batch of epoxy in the paint tray. I like to use foam rollers to spread the epoxy (**Figure 9-10**). They seem to wet out the cloth about as fast as any method I've used.

Figure 9-10

I started on the side of the keel and then worked my way out from there. As I wet the cloth on the bottom, the roller had a tendency to pull the cloth away from the side of the keel and cre-ate bubbles (**Figure 9-11**). After the bottom is wet, use the roller to push the cloth back in con-tact with the keel (**Figure 9-12**).

Figure 9-11

Figure 9-12

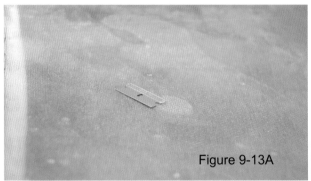
Figure 9-13A

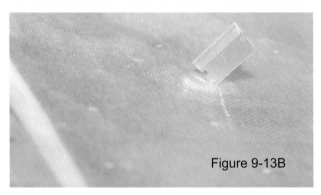
Figure 9-13B

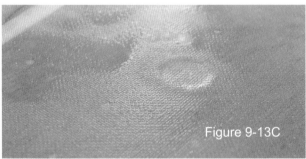
Figure 9-13C

If the epoxy is starting to get tacky it will be easier to push out the bubbles. It's not a big problem if the epoxy dries with those bubbles there, but you should be able to push them out. I found a small bubble caused by outgassing and a small pinhole (**Figure 9-13A**). I used a razor blade to

cut the cloth and then pushed it down into the tacky epoxy (**Figure 9-13B**). You can use this technique to fix the keel bubbles like **Figure 9-13A** as well.

As epoxy cures it goes from wet, to tacky, to "green," and to fully cured. This can be a matter of hours or overnight depending on the temperature. "Green" epoxy hasn't fully cured but has lost any tacky feel. At this stage the cloth is easily cut and peeled away from the hull; which is what I have done in **Figure 9-14A**.

Next, pull the blue tape (**Figure 9-14B** and **C**) and trim the extra cloth. In **Figure 9-15** notice that I left the wild cloth dry because it's easier to

Figure 9-14A

Figure 9-14B

Figure 9-14C

Figure 9-15

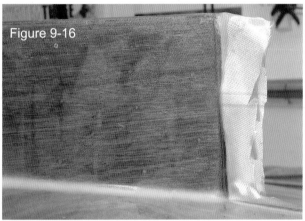

Figure 9-16

Figure 9-17

trim and less messy. A sharp single-edge razor blade or mat knife will do a great job in trimming all the extra cloth (**Figure 9-16**). **Figure 9-17** shows the boat ready for the next layer of 9 ounce cloth.

I changed the way I put the next layer of cloth on the boat. Instead of laying the cloth athwart ship I decided to do the **keel section** and then **hull bottom** and **side**. By eliminating the **keel section**, the 50-inch wide cloth covered the **hull bottom** and **hull side** running fore and aft.

The temperature was starting to get warmer and I felt this divided the hull into more manageable sections. Actually, if you find yourself facing ever-warmer temperatures there no reason you couldn't put the first layer of cloth on like this.

First I cut two strips about 22 inches wide (**Figures 9-18A** and **B**), draped them over the keel section with about an inch overlap and trimmed it right above the **hull bottom** and **keel side** joint (**Figure 9-18C**). I taped the sections down and smoothed them out (**Figures 9-18D** and **E**) so they were ready to wet out.

Figure 9-18A

Figure 9-18B

Figure 9-18C

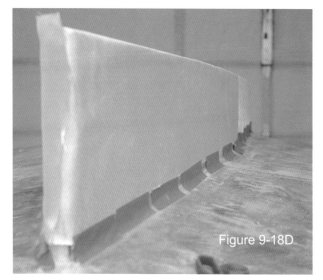

Figure 9-18D

Figure 9-18E

Figure 9-19

Figure 9-20

If I had it to do over I think I would have first put blue tape on the **hull bottom** about 4 inches out from the **keel side** and then draped the cloth so it overlapped the blue tape. Basically, just like I did with the first layer of cloth on the bottom. That way I could have trimmed to the blue tape and then lapped the cloth on the **hull bottom** up **keel side** giving me some extra cloth on that joint.

Wetting out the cloth on the keel didn't take long at all, which was what I wanted, and when the epoxy cured I draped the **hull bottom** and **hull side** (**Figure 9-19**) and wet that out (**Figure 9-20**).

When both sides of the boat were done I trimmed the excess cloth (**Figure 9-21**) and put two layers of tape down to cover the seam between the cloth on the **keel side** and **hull bottom**.

At this point all the cloth and tape was on the boat and the prep work for filling the weave in the cloth started. This involved sanding the edges of the tape down plus any rough areas that can be found. You can see the tape edges and epoxy runs in **Figure 9-22**.

In **Figure 9-23A** the bottom has been sanded and is ready for you to start filling the weave with

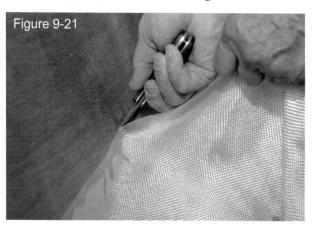

Figure 9-21

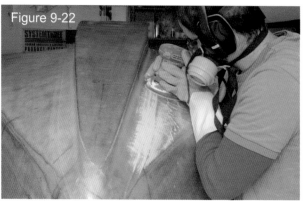

Figure 9-22

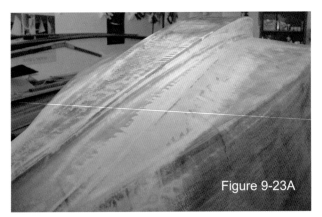

Figure 9-23A

Figure 9-24A

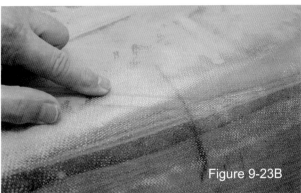

Figure 9-23B

Figure 9-24B

epoxy. The goal with this sanding is just cleaning up edges and rough spots and not to sand into the cloth. The area at the end of my finger in **Figure 9-23B** shows a spot where the cloth has been sanded away. A small area like this doesn't matter, but sanding the entire bottom like this would diminish the strength of the cloth. You want to fill the weave not sand it smooth.

I like to use graphite mixed into epoxy to fill the weave on the bottom or any high abrasion area. I tend to mix more graphite than some builders use and I'll add graphite until I get a heavy cream consistency. **Figure 9-24A** gives an idea about how thick I mix the epoxy. Notice the drip in the lower right hand corner. With epoxy this thick, care has to exercised when coating vertical surfaces like the **keel sides**. If you add too much too quickly it will sag and sags are no fun to sand off. The finished bottom should look like **Figure 9-24B**.

Do you have to add graphite to the epoxy? No but many builders think the added graphite increases the abrasion resistance of the epoxy. My experience is that it certainly seems to but I have

Figure 9-25

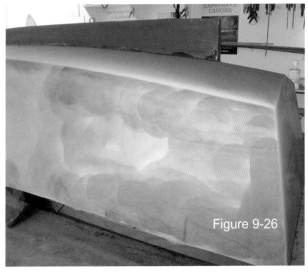

Figure 9-26

Figure 9-27

never seen any tests to verify this. So consider my opinion as anecdotal evidence only.

I coated the bottom and then coated the **hull sides** with straight epoxy. It will take at least two coats of epoxy on the **hull sides** to fill the weave. Watch for runs and sags as you go because those are hard to sand off. And sanding everything smooth is what you will do (**Figure 9-25** and **9-26**). Finish with at least 180 grit paper and 220 wouldn't be unreasonable.

A small caveat if you add graphite to the epoxy. You will need to have a very good dust collection system on the sander because the dust will get onto and into everything and it is hard to get off once it's there. Actually you'll need a good dust collections system even if you don't add graphite because epoxy dust is just as invasive.

In fact you may want to clean out your shop after you finish all the sanding and before you move to the next step. A good cleaning, and by good cleaning I mean vacuuming everything in the shop, not just the floor, will keep all that dust from winding up on your freshly primed hull, which is the next step. I have two air scrubbers that I run whenever I sand and I still had dust everywhere.

There's nothing fancy about priming the hull. You just roll it out with a foam roller (**Figure 9-27**). I added several coats of primer, sanded that smooth (**Figure 9-28**), and then enjoyed an imaginary voyage in the boat I just finished priming.

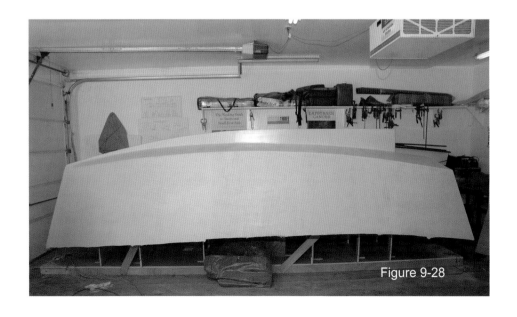

Figure 9-28

10

Centerboards from Start to Finish

When I returned from my imaginary voyage in the primed hull, I discovered that the white primer had highlighted some unfair areas on the bottom and on the sides. I was expecting this discovery and you should as well. It would have been unrealistic to assume the hull was perfectly fair at this point. And really, that was the main purpose of this first coat of primer; to highlight areas that need work.

So that's what I did. I highlighted the areas with a lead pencil (Don't use a marker or ball point because that will bleed through the paint). It took me a couple of hours of looking at the hull from different angles and with the light at different angles. That way I could go back and find those spots that needed work when I had a few minutes of down time. I knew there were going to be some spare moments with the next step.

The next step was installing the centerboard cases, but there was a great deal that preceded installing. So let's go back to the start and work our way forward.

First of all, both these boats use tandem centerboards and when you tell people your boat has not one but two centerboards they will look surprised and ask you why. Tandem boards, either fore and aft or side by side, are unusual. There is a reason tandem boards are not the norm. Like everything else in boatbuilding, tandem boards have advantages as well as disadvantages and until recently the bad outweighed the good. Let's start with the disadvantages.

Up to the inclusion of epoxy in boatbuilding, a centerboard case could be a leaking hole in the bottom of your boat. They could be made watertight at first but sooner or later most would start to leak. When the leak became bad enough you had to either haul out and fix it or get rid of the boat, leaving someone else to deal with it.

Given that scenario it's easy to see why people were very reluctant to put yet another hole in the bottom of their boat. Of course, there was the added negative that it was twice as much work putting in that extra hole that was going to leak.

But in spite of those negative points some designers did draw and build boats with tandem boards. Spaulding Dunbar was one of those designer/naval architects who did a few boats with two boards and I studied his work very closely. What I found convinced me that tandem boards did have worthwhile advantages.

Probably the biggest advantage is the ability to fine tune the helm of the boat. More specifically, by raising and lowering the two boards it is possible to move the center of lateral resistance of the hull in relation to the center of effort of the sails. This was the main reason I chose tandem boards.

Another reason was that tandem boards allow the cases to be located where they were less intrusive. In a small boat, it is hard to find something more intrusive than the centerboard case right in the middle of everything.

And finally, two boards tend to give boats better windward ability in shallow water. They work more effectively than one deep board that has been drawn up into the case. And of course, the Sea Eagles are designed as beach cruisers.

With both boards down, the Sea Eagle 16.5 has almost 3 square feet of centerboard and draws only 28 inches. It would be difficult to have a single board with 3 square feet of surface under water and still draw 28 inches. *It's important to note that both boats have a long shallow keel and the boards are meant to supplement the keel and not be the sole source of lateral resistance.*

These are all good points. But when put on a balance with the big leaking hole, the scale always tipped in a dramatic fashion until epoxy took the leaking hole out of the equation. With the big leaking hole off the balance, the scale tips in the other direction, in my opinion, and that's why these boats have tandem boards.

So that takes care of the WHY part of tandem boards; now let's look at HOW I put tandem boards in the Sea Eagle 16.5.

The forward centerboard case fits between **fixed** bulkheads so the first thing that must be done is get the **exact** measurements between bulkheads # 2 and #3. This means crawling under the boat and making a series of very careful measurements with an expanding tick stick or story stick. **Figure 10-1** shows a very simple shop-made expanding tick stick/story stick and a story stick made with Veritas Bar Gauge heads. If you use the simple tick stick (there is absolutely nothing wrong with the simple one) be sure to use spring clamps that are very strong. You do not want **any** movement after you have expanded the story stick to get the measurement.

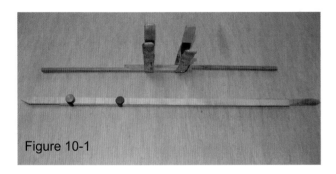

Figure 10-1

I started at the bottom of the boat and worked towards the sheer (good lighting under the hull will help insure accuracy). I centered the story sticks on each bulkhead centerline, locked the two sticks together, carefully removed the story stick, and then used a 48-inch ruler to get the dimension. I recorded the distance to a 1/16 or if it was slightly more, a 1/16+, for extreme accuracy.

I took a measurement about every 6 inches and that gave me an excellent picture of the space between the two bulkheads. I did find the space at the bottom of the boat was slightly smaller than the space at the sheer. I didn't expect to find the distance **exactly** equal from top to bottom and you should probably expect the same.

Once you have all the measurements done and carefully recorded go back and **re-check** everything. Take your time and be very meticulous. Remember the old adage, "Measure once cut twice.

Measure twice cut once." I promise the last thing you want to find is a very complex centerboard case that doesn't fit.

Then, using my meticulously taken measurements, I determined the inside dimension of the centerboard case. **Figure 10-2** gives the construction layup of the case. Notice I used a 4mm plywood plate over the ends of the case. I felt this was important to help completely seal and strengthen the case.

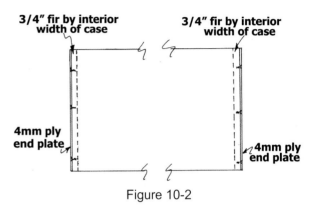

Figure 10-2

That meant I determined the inside length of the CB case by subtracting 8mm (4mm each end), 1½ inches (¾-inch spacer at each end), 8mm (4mm at each end on the inside of the case), and ¼-inch (1/8 play at each end) from the distance between #2 and #3 bulkheads (**30 inches in my case**). I left 1/8-inch play at each end and I was glad that I did. Plywood is never exactly 4mm or 6mm just like a 1X4 isn't exactly a 1X4. It is always slightly less. So, measure the material carefully. It only takes two 1/32 errors in measurement to add 1/16 to a fitting, and that 1/16 could be the difference between being happy and very sad.

Now that I had an accurate **interior** dimension for the forward centerboard case I turned my attention to making the cardboard mock up of the centerboard itself. You will use **Figure 10-3A and B** to make your mock up. If you make it slightly oversize you can cut it down until you get the fit you want. Then you can make the plywood mock up.

In **Figure 10-4A** stations #2 and #3 and a baseline have been lofted on a piece of scrap plywood. Notice that the bottom of the boat **is not** the

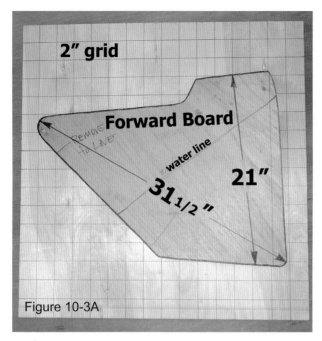

Figure 10-3A

2" grid

Forward Board

water line

31 1/2 "

21"

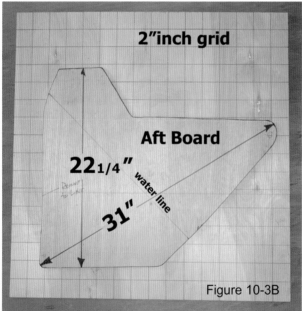

2"inch grid

Aft Board

22 1/4 "

31"

water line

Figure 10-3B

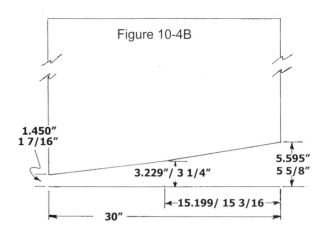

Figure 10-4B

1.450"
1 7/16"

3.229"/ 3 1/4"

5.595"
5 5/8"

←15.199/ 15 3/16→

30"

same as the baseline. The keel is curved here unlike the keel at the aft centerboard case, which is flat. **Figure 10-4B** gives you the dimensions for lofting the bottom and **Figures 10-4C** and **D** are photos of how I lofted the curve of the keel. The numbers in **C** and **D** are decimals to 1/64-inch and were taken from the program I used to design the sea Hawks. I rounded those numbers up or down 1/32-inch to get the dimensions in **Figure 10-4B**. The keel in your boat may vary slightly from the original Sea Eagle 16.5 but as long as stations #2 and #3 are very close to 30 inches apart the difference will not matter.

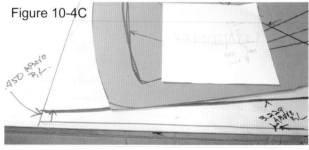

Figure 10-4C

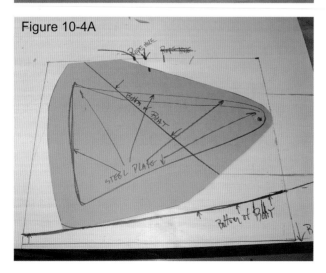

Figure 10-4A

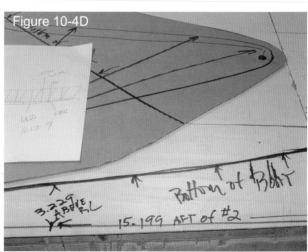

Figure 10-4D

70

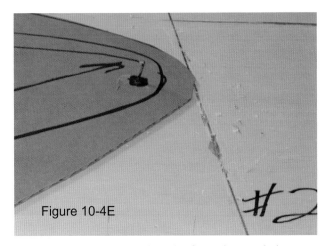

Figure 10-4E

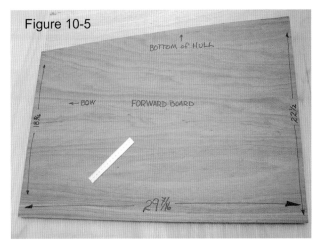

Figure 10-5

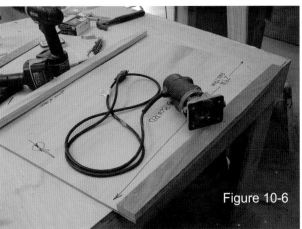

Figure 10-6

Figure 10-4E is a detail of **10-4D** and shows a nail at the point of the centerboard pin. It may take you a bit to find the exact spot for the pin so use a finish nail temporarily. Here's where some hand fitting will be required but take your time and make sure the cardboard centerboard is a good fit. When you have that established, you can make a plywood version from the cardboard pattern. I used 6mm plywood scrap but something lighter will work.

Once the plywood pattern is completed check the fit on the mock up one last time and then start on the case itself. This can appear a bit intimidating but it's really simple as long as you check your numbers carefully.

Take the overall dimension between #2 and #3 (**remember my distance was 30 inches**) and deduct 8mm (the combined thickness of the end-plates—**be sure to measure the exact thickness of these**) plus ¼-inch (1/8-inch play at each end) and that will give you the **outside or exterior** length of your centerboard case. Now cut two rectangles 24 inches high by (insert your length dimension here), and temporarily screw them together.

In my case I screwed two 24-inch by 29 7/16-inch rectangles together and marked the outsides with bow and bottom. Next I lofted the curve of the keel (just like I did on the mock up), struck a line and made my cut with a saber saw (**Figure 10**-5).

At this point I took both of the sides, crawled back under the boat and made very sure that they

fit between the bulkheads 2 and 3. **You do exactly the same thing**. Because, in spite of all my careful measuring I still had to cut an extra 3/16-inch off the boards so my final size was 29¼ inches long by 24 inches high.

Satisfied that the sides of the case would fit between the two bulkheads, I added the framework to the outside of both. I found it easier to put the bottom curved piece on first. I rough cut a piece of 18mm plywood (two 9mm pieces laminated together) and then used a router with a flush trim bit for the final cut (**Figure 10**-6). The rest of the framing was solid fir and it was screwed down with 6X¾ screws (**Figure 10**-7A). **Figure 10**-7B shows the framing dimensions for the aft case. The framing for both cases was the same. Once you have it screwed down, pull it off and epoxy all the framing in place.

Now you're ready to check the fit of the plywood pattern. In **Figure 10**-8A I took some ¾-inch thick stock and outlined where it would go

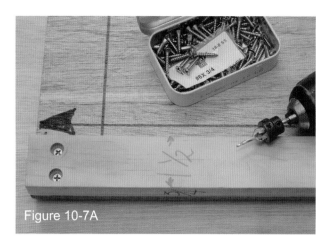

Figure 10-7A

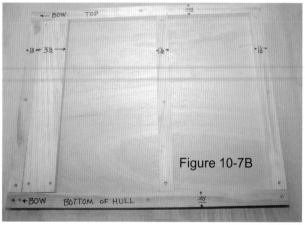

Figure 10-7B

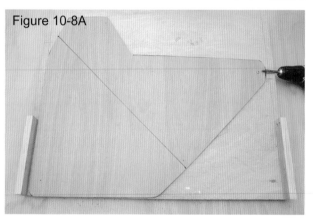

Figure 10-8A

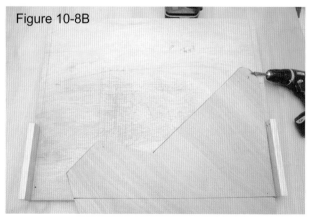

Figure 10-8B

Figure 10-8C

inside the CB case. This told me whether I needed to trim any off the plywood pattern or move the location of the CB pin slightly.

Notice the amount of centerboard left inside the case in the lowered position (**Figure 10-8B**). It is important to have a good amount of the centerboard left in the case. The greater the amount of board outside the case, the greater the mechanical advantage the board has as a lever should you strike something underwater. A damaged centerboard or damaged centerboard case is an experience you absolutely want to avoid.

Figures 10-8A and **B** established that it all works and the CB pin was in the correct place, so I drilled a small pilot hole at that location (**Figure 10-8C**). A close look at **10-8C** shows about ¾-inch of material surrounding the hole in the centerboard itself. Care should be taken to not put the hole for the CB pin too close the edge of the board. I used a stainless steel CB pin 3/8-inch in diameter so that left about a ½ of material surrounding the pin. Less than that is not a good idea.

My next step was to calculate the interior width of the centerboard case. **Figure 10-9** shows how the case is constructed. *Notice there is a piece of 6mm plywood on each side of the case in addition to the 9mm plywood. This 6mm plywood is part of an inner case (for a lack of something better to call it) that is glued in place after the hole in the bottom has been cut.* So I added 12mm (2 X 6mm), ¾-inch (width of the steel plate centerboard and two

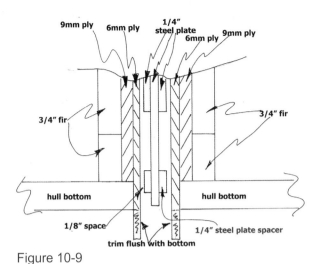

Figure 10-9

¼-inch spacers on each side of the board), and ¼-inch (1/8-inch space on each side of the board) for a total of 1½-inch width. **In retrospect I found that 1/8-inch wasn't quite enough on the aft case and an additional 1/16-inch allowance would have been better.**

With that dimension established I cut two pieces of ¾-inch fir 1½ inches wide and screwed them to the case (**Figures 10-10A** and **10-10B**) using #8 X 1½ stainless steel screws. I also carefully marked the location of those screws for later

Figure 10-10A

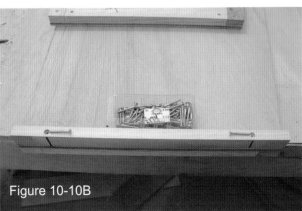

Figure 10-10B

reference.

The location of those screws is important because when you clamp the case together they are covered up. Use strong powerful clamps here because any case movement would create problems. It is also important to make sure the case is square vertically. That is the sides of the case are even and the case sits flat on a level surface. Use a square to check this after you have the case securely clamped together.

In **Figure 10-11A** I have clamped the case tightly together and I'm transferring the location of the spacer to the outside of the case using some scrap off the end of the spacer. This allows me to center the ¼ X 20 stainless steel through bolts in the center of the spacer (**Figure 10-11B**). In my case I used 3½-inch hex head bolts but you may need a slightly different length depending on the

Figure 10-11A

Figure 10-11B

overall width of you case.

I also wanted to recess the bolt so I used a Forstner drill bit to give me a flat bottomed recess (**Figure 10-11C**). *Be sure the recess is wide enough for the washer.* An extra long drill bit was used to pass though the case (**Figure 10-11 D**). The location of the bolts were also marked, showing them going all the way through the case. Notice the through bolt is offset from the location of the screw in the spacer. Three bolts should be plenty unless your case is warped, and you shouldn't have a warped case.

Figure 10-11C

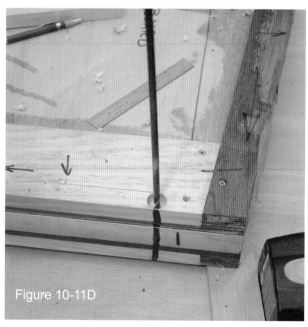

Figure 10-11D

Once you have the case bolted together tightly, check for square and draw some registration lines on the end of the case. Those lines you put marking the location of the bolts will serve as registra-

tion marks. This is important because you will take the case apart and reassemble it before final glue-up.

With the case securely bolted together, it's time to transfer the hole for the centerboard pin to the other side of the case (**Figure 10-12A**). It will be best if you use a portable drilling jig like the one in **Figure 10-12B**. This will help insure the pilot hole on the other side of the case is in alignment with the original hole.

The second step is to use a forstner bit to drill a recessed hole on each side of the case centered on the pilot hole (**Figure 10-12C**). The portable drilling jig will make this job much easier.

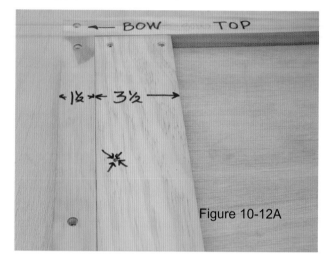

Figure 10-12A

Figure 10-12B

There is a reason why I used a recessed hole in the second step. Way back in the late 1980's I read an article in *WoodenBoat* by Sam Manning about centerboard cases. In the article he describes a

Figure 10-12C

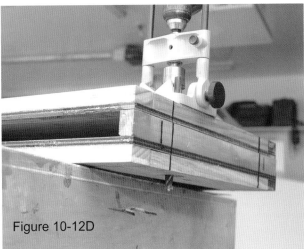

Figure 10-12D

Figure 10-12E

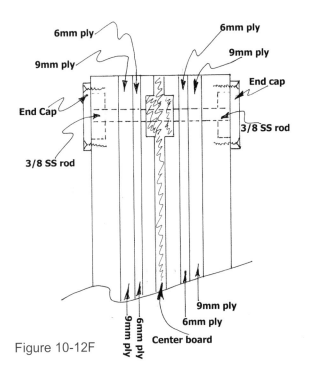

Figure 10-12F

"floating centerboard pin" as the best and most trouble free method for putting a pin through the case. I did a few exactly like his drawing and decided that a recess filled with sealant was a slight improvement of his excellent method.

The third step in this method is to drill a hole slightly larger than the centerboard pin. Basically you are enlarging the pilot hole so it's about 1/32-inch larger than the pin. In my case the pin was 3/8-inch stainless rod, so my hole was 13/32-inch. Again the portable drilling jig will be most helpful in getting the perfect alignment (**Figure 10-12D**).

A close look at **Figure 10-12E** shows that I changed my mind about the size of the centerboard pin. Originally I thought I would use a ¾ pin and drilled the hole accordingly. Why I settled on a ¾-inch pin I have no idea, but once I drilled the hole I knew ¾ was way too big, but what was done was done.

I certainly didn't want to remake the case, so I plugged the hole with a ¾-inch dowel glued in place with epoxy and then re-drilled the hole at 13/32. So remember 3/8 stainless rod is plenty heavy for the pin and I believe I'd make the recessed hole 1⅛" or 1¼" maximum. The smaller recess would use less sealant. **Figure 10-12F** is a cross section of the centerboard case and shows how the endplate captures the pin and creates a watertight seal as well.

The fourth step is to cut the pin to the right length. In my case it was about 3¼ (**Figure 10-**

12G), but the exact dimension for your pin will be slightly different. Ideally the pin should be a 1/16 shorter than the width of the case but an 1/8 is less likely to turn out too long for some reason. What you don't want is a pin that is so short it can slide far enough to slip one side of the case or so long the endplate won't lie flat and therefore isn't watertight.

Figure 10-12G

So the fifth step in this process will be to disassemble the case and make sure the plywood pattern for the centerboard works using the 3/8-inch stainless pin. Check that nothing binds and is an allowance for the 4mm ends of the inner case. When I was satisfied that it all worked with the pin in place, I cut the steel plate.

If you are going to have a welding shop cut the plate from the pattern, you will want to start this process early on, maybe even as soon you get the bulkheads locked into place. Do this and you know the measurements won't change. This is a good job while you wait for the laminations to dry.

That way you'll have everything ready to go into the boat at this point. It is frustrating to have work come to a halt while you wait for someone else to get a part ready.

Having the shop just cut out the centerboard plate and weld on the spacers, means it will need to be cleaned up with a grinder when you get it back depending on how the plate is welded. Chances are it will need some hand fitting with a grinder (**Figure 10-13**). Please note the face shield, heavy gloves, and long sleeve shirt. **All are essential safety gear and do not do this kind of work without them.**

Figure 10-13

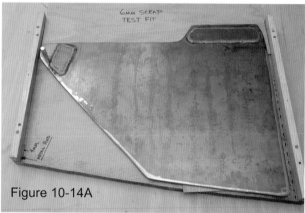

Figure 10-14A

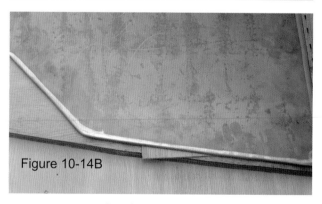

Figure 10-14B

Figure 10-14A shows the centerboard plate in place with the pin. Move the plate back and forth to be sure it is well clear of the ends **with the 4mm inner case in place.** Notice the 6mm piece of scrap plywood under the plate and that in **Figure 10-14B** the edge of the board that will extend out of the case has been rounded and smoothed out to a fine point

Figure 10-14C

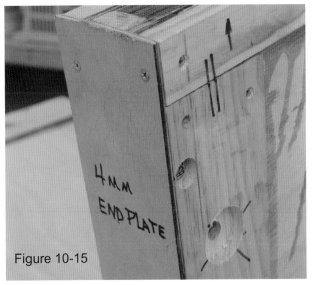

Figure 10-15

Figure 10-14D

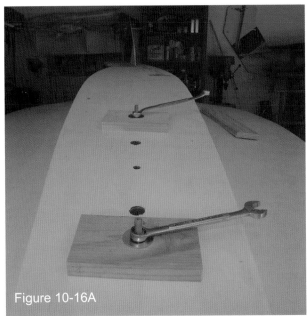

Figure 10-16A

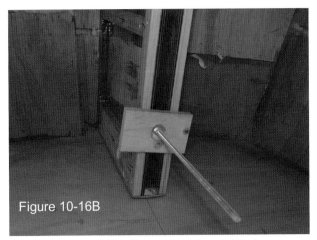

Figure 10-16B

Pay particular attention to the area at the pin (**Figure 10-14C**). Slide some scrap 4mm between the end of the plate and the spacer. Rotate the centerboard plate to be sure nothing binds. I had to do some grinding here to get enough clearance.

I also had to do some grinding on the spacers because some 6mm on top of the board showed only a 1/16-inch clearance (**Figure 10-14D**). Be sure you check this dimension very closely. Not enough clearance will cause the centerboard to bind against the side of the case. You'll want to fix any problems now before the cases go together with epoxy and before they are epoxied in the boat.

When I was satisfied that the steel boards worked in the cases, I reassembled them and added the 4mm endplates (**Figure 10-15**). Now the cases were the exact finished length and ready to be put in the boat so the slot could be cut in the bottom of the hull.

Figure 10-16A shows 5 holes drilled on centerline. This is best accomplished from under the boat. The holes with the 36-inch long 5/8 all-

Figure 10-16C

Figure 10-16G

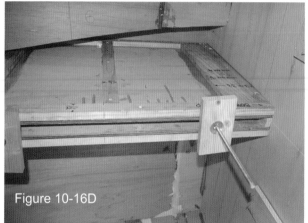

Figure 10-16D

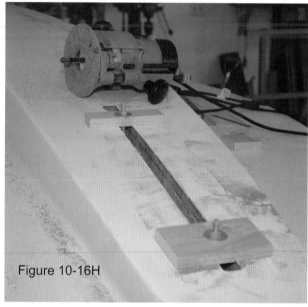

Figure 10-16H

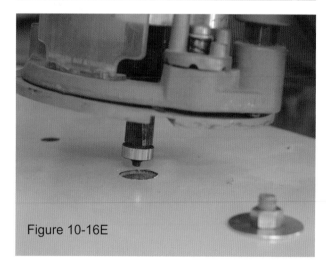

Figure 10-16E

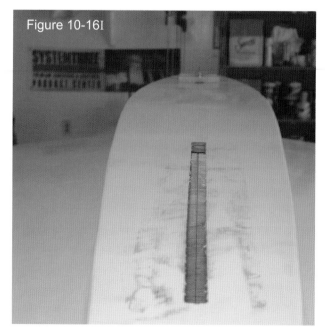

Figure 10-16I

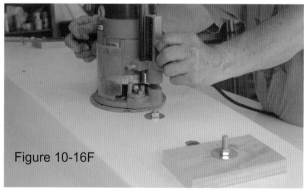

Figure 10-16F

thread in them are as close to the bulkheads as the drill would go. The three other holes allow for the router to drop in and cut a slot while the two rods support the case and clamp it in place (**Figure 10-16B** and **C**).

It is critical that the case be on centerline, so take your time here. Good lighting and flash lights will be required to make sure it is all centered up. In **Figure 10-16D** the case is well centered at the base and at the top. I tightened the nuts until I was absolutely certain that the case was pressed hard against the bottom of the hull. Another pair of hands here will not only be welcome but probably a necessity.

A careful check showed nothing had shifted while cranking down the nuts and I dropped the trim router bit into the hole and cut a section of the slot (**Figure 10-16 E, F,** and **G**).

This process takes three all-thread rods. You cut a portion of the slot then place the third rod in the slot, tighten it down, and drop one of the other rods. This keeps the case from moving while the entire slot is cut with the router (**Figure 10-16H**). **Figure 10-16I** shows the slot perfectly centered against the centerline on bulkhead #3, and the blocks and all-thread set up the cut the rear centerboard slot.

With the slot cut I dropped the case and started building the inner case. The first step was to mark the spacer and then strike a line at both ends so I could get an accurate measurement between the two (**Figures 10-17A** and **B**). and then locate the 6mm so it didn't interfere with the case going together again (**Figures 10-17C** and **D**). These were screwed in place without epoxy (that comes later). You will want to drill the hole for the centerboard pin through the 6mm before you epoxy the sides in place.

Next, I located the stop rod for the centerboard plate (**Figure 10-17E**). The purpose of this pin is to keep the plate from hitting the forward end of the case. As strong as this case is, it would be possible to beat it apart by allowing the board to slam the forward end of the case. I've had enough boats with heavy centerboards to know

Figure 10-17A

Figure 10-17B

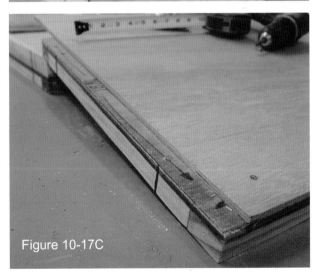

Figure 10-17C

that sooner or later that centerboard pennant is going to slip and the board will come down with a bang against the forward end. It's going to happen, you can count on it. The stop rod absorbs the energy of the blow rather than the end of the case.

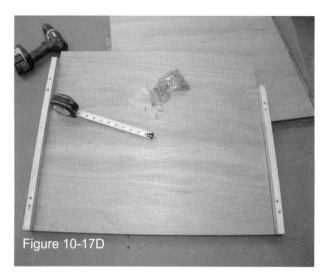

Figure 10-17D

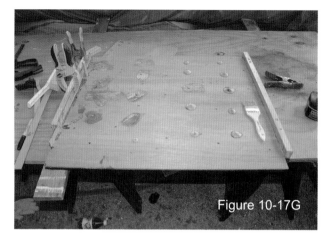

Figure 10-17G

Figure 10-17E

Figure 10-17H

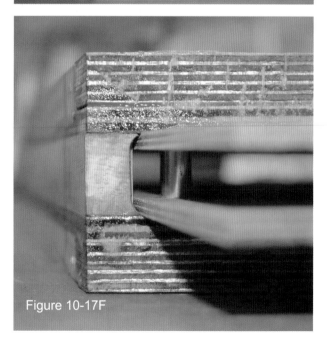

Figure 10-17F

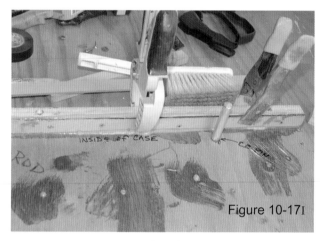

Figure 10-17I

In **Figure 10-17F** I've dry assembled the case with the 4mm (just barely visible) and the 6mm sides. This was to make sure the stop rod was the correct length. This is important because if the stop pin is too long the case won't fit together when it's bolted up. If it's too short then the first time or two it takes a blow the stop rod will fall out.

The next step is to epoxy the inner case in place. Notice in **Figure 10-17G** the 4mm extends

Figure 10-17J

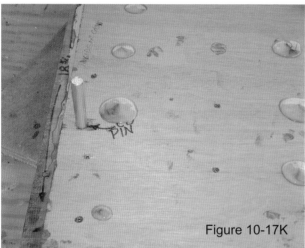

Figure 10-17K

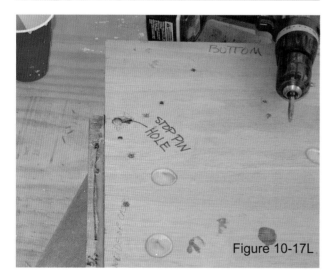

Figure 10-17L

the same laminating technique of drill holes on a grid and setting a number of screws. In **Figure 10-17 H** the hole for the stop rod has filled with excess epoxy. This is good because you will re-drill the hole a bit later and the epoxy seals the plywood against water.

While I didn't care if the stop rod hole filled with epoxy I didn't want the centerboard pin hole to fill up with epoxy so I inserted the pin during the glue-up (**Figure 10-17 I**). Also in **10-17 I** there hasn't been any clean-up done. It is critical that **all the excess epoxy is cleaned up**.

In **Figure 10-17 J** the aft 4mm strip is about to be epoxied in place. Once the aft 4mm piece was epoxied in place and **all the excess epoxy was cleaned up** this side of the case was finished. I cut the 4mm flush with the top of the spacer which meant that I had to measure the combined width of the 4mm and the spacer and adjust the width of the 6mm on the other side of the case. Actually, I forgot to do that, so when I tried to bolt up the case, of course, it wouldn't fit. The extra thickness of the 4mm kept the sides from fitting together.

There will be moments like this in boatbuilding. If you are lucky there will not be many, but sure as the sun comes up in the morning, there will be some. The important thing, when these moments arrive, is not to panic and do not despair because just as there will be problems and mistakes, there will be solutions to those issues.

In this case, I believe I put that half of the case on the table saw, adjusted the depth of the cut to 6mm plus a very small amount, and took a 4mm strip off each end of the 6mm. The cut at each end allowed the extra 4mm strip on the spacer to fit. There are several other ways that would have worked just as well, but the important thing is not to panic.

If you look closely at **Figure 10-17 K** you can see that the 6mm side comes right to the spacer. It wasn't until I had everything cleaned up and attempted to bolt up the case that I discovered what had happened. Also notice in **Figure 10-17 K** that the centerboard pin is in place during glue-up.

Just like the other side of the case, the pin

well below the bottom of the centerboard case along with the 6mm. This is important and it should be more than the thickness of the hull by at least an inch or so.

Also in **Figure 10-17G** you can see that I used

Figure 10-17M

Figure 10-17N

Figure 10-17O

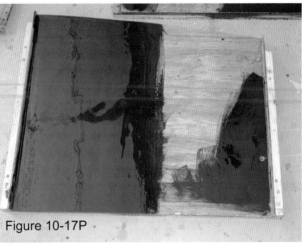

Figure 10-17P

helped keep the hole free of epoxy and made sure everything was in alignment. And just like the other side, this stop rod hole filled with epoxy as well (**Figure 10-17 L**). On this side of the case, clean-up is even more important and the clean case should look like **Figure 10-17 M**. Also in **Figure 10-17 M** I've drilled out the stop rod hole with a 3/8-inch forstner bit. Be sure to re-drill so the stop rod is supported by the full depth of the 6mm side. In other words, make sure the hole is a full 6mm deep.

You'll have to not only re-drill the stop rod hole but the holes for the through bolts as well (**Figure 10-17 N**). The good news is the cases are almost ready to put in the boat. After you do a dry fit bolt up with the stop rod and centerboard pin (this is where I discovered my mistake) there are just a couple of more steps left.

I coated the inside of the case with un-thick-ened epoxy and then did a test fit of the center-board plate (**Figure 10-17 O**). I found the area between pin and the end of the case a bit too tight and took off some of the plate with a grinder. Also now is a good time to mark on the top of the case where the block for the centerboard pennant needs to be. **Do a test fit for both cases**.

I added a mixture of graphite and epoxy to the sides of the cases after I could see where the board was going to abrade the side of the case (**Figure 10-17 P**). While some may feel that this step is not all that necessary, I recommend doing it. The graphite seems to make everything slide a bit smoother and also seems to be a bit more abra-sion-resistant than epoxy alone.

This is probably a good time to stress the im-portance of coating everything with multiple lay-ers of epoxy. Once these cases are epoxied in the boat, **they are a permanent part of the boat.** So you want to make sure the cases don't develop a problem because corners were cut during the con-struction process. **Build the cases to last as long** as the hull because they are part of the hull. Encapsulate everything in multiple layers of epoxy.

After the multiple coats of epoxy have hardened, dry bolt the case together one last time. The inner case should fit together like **Figure 10-18**. If it does then you're going to want to test the fit in

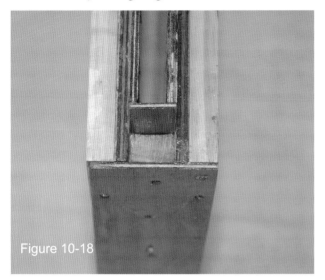
Figure 10-18

the boat. But before the case will fit in the slot you have to square the corners of the slot. The router left the corners slightly rounded (**Figure 10-19**) and you need to take a Japanese saw and a chisel to square up the corners. Once that's done, slide the case into the slot. It will be tight but it should slide in. If it doesn't, stop and figure out why (perhaps the corners aren't square enough or you may need to take a small amount off the inner case). But it should fit because the slot is exactly the same dimension as the outside dimension of the inner case.

Figure 10-19

Once it fits, slide it out and epoxy the case together with peanut butter thick epoxy. Again, be sure to clean up the squeeze out. That is important. Also it will be a good idea, when the epoxy has hardened, to put the centerboard plates in the cases and once again check to see that it moves easily in the case before the case goes in the hull for the final time.

I did a great deal of checking and rechecking each step of the way. I found each time that some small adjustment was needed, so I was always glad I took the time to double check the fit of everything. This is a complex process so take the time to check and recheck. You will not be sorry you did.

With nothing more to check, I put stilts on the backing blocks (**Figure 10-20**) to accommodate the inner case sticking out beyond the bottom of the boat and buttered the case with an enormous amount of peanutbutter-thick epoxy (**Figure 10-21**). The ends of the case and the bulkheads were coated with un-thickened epoxy. The thickened epoxy was applied with a baggie.

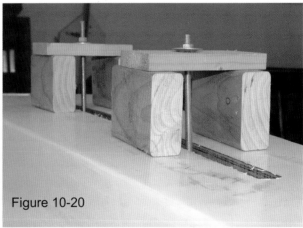
Figure 10-20

Figure 10-21

This is one of the few jobs that really can't be done alone. I suppose that with enough fore-thought it could be done, but it will be far easier with another person's help. Do a couple of re-hearsals so they know what you want them to do and then butter up the case. I think it goes with-out saying that you want epoxy with a very long pot life for this job.

I did find the job easier with a temporary brace under the hull to support the case while it was screwed in place with the all-thread. It takes some time to get the blocks on the underside of the case set, and the brace took the load until they were in place.

Another thing I found helpful was a tyvek suit and hat. There was a great deal of epoxy, and all that squeeze-out dripped and fell down on what-ever was under it and that will be you.

The tighter the case was screwed against the bottom the more squeeze out and you want to apply a great deal of upward pressure with the all-thread. You are certainly not going to break the case or the hull, so when you just can't turn the nuts any farther you can figure it has bottomed out against the hull. I put a hash mark on the inner case that matched the thickness of the hull so when that appeared I knew the case was flush against the bottom of the boat.

With the case firmly against the bottom it was time to clean up, clean up, and clean up (**Figure 10-22**). This can be a bit more relaxed pace, but you don't want the squeeze out to cook off before you can get it picked up. Now crawl out from under the boat and take a well-earned break. The good news is that the forward case is in place and the aft case is easier.

Figure 10-22

It took my son and I slightly more than four hours to get both cases epoxied in the boat. We finished out the day with easy jobs and by the next morning the inner cases were ready to cut flush with the bottom of the boat (**Figure 10-23**). I used my trusty Japanese saw and the 6-inch ran-dom orbital sander with 80 grit paper to smooth everything down.

Figure 10-23

If you look closely at **Figure 10-23** you can see there is a sharp edge on the inside of the case. That sharp edge needs to be rounded over because you are going to put fiberglass tape on the case. I used a rabbet plane to do the round-over but a file or block plane will work as well (**Figures 10-24A** and **B**).

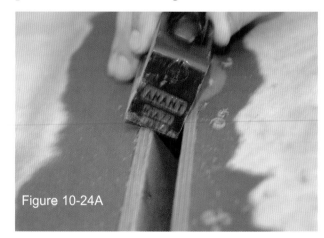
Figure 10-24A

The next step requires a bit of care but it's very simple. Three inch wide, 9 ounce fiberglass tape is set in epoxy over the edge and on the inside of the case. The only issue will be making sure the tape lies absolutely flat against the inside of the case. Remember, there isn't that much room on

Figure 10-24B

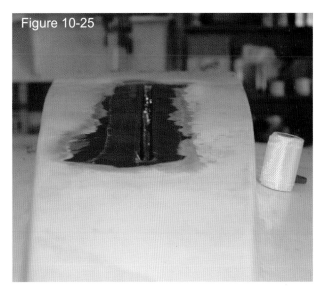

Figure 10-25

the inside and you don't want the tape dragging on the centerboard plate.

I used two layers of tape. The first extended down inside the case about two inches and over the bottom about an inch, The next layer extended down about an inch and over the outside of the hull about two inches. That gave a total of 18 ounces of cloth that sealed and supported that joint and covered that seam (**Figure 10-25**). Once the epoxy had gone off, I sanded the tape smooth and got the surface ready for the final coats of paint.

It was a good feeling to know that water will have to work hard to find its way into the hull through those cases.

NOTE: At some point, once the hull is turned over and before the interior goes in, you will want to put both boards in the cases for another trial fit (**Figure 10-26**). Fixing an unexpected problem with the fit will be much easier with easy access. It will also be a good time to sort out exactly where all the pulleys go.

Figure 10-26

11

Things to Finish Just Before Turnover

Putting in the centerboard cases was probably the most complex process about building the Sea Eagles. It was certainly one of the most exacting tasks to be sure. With that in mind the next few steps will be a piece of cake.

Most of what needs to be done is simple painting. Jobs like the finish coats of paint, adding a boot strip and perhaps anti-fouling paint. Even though it's simple painting there are some lessons I've learned over time, mostly the hard way.

First of all, take a very hard look at the primer coat. If there are numerous and obvious flaws now is the time to correct those problems. Don't deceive yourself into thinking the paint will cover them. The final coats of paint **will not** hide those flaws, if anything it will accentuate them. This is the level that will make or break your final finish. If the primer is smooth and looks good then the paint will flow out beautifully and look great.

Over the years I've developed a feel for what I think needs to be fixed and what is so minor I won't be able to see it once the boat is in the water. But what would be a minor flaw for me would not pass for another builder. It boils down to: There is no easy answer, no definitive yardstick to measure against. You are going to have to decide what needs to be fixed and what you will let slide. But I recommend that you try to find a happy medium between a flawless hull (which will take hundreds of hours and still not be achieved) and a poorly done finish that you feel needs an apologetic explanation. You know- the level of finish that is the Goldilocks Finish.

And if that wasn't vague enough just remember these are boats that will be used, and as they are used they will acquire dings, scratches, and small dents. After a year on the water a small flaw that you agonized over will have disappeared among scratches and dings.

Now let's paint a boat.

I use a painting method called rolling and tipping. You roll out the paint with a foam roller, just like the one you primed the hull with, and then drag a dry brush across the wet paint to break the stipple from the roller. If your surface is smooth (sanded with 220 grit paper) the paint will flow out and the brush marks will disappear. It will look like the surface was shot with a spray gun.

That seems simple enough and it is. But there is a variable that makes the learning curve a little steeper and that variable is the temperature. If it's very hot the paint will dry too fast to flow properly and if it's too cold the paint won't dry. I've found that higher temperatures present more problems than lower temperatures. Most paints operate best between 60 and 75 degrees (F) and most, if not all, tell you not to use them below 50 degrees Fahrenheit. Most will have accelerators to speed drying in colder temps and retarders to slow drying in higher temps.

I have to deal with the higher end of the temperature range because I live and build boats in Texas. I also think it's harder to make rolling and tipping work at the upper end so that's where I'll focus mostly.

Figure 11-1 shows the foam roller, roller tray, and a small section of the hull being rolled out. In the tipping part of the process (**Figure 11-2**) a dry brush is lightly dragged back across the fresh paint towards previous rolled out section. The first thing to notice in **Figure 11-3** is the band of stip-

Figure 11-1

Figure 11-2

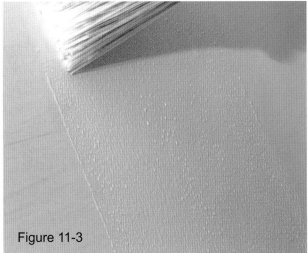

Figure 11-3

Figure 11-4

ple from the roller. There is a clear line of stippled fresh paint and the last section of paint. It's easy to see where one starts and the other ends.

In **Figure 11-4** the band ends where the brush has been pulled across and the fresh paint blends into the paint of the previous section. There is no line separating the fresh section from the last section. Everything is working just right in **Figure 11-4** and that is what you should see. One section blends into the other and it's impossible to distinguish one section from another. What makes rolling and tipping work is one section blending seamlessly with the last for the whole boat. But if the paint dries too fast you would be able to see where the fresh paint didn't blend in with the last section. You would have a dry line and you'd have to add some retarder or an additive to the paint to slow down the dry time and get back in the zone.

It's not hard to hit the zone and stay there for the whole boat but it does take a bit of practice. So learn on the bottom of the boat. You have to paint the bottom anyway so paint that section first. Do a coat or two on the bottom of the keel and slowly work your way topside. You'll be surprised how little time it takes to do an acceptable job. Once you're doing a good job on the bottom, move to the sides of the hull.

I've learned that if I work in small sections I can avoid dry lines. Another pair of hands is great, but if you have to work by yourself then small sections will be mandatory. I found that a single roller width from the bottom chine to the sheer, like **Figure 11-1**, was about the maximum I could do and not get a dry line. I did try small sections of a square foot or two moving down the hull, but that never gave the seamless look I needed. It always had a patchy look when it dried.

Also remember that several light coats are much better than a heavy one. A heavy coat will run or sag and that is always a problem. Get the feel for how much paint to carry in the roller while you're working on the bottom and don't deviate from that amount. The more consistent your application can be the better your results will be.

By the time you finish the second full coat on the boat you have it down cold. The final full coats will look like it was shot with a spray gun.

And while that final coat is drying you are going to have to make a decision about an anti-fouling paint. I didn't put one on at this point and that was a mistake. I thought because the boat would live on a trailer I didn't need the anti-fouling paint. I was amazed how fast things grew on the hull. So I recommend that you pick an appropriate anti-fouling paint and apply it now while the boat is upside down. I wish I had.

To do that you'll need to establish the waterline on the hull. Remember that the flat part of the keel is the baseline, so all you have to do is establish that line and measure down 16 inches. In **Figure 11-5** I used plywood to carry the flat of the keel (the baseline) out to the side of the hull, measured down 16 inches, and set up a story stick. Be sure that the angle between the floor and the side facing the hull is a true 90 degrees.

Figure 11-5

Next I used a level to true up the pointed tick stick and set it on one of the marks (**Figure 11-6**). Now all that was left to do was move the tick stick down the hull, putting marks every 6 inches or so, on both sides of the hull. This established a waterline completely around the boat from the baseline. Now connect the dots with tape and you're ready to paint the bottom (**Figure 11-7**).

You have no doubt noticed that in the photos my hull is not yet primed. I used this method to establish what area I covered with epoxy and graphite. I then primed and painted my hull and, much to my regret, turned it over without bottom paint. Let me again suggest that you not

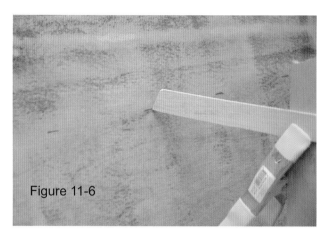
Figure 11-6

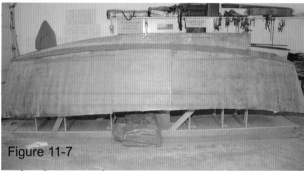
Figure 11-7

make that mistake.

I think it's important to mention something about bottom paint or anti-fouling paint. It works because it is toxic to creatures living in the water. It should be obvious then that it is also toxic to you. Handle and apply it with extreme care.

After you have applied the anti-fouling paint, using extreme care of course, you will want to add a boot stripe. A dark boot stripe helps a white hull stay looking clean because the white or light color, as the case may be, starts above the splash zone.

To line off the boot stripe simply drop the pointed tick stick down about 4 inches toward the sheer and place a series of marks around the hull. Connect the dots with tape and paint your boot stripe.

With the boot stripe done you have one more small job to do before starting the turnover process. You need to take the measurements for the skeg so it can be lofted out full size.

I used a straight, fairly heavy board to extend the line of the keel bottom so a plumb bob (in my case a tape measure) just touched the top of the transom (**Figure 11-8**) and recorded that measurement (47 inches). I measured out from

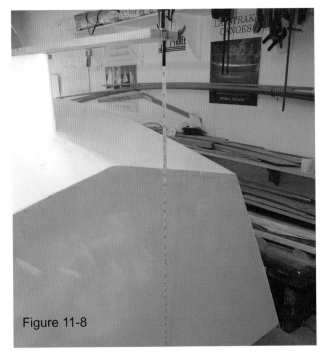

Figure 11-8

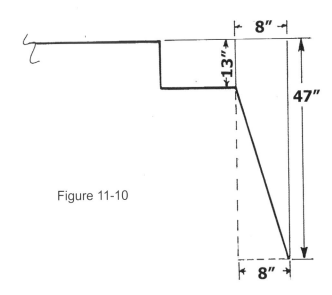

Figure 11-10

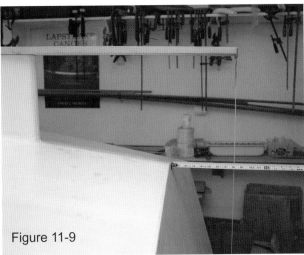

Figure 11-9

bottom of the transom to the plumb bob and recorded the distance (**Figure 11-9**). That gave me an 8 inch by 47 inch base rectangle. Next I measured down from the board on the keel bottom to the bottom of the transom and that distance was 13 inches. These dimensions gave me a base rectangle that established the slope of the transom (**Figure 11-10**). You will need to take the measurements directly from your boat as they will be slightly different than my boat and you want this to be fairly exact.

Now I could lay out and loft the skeg full size. And with that information safely recorded I could start the long awaited turnover process.

12

The Big Turnover

As you look at your upside down hull, it's good to remember that over the ages humans have successfully moved very big, very heavy, objects with very little in the way of tools. The huge blocks for the pyramids and the enormous statues of the Easter Islands all rolled over cylinders. So learning from these early builders I bought a few sections of steel plumbing pipe and set about to turn over the hull.

Just slide at least three sections of pipe under the strongback (**Figure 12-1**), attach a bridle to the front (**Figure 12-2**) and start out the door. It was amazing how easily the whole unit moved. I had been prepared to hook everything to my son's small truck but that proved unnecessary until a section of the strongback cracked and started to drag.

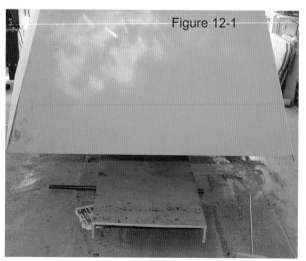
Figure 12-1

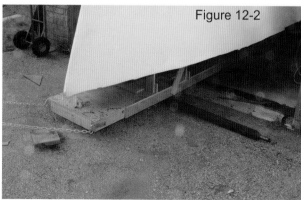
Figure 12-2

There were some minor glitches like the small drop from the garage floor to the surface of the driveway (**Figure 12-3**) but that was easily overcome by using a larger diameter size pipe, in this case an old drive shaft. Also we had to ooch the stern over with a pry bar to make a rather sharp turn (**Figure 12-4**).

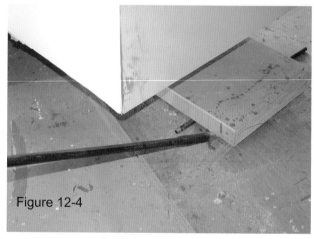
Figure 12-3

Figure 12-4

I was very relieved that the boat made the turn because the alternative was a great deal of extra work I hadn't planned on. The lesson there was better planning at the start. I did know that I could get the boat out of the garage before I started building but I don't think I looked quite hard enough. Of course if you have a straight shot out there is no problem at all.

Figures 12-5, 6, 7, and **8** show the progress as the hull moves out of the shop and turns under the canopy. I could have done this by myself but this is another time where an extra pair of hands made the job much easier and safer. There were a number of moments during the move when I was

Figure 12-5

Figure 12-6

Figure 12-7

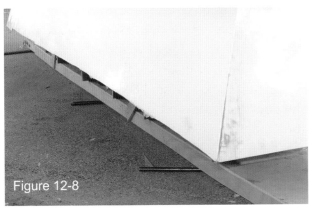

Figure 12-8

very grateful for the extra help. It took my son and I about an hour move the hull out of the shop and get under the canopy.

Once under the canopy we started building the cradle to rotate the boat. I think this is a good time to say a few words about the cradle and turning the hull in general.

During the life of the boat, the turnover will probably put the boat at greatest risk. There are a number of things that can go wrong and the boat or someone can be hurt or damaged—the bigger the boat the great the risks.

I used 2X6's and 2X4's to build the cradle and you should as well. Ignore the advice of the "dock admirals" who tell you that 2X6's and 2X4's are overkill and an unnecessary expense. The last thing you want is for the hull to break loose because the cradle cracked or collapsed completely. If this happens, about the best you can hope for is a slightly damaged hull and things quickly get worst from there.

So with that major caveat ringing in your ears, here is how I built the cradle. In **Figure 12-9A** my son has set up two 2X6's clamped together at station #4. Notice that the vertical 2X6 rests directly on the ground and directly against the side the hull and the horizontal 2X6 rests directly on the keel bottom. The 2X6 will be clamped to the horizontal to match the vertical piece. These will be through-bolted together and form the frame used to capture the hull at station #4.

Figure 12-9A

A second 2X6 horizontal piece was added at the sheer and the rest of the framework was 2X4's (**Figure 12-9B**). We just invented this as we went along so there's no right or wrong way. The goal was to tightly brace the hull so it could not move as the cradle was rotated. **Figures 12-10** and **11** show more angles of the cradle at #4. We added foam between the cradle and the frame to protect the finish on the boat, and it will be a good idea for you to do the same.

Figure 12-10

Figure 12-9B

Figure 12-11

Figure 12-12

There was also 2X4 bracing that tied the cradle to the bulkhead. This is important because it locks the cradle in place (**Figures 12-12** and **13**). You will want to do this at all three frames.

When you have finished the frame at #4 move to station #5. You need to have #5 in place before you can do the frame at #3. **Figures 12-14A** and **14B** show how we placed the 2X4's at station #5. Again there's no right or wrong way to capture the hull as long as it is captured and cannot move. We did this one just a little different than #4.

Figure 12-13

Figure 12-15A

Figure 12-14A

Figure 12-15B

Figure 12-14B

Figure 12-16

The frame work at #3 is a bit more tricky because the keel is not on the same level as #4 and #5. Actually there is 3/16-inch difference between #4 and #5 but we decided to treat them as level.

Start the frame at #3 by screwing a couple of 2X4's to the 2X6's at #4 and #5. Then clamp a 2X6 on station line to those 2X4's as shown in **Figure 12-15A** and **15B**. That puts the 2X6 on the same level as the other two and you can attach the vertical 2X6's so they rest on the ground (**Figure 12-15A**). **Figure 12-16** shows how the rest of the bracing was done and how we captured the spacer between the keel and the 2X6 cross piece.

Next tie all the frames together with a 2X4 (**Figure 12-17**) and add plywood braces at the bottom joint. This photo was taken facing aft on the right hand side of the boat. I decided those corners, which would bear the entire weight of the boat on the first rotation, needed to have some reinforcing.

Figure 12-17

It occurred to me at some point that all the 2X6's would have to be trimmed so they didn't rest on the ground. Even with the strongback raised and rolling on the pipe, the driveway was uneven enough that a leg might drag. The sawdust by each leg is from the cut off.

It took most of the day for my son and I to get the boat out of the shop and the bracing on, so don't wait until the turnover day to get this done. I suppose we could have added the cradle inside the shop but it would have been very tight getting the boat through the door. If you decide to or you must build the cradle inside the shop, be sure to check and recheck that everything will fit through the door. You don't want to have the boat stuck inside the shop on turnover day.

I managed to lure four friends out to my shop on turnover day with the promise of barbecue and ample carbonated beverages. With my son and I, that made six able bodies to roll the boat.

Set the day well in advance, at least a week, and then deliver on your promise of food and beverages. If you plan to serve beer, do not, let me repeat, do not serve the beer until the rollover is done and

the boat is back in the shop. It doesn't take much imagination to see why that's a good idea.

More good ideas are dry runs and very clear communication about the plan of action. That means you must have a very clear idea about how to turn over the hull. This is not something you want to invent as you go.

I drew the cradle out to scale so I could see exactly how many feet I needed for the rollover. You don't want to have to stop mid-roll because it has become obvious that the boat will end up in the flower garden or won't quite clear a tree. Poor planning will get people hurt.

In **Figure 12-18** the boat is in position and everyone has been assigned a job and place and I've attached a belaying rope (the white rope at the bottom right of the photo) to a dead man (a stout tree to the right). I had three people on the lift side and two on the catch side. The belaying rope would act as a safety net should something go wrong and the process have to be stopped mid-roll.

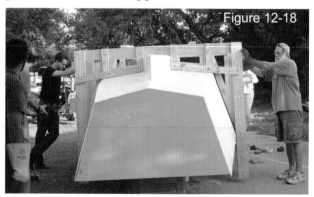

Figure 12-18

As it turned out, nothing had to be stopped mid-roll and the boat was turned on its side without a problem (**Figures12-19, 20, 21,** and **22**). In **figures 12-21** and **12-22** you can see the importance of the belaying rope. At the height of the arch, the legs of the cradle were too high and everyone had to shift their hands to the strongback. I was able to support the weight of the boat and take the strain off the catchers. The belaying rope kept the hull under complete control during the first part of the rotation.

With the first half of the rotation complete, now is the time to remove the strongback. You have great access to it and a Sawzall will make fast

Figure 12-19

Figure 12-20

Figure 12-21

Figure 12-22

Figure 12-23

Figure 12-24

Figure 12-25

work of the job (**Figures 12-23** and **24**).

Once the strongback was cleared out of the way, we were able to drag the hull back a bit and finish the rotation (**Figure 12-25**). It takes more space to rotate the hull than you might think (it certainly took more space than I thought), and that's why the scale model of the cradle is important.

The truck played an important role in the turnover but your neighbor may not like you driving across flower beds or lawn. Plan ahead and know exactly what you need to do at each step. You don't want to have to solve unforeseen problems while your turnover crew stands around.

When the hull was in the right place and the belaying rope had been moved to the new loca-

Figure 12-26

Figure 12-27

Figure 12-28

Figure 12-29

Figure 12-30

Figure 12-31

tion I explained the plan to everyone and what everybody's job was. If there was a problem they all knew what they were to do and their escape route. I can not express just how important this kind of communication is.

Again, I had three lifters and two catchers because once the hull starts its downward path, gravity and the belaying rope do most of the work (**Figure 12-26, 27,** and **28**).

I experienced a great deal of relief when the hull was right side up because we only had one more somewhat difficult job left. Originally I had planned to cut the cradle out from under the hull and then roll it back into the shop. But it was decided that tilting the hull back and walking the cradle out from under the hull was simpler and faster (**Figures 12-29** and **30**).

The only problem we had getting the hull back in the shop was a simple one. The hull could be pushed so fast on the pipe that the pipe movers had trouble keeping up (**Figures 12-31, 32,** and **33**).

I left the hull sitting on the flat part of her keel and put some temporary bracing at station #5 and at the stern (**Figure 12-34**). I also braced the keel at the bow. Make sure the bracing is solid and doesn't move as you get in and out.

This is important because you don't want the hull to rock and move every time you step in. Notice the large box step at station #5. I found this to be a more secure step getting in and out of the hull. Given how many thousands of times you will do just that, take the time to make it very easy.

Once the shop was quiet and everyone had left I climbed into the boat and sat down with my back against the hull. This was a very satisfying moment for me and I suspect it will be for you as well. Take the time to enjoy the moment.

Figure 12-32

Figure 12-33

Figure 12-34

Finishing out the Interior

It always seems like I'm halfway finished when the hull is turned over and work is starting on the interior. After all, building the hull is half the job, right? Well, the truth of the matter is, with the hull turned over, I was about twenty five percent done.

I mention this because thinking that you are at the halfway point can lead to unrealistic expectations. You begin to say to yourself that the boat will be finished in time to launch by March or June or September when, in fact, that may not happen.

Try to avoid this trap because it makes you impatient and creates disappointment. Just continue to work at a steady pace and look at each task as a separate job and take satisfaction in its completion.

There are a great many different tasks with the interior and many times you'll be working on several at once. Finishing out the inside is not as linear as building the hull. If I described building the interior like I actually built it you would get lost in all the muddled details.

To keep that from happening I have broken this next part of the building process into sections like the cockpit, the tabernacles, the spars, and so on. Each one is treated separately but in most cases they are being worked on at the same time.

For example putting the ballast in the keel needs to be done before you put on the cockpit seats and sole, but you won't find anything about the ballast in the section on the cockpit.

So as you read the next section understand that many of the tasks are dependent on others and you don't want to jump ahead creating problems for yourself.

An example of this kind of jumping ahead is putting on the decks and enclosing the cockpit before the cuddy and quarter berths are finished out.

This is what I did because I wanted to take the boat with me when I taught for the summer at Great Lakes Boat Building School in Michigan's Upper Peninsula. I skipped ahead because it was important at the time. It worked, but it made finishing the cuddy and quarter berths far more difficult.

I strongly urge you to resist this temptation. As you work keep in mind that almost all the tasks are interdependent and you'll do just fine.

13

Taping the Hull and Bulkheads

Your first job is to add heavy fillets and tape to the hull chines and bulkheads. This is a straight forward process that you should be very familiar with by now—unthickened epoxy, peanut butter epoxy, and fiberglass tape wet out with unthickened epoxy.

Figure 13-1 shows a heavy fillet being applied to a bulkhead with a baggie. A little planning here will make life easier for you a bit later. Some of the bulkheads are cut away from the hull so you need

Figure 13-1

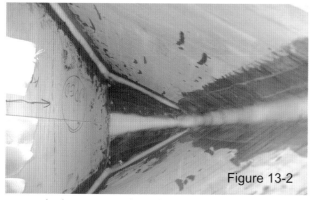

Figure 13-2

to mark those areas that don't get a fillet and tape.

In **Figure 13-2** the bow section has been taped over a heavy fillet. I staggered three layers of 9 ounce tape over the fillet in the bow and keel. The **bottom/ side** chine also has three layers of 9 ounce tape staggered over the fillet. It's very important to make this joint very strong over the entire length of the hull. The face of the bulkhead was left bare as

Figure 13-3

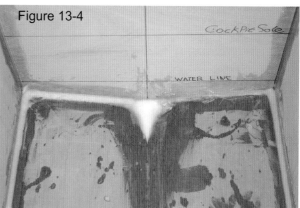

Figure 13-4

the bracing for the tabernacle would be added later.

The box keel was heavily taped as well. In **Figure 13-3** multiple layers of tape were applied to the keel and the bulkheads. Like the **bottom/side** chine these joints should be well reinforced with three layers of 9 ounce tape and heavy fillets.

Figure 13-4 shows the aft side of #7 bulkhead with the space at the very end of the keel filled with thick epoxy. Three layers of tape were applied to the centerline joint and the bulkhead was taped all around with a single layer. In the photo, the sides of the motor well are in place with fillets but no tape. I didn't tape this side of the motor well/ transom braces. The other side was taped.

Let me say once again that much time and labor will be saved if you take the time mark those areas that do not get fillets and tape. You will want to make sure to clean up all the extra epoxy and keep the tape as smooth as possible, especially in the cuddy cabin area. If you are tempted to leave a small lump of epoxy or think you'll clean it up later, just remember how hard it was sanding the outside of the hull. Sanding the inside is even harder, so clean up, clean up, and clean up.

14

The Cockpit Plus

Looking at your boat with all the bulkheads in place and uncut (**Figure 14-1**) is much like looking at an unedited movie—all the parts are there, but where do you star?. Like the film, it's best to go back to the start.

Remember when you were doing the layout for the strongback and you transferred the waterline and the cockpit lines to each bulkhead (**Figure 14-2**)?

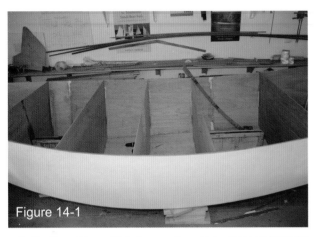

Figure 14-1

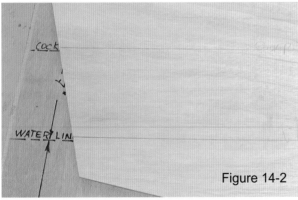

Figure 14-2

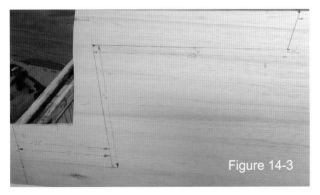

Figure 14-3

Well now you're going to take that information and lay out the cockpit on the bulkheads using those baselines. In **Figure 14-3**, the side of the cockpit bench is 11 inches from the centerline, the top of the bench is 14 inches up from the cockpit sole and the top of the bench seat is 18 5/8 inches. **Figure 14-4** shows the combing to be 7 3/8 inches and the slope of the seat is determined by a line 1 inch out from vertical or 90 degrees.

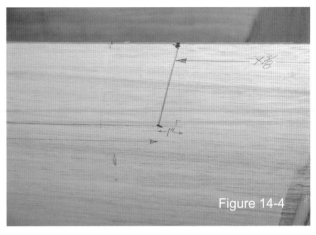

Figure 14-4

Figure 14-5, 6, and **7** are overall shots of bulkheads #3, #4, and #5. In **Figure 14-5** the bulkhead has not been trimmed to the lines but in **Figures 14-6** and **7** the bulkheads have been trimmed down to the lines. Also notice that on bulkhead #3 the cockpit sole is 8½ inches above the waterline and 8 inches and 7½ inches on bulkhead #4 and Bulkhead #5. This is important because you want the cockpit sole to slope down toward the motor well.

Figure 14-8 shows bulkhead # 6 (remember my bulkhead #7 is your bulkhead #6 because I dropped #6) with the cockpit sole at 7 inches above the waterline. Also notice that there is a change in the slope of the combing as well. It is 1 7/8 rather than 1 inch.

In **Figure 14-9** cleats have been placed on the lines and a trim router with a flush trim bit will be used to cut the bulkhead to the line. In the background #5 has already been trimmed using the router. This is a very fast and easy way to trim the bulkheads to the line and the tool saves hours of hand work.

Figure 14-10 shows the other side of #4 with the bulkhead trimmed. These cleats are just tem-

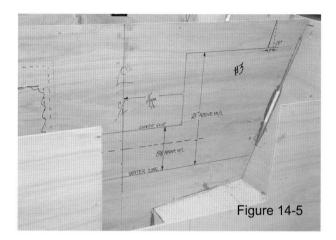

Figure 14-5

Figure 14-9

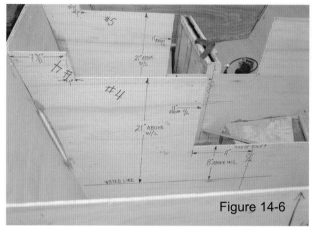

Figure 14-6

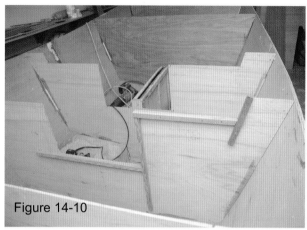

Figure 14-10

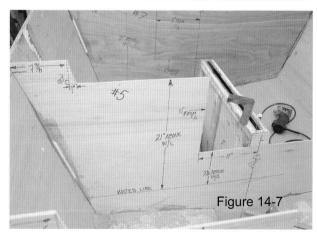

Figure 14-7

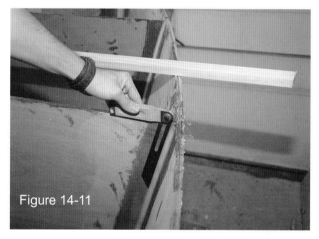

Figure 14-11

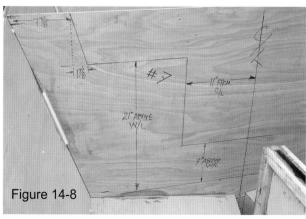

Figure 14-8

porary and the permanent cleats will be epoxied in place a little later. More care was taken fitting the permanent cleats, and I used a bevel to get a close fit (**Figure 14-11** and **12**).

I used ¾ X 1½-inch fir for most of the cleats. This gave plenty of glue surface and strength. **Figure 14-13** shows the permanent cleats epoxied in place. If you look carefully at #3 you can see where I have started to cut out the bulkheads.

Most of the permanent cleats are in place in **Fig-**

Figure 14-12

Figure 14-15

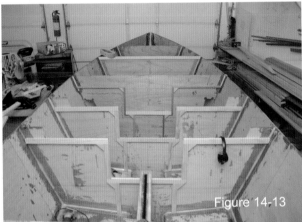

Figure 14-13

Figure 14-16

Figure 14-14

Figure 14-17A

ure 14-13, but I wanted the cockpit sole to extend under the bench seat to create storage for the outboard motor gas tank. This called for some extra cleats for the sole to rest on. If you look closely at **Figure 14-14**, you'll see where I added additional cleats to the faces of #5 and my #7 (your #6). This gives the cockpit sole a lip to rest on. **Figures 14-15** and **14-16** show a more detailed view of the cleats.

You can also see where I wrote "gas tank here" on the side of the hull in **Figure 14-14**. I wrote myself a great many notes on the boat about what to cut out and what not to cut. This is a good idea and helps minimize confusion and mistakes. Cutting out the wrong panel can be fixed but it takes time and materials to correct.

Figure 14-17A shows the cutting process under way on bulkhead #3 and my "no cut" notes are clearly visible on those sections that were not to be cut. As you can see the trim router will not cut cer-

Figure 14-17B

Figure 14-18

Figure 14-19A

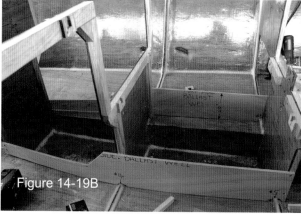

Figure 14-19B

Figure 14-20

tain areas and those were cut by hand (**Figure 14-17B**).

In **Figure 14-18** I've cut out #2 with the trim router and will come back to even up the area on the side of the hull by hand. I did that job with a Japanese saw but a Sawzall would make fast work of it as well. Notice the cleat at the top of #2. I added a cleat to the other side so the plywood was sandwiched between the two cleats.

The photo in **Figure 14-19A** was taken at #4 facing aft and shows that #4 was cut away on both sides and #5 was cut away on the right hand side of the photo, but only partially cut away on the left hand side. It's important to cut out the lower section of #5 to give access to the centerboard case. You can see that #7 was left almost completely intact. Also you can see that I left a remnant of the bulkheads to form a rib on the hull side. I felt this was necessary to add strength to the side of the hull.

When I had completed cutting the bulkheads I added the ballast well (**Figure 14-19B**). I used 9mm plywood and epoxied both sides in place. The aft section (the bow is to the left in the photo) is higher than the forward section. I left the forward section lower because this was the location for the batteries and high sides would mean difficulty in getting the batteries in and out of the boat when everything was closed in.

You will need to add the ballast before the decking is added (see section on ballast). Also, it will be easier to get the boat on the trailer if you put it on the trailer **before** you add the ballast.

Figure 14-20 is another view from #2 facing aft. The hatch is in place between # 2 and #3 (see sec-

Figure 14-21

Figure 14-22

Figure 14-23

Figure 14-24

tion on hatch) and the interior has been coated with unthickened epoxy. All the brackets that hold the bracing for the decking are also in place. **Figure 14-21** is a close-up of my #7 (your #6) with the "no cut" area clearly marked and the brackets for the deck bracing epoxied in place.

Once all the bulkheads are cut out it will be time to turn your attention to the bracing that goes under the cuddy and quarter berth sole. Unfortunately this involves a great deal of hand fitting. The good news is that the decking is not on, so it will be much easier for you than it was for me (remember I jumped ahead to take the boat to Michigan for the summer).

All this hand fitting will be also be easier if you have a small spirit level. I found that both 18-inch and 6-inch long levels work great for keeping the bracing level. I also used a great deal of scrap plywood making and remaking patterns.

In the section between #1 and #2 (**Figures 14-22, 23,** and **24**) start at the forward brace and carry that level line aft. Mark the location of each cross brace on the hull because just a slight movement fore or aft will change the fit. Do one side and then carry that level line to the other side. When you have a good fit for all the pieces that run athwart ship, tie them together with spacers as shown in **Figure 14-22.** This will hold it all in place while the epoxy cures and supply additional support under the plywood. But don't epoxy anything until both sides are in place and you can check for level. Be sure to check level fore and aft as well as athwart ship. I used two pieces of 9mm plywood to cover this section (see section on finishing the cuddy and quarter berth).

The section that is the quarter berth needs to be leveled out too. If you don't create a level area here, sleeping will difficult at best, as you always roll toward the keel. After all the hand fitting you did in the section between #1 and #2 this will be simple (**Figure 14-25**). I used fir slats and plywood in this area but plywood only would work equally well (see cuddy and quarter berth section).

It will be much easier to paint this area before the decks go on, as well. You may want to spread a

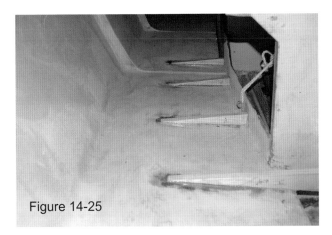

Figure 14-25

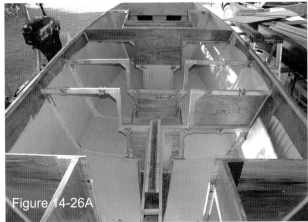

Figure 14-26A

Figure 14-26B

Figure 14-26C

drop cloth to cover the area after it has had the final coats of paint because there will be some epoxy drips when the decks are put in place. The drop cloth will make cleaning up a matter of picking up the cloth rather than sanding and touching up the paint.

Figure 14-26A was taken standing in the motor well facing forward. This is yet another view of the interior and shows all the structure that has been cut away. It will help give you a good idea of what

stays and what is cut away. Consider this the "bones" and the decking the "skin." The only "bones" missing are the deck beams that run fore and aft. The brackets for these ¾ by ¾ fir beams can be seen in **14-26A** and in the detail photo **Figure 14-26B**. Please note the cleats attached to the aft centerboard case (**Figure 14-26C**). This gives the cockpit sole something solid to screw into at the aft end of the centerboard case and along the sides. Everything is square to the centerboard case but it does look out of square because the camera is slightly off centerline.

With all the "bones" in place a quick look at the curved hull tells you that some hand fitting of the "skin" or decking is involved in the next step. So grab your story sticks and some scrap plywood.

The trick here is to have the scrap plywood square to the width between the bulkheads so you can place one end against the hull. Mark where the outside edge falls on the cleats and take a measurement with the story stick as in **Figure 14-27**. Transfer that information to another piece of scrap ply, draw the curve and cut it out. In Figure **14-28A** the information from the first scrap of plywood has

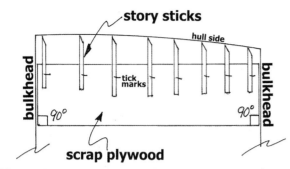

Figure 14-27

Figure 14-28A

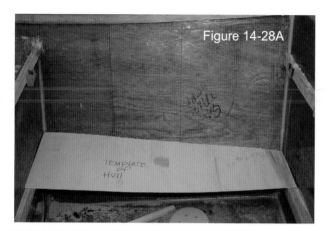

Figure 14-28B

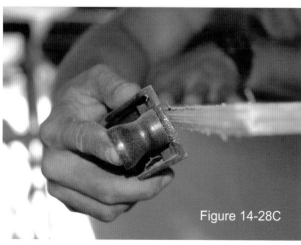

Figure 14-28C

Figure 14-28D

been transferred and the curve cut. A test fit in shows a good fit, so the curve is transferred to marine plywood (**Figure 14-28B**). A bevel was planed on the curved edge (**Figure 14-28C**) and it was put up for another test fit. When a satisfactory fit is achieved, then I moved on to the next sections.

The main section of the cockpit sole is quite simple and just requires you measure over from the centerline at each station or bulkhead (**Figure 14-28D**). When all the decking or "skin" has been fitted then it's time to put it in permanently.

The "skin" or deck goes on in a very specific order. First the cockpit sole went on, then the bench sides and then the bench seats. In **Figure 14-29A** a baggie is used to spread the peanut butter epoxy over the deck beams and cleats. Notice the Tyvek suit. It will be impossible for you to lay down the decking and not get epoxy on you and your clothes. Because you really, really need to keep epoxy off of your skin, you need to wear a Tyvek suit when you do this job. You want epoxy with a fairly long pot life for this job and of course, you will have done at least one dry fit before moving to epoxy.

Figure 14-29B shows how the bracing at the aft end of the centerboard case fits under the cockpit sole. It was much easier to cut the curved piece without the notch around the case.

I used #8 X 1¼ stainless steel screws to fasten the plywood in place (**Figure 14-29C**) and then moved on the section on the other side of the centerboard case (**Figure 14-29D**). Notice the heavy fillets on the first piece that was put in. These fillets are very important for a leak-proof cockpit sole.

Let me add a short note about the curved sec-

Figure 14-29A

Figure 14-30

Figure 14-29B

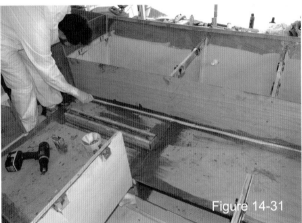

Figure 14-31

Figure 14-29C

Figure 14-29D

tion of cockpit sole. I didn't place any bracing under the curved edge. It had a large fillet above and on the underside along that curved edge. Because this area was covered with a bench seat and it would not have to support any weight I felt this was strong enough.

Next the sides of the bench were added (**Figure 14-30**). I used 6mm plywood for the sides and spring clamps held everything in pace while I screwed it down. Be sure that the back side (inside the hull) of this joint lines up. If your 6mm plywood has a little warp to it there can be small problems with getting a good fit.

In **Figures 14-31** and **32** the port side has been screwed in place and those large very important fillets added to the joints. **Figure 14-33** gives you a very good look at the cockpit sole completely in place. You can see the beams for the port bench seat in place and the starboard bench seat has fitted.

Use the same method you used to fit the curved cockpit sole to fit the curved bench seats. The story sticks and scrap plywood will save expensive mis-

Figure 14-32

Figure 14-33

Figure 14-34

Figure 14-35

Figure 14-36

takes and when both bench tops are in place your cockpit should look like **Figure 14-34**. Also, if you look closely at **14-34** you can see an additional strip of plywood epoxied to the sheer. I added that strip to give the combing extra glue surface. The combing will be added next, so this strip needs to be in place.

The first step is to make the blocks that will form the frame work for the supports (**Figure 14-35**). Use scrap plywood to do the layout and then use good plywood. Remember that the slope is 1 inch forward of a 90 degree angle. Fir cleats establish the angles on the bulkheads. Notice there are holes in each of the blocks. These holes allow air and moisture to escape this small enclosed area. You definitely do not want to seal this area up completely. If you look closely at the bulkhead, you will see a small hole that opens into the cuddy area.

Once you have the blocks epoxied in place you will need to put the decks on before you can finish

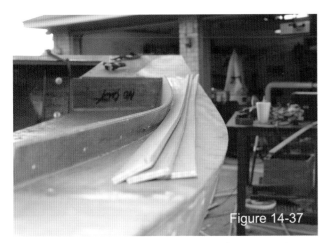

Figure 14-37

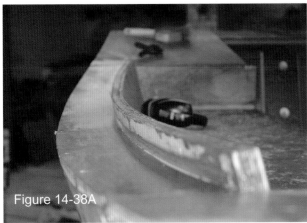

Figure 14-38A

Figure 14-38B

Figure 14-39

the combings (see deck section). With the decks on then fit the sloped piece (**Figure 14-36**). This will take some hand fitting like a good deal of the cockpit. I used 9mm for this piece and found that I didn't think that provided enough thickness. So I added several layers of 9mm on the outside edge to beef it up (**Figure 14-37**).

This meant cutting a bevel on the plywood and then clamping the layers in place (**Figures 14-38 A** and **38B**). This thicker section was rounded over

and a small breakwater was added to the forward section (**Figure 14-39**). The sole purpose of the breakwater is to keep water that runs along the deck out of the cockpit.

The angle of the breakwater between the hatch and the combing was completely arbitrary. In **Figure14-39** you can see a line I drew on the deck. That was supposed to be the placement but for some reason I moved it back some.

This portion of the interior was very complex, and in some cases, like the combing, interdependent with others. As you work along on the interior, in many cases it will seem as if there is just no movement and this can be discouraging. But then one day one small job is completed and a bunch of others fall into place and you take a giant leap forward. Keep that in mind when you feel like you are running in molasses.

15

Pouring the Ballast

You would think that of all the different tasks in building this boat pouring the ballast would require little or no thinking or planning. Sorry, even this requires some planning and thought.

First, I think it's important to define ballast and what it includes. A very general description of ballast is anything that adds weight to the bottom of the boat like the steel centerboards and centerboard cases, the batteries, and of course, the lead and concrete. I might also add that the layers of plywood, cloth and epoxy on the bottom contribute to the ballast as well.

The point being, that you have to keep track of all that or the boat will weigh too much. I weighed the centerboards and the centerboard cases and I knew what the batteries weighed. Those were totaled up and deducted from the 600 pounds of ballast. That meant I put 350 pounds of fixed ballast and 150 pounds of trim ballast in place.

I had hoped to use concrete as the sole source for fixed ballast, but I changed my mind and decided to use mostly lead with a small amount of concrete. I discovered later that lead was becoming increasingly harder to come by and therefore increasingly expensive. Actually, it had become very expensive.

I did stumble across a reasonably priced source for lead, but it takes advance planning to accumulate enough for the ballast. What I discovered were the little lead weights used to balance tire rims. When tire stores rebalance tires they throw away the old wheel weights and put on new ones.

A 5 gallon plastic bucket of "thrown away" wheel weights tips the scales at about 125 pounds. I was able to negotiate a very reasonable price for a bucket of weights at pennies per pound instead of dollars a pound.

The advanced planning comes in finding a tire store that will sell you the used wheel weights and then collecting them. I found the small independent stores receptive to the idea while the big chain stores had corporate policies that prohibited them from selling me the weights.

Not only do you have to find a store willing to sell you the weights but you have to allow enough time for the store to collect enough weights. A busy store can take 3 to 4 months to fill a 5 gallon bucket. That means you must start this process about the time you lay the keel (start construction on your boat).

Because you laid your keel way back when, at this point you should have three 5 gallon buckets of wheel weights and two bags of ready mix concrete sitting ready to go in the boat. Also, you should have the boat sitting on the trailer). I strongly advise to **not** add the ballast until you have the boat on the trailer.

The first step is to level the trailer (this is much easier than trying to level the boat) both athwartship (**Figure 15-1**) and fore and aft (**Figure 15-2**). If the driveway or surface the trailer sits on is fairly level then a shim under the wheel will do but you may have to use a jack and blocks for big differences.

Figure 15-1

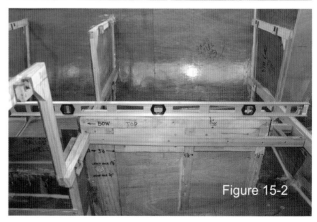
Figure 15-2

Figure 15-3 shows the forward section of the keel box (the bow is on the right of the photo) with stainless screws surrounded by epoxy in the side of the keel. I think a much better way to do this is to add the screws to a separate strip and then epoxy that to the side of the keel. The real danger with screwing directly into the keel is running a screw all the way through the keel side.

Next my son and I weighed out 25 pounds of wheel weights (**Figure 15-4**) and poured them into the forward keel box (**Figure 15-5**). These were tamped down like grapes to compress the weights and make a denser package. We worked in 25 pound units until we reached the desired amount of ballast.

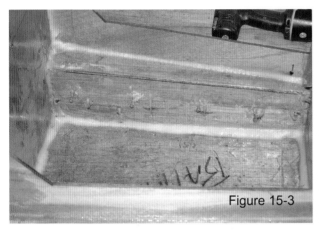

Figure 15-3

Figure 15-4

Figure 15-5

I could have melted the lead and made small pigs that would have been compact and kept the weight of the ballast lower, but I didn't do that and you shouldn't either. In fact, let me be more direct—**Don't do it!** Melting lead is very dangerous. If there is any water on the wheel weights being added to the molten pot, the water will cause an explosive reaction and spray molten lead all over you and anything close to the pot. If that isn't scary enough, molten lead gives off highly toxic fumes that require a special respirator *and* it's more than likely just downright illegal in your area.

The forward compartment had 120 pounds of lead poured in and then we added 20 pounds of concrete (We actually added 40 pounds of concrete to compensate for the water that would evaporate) for a total of 140 pounds of fixed ballast. I had held back 150 pounds of ballast (batteries) for moveable trim ballast. It is always a good idea to hold back some ballast for moveable trim because the boat may float a bit differently than you think.

The amount of fixed ballast you add will vary some from my amounts and that's why you need to keep accurate records of weights. **Figure 15-6** is how I did the calculations on the ballast and is the corrected post launch figures.

After I launched the boat I found I had too much weight toward the stern and should have added at least 50 pounds to the forward section. In other words I should have had 50 pounds less in the aft section and 50 pounds more in the forward section. I was able to have the boat float level because I could move the trim ballast where I needed it. If you do all the math carefully the boat should float fairly close to her lines when she is launched

Figure 15-6

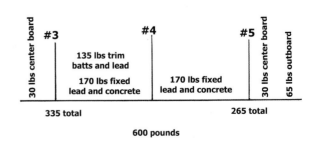

Figure 15-7

Figure 15-9

Figure 15-8

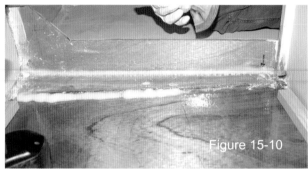

Figure 15-10

but you really won't know until she is in the water. That's when you plan on permanently placing the trim ballast.

In **Figure 15-7** we have added the wheel weights and in **Figure 15-8** we have not only poured in the concrete but put the date and my initials. Wet concrete seems to bring out the six year old in us all.

Depending on the time of year the concrete will take a while to completely cure and dry out. Two weeks is probably a safe average if the temperature is around 75 degrees.

I would wait as long as possible before adding the plywood over the top (**Figures 15-9** and **10**). The plywood covering will give you something to screw into for the batteries and just as importantly, help keep the concrete and lead in place should disaster strike and the boat find herself inverted.

More than one boat has come to an unhappy end because the ballast shifted, and this is a good thing to keep in mind as you secure the plywood and cleats to the bulkheads.

16

The Hatch

I suspect that some builders will wonder why I chose to use a large hatch rather than a companionway to access the small cuddy. There were a couple of reasons really, but the main reason was that a hatch is watertight (more or less) and therefore better at keeping water from getting below decks.

There is a great deal of volume below decks and unless that gets flooded these boats should stay afloat in a hard chance. Does that make these boats unsinkable? Of course not, any boat can sink and the floor of the ocean is littered with boats that were supposed to be unsinkable and very seaworthy.

So, a hatch is watertight (more or less) and a hatch is a little simpler to build than a good, somewhat watertight companionway. Actually, compared to some of the other tasks you've accomplished the hatch is very straightforward and simple.

The first thing I did was establish how big to make the hatch. I'm a big believer in doing a full size mock-up when possible. I found a scrap piece of plywood, cut out a 24 X 40 inch section and laid it up on the boat (**Figure 16-1** and **16-2**).

This let me determine if I had enough room to easily get in and out of the cuddy. After a bit of study, I decided that 24 X 40 was too big and reduced the hatch to 23 X 33½. But after sailing the boat I'm sorry I didn't leave the width at 40 inches.

The hatch size was arbitrary, and you may decide to use a different hatch size. Whatever the dimension of the hatch you settle on, be sure to do the mock up and don't make this a snap judgment.

Notice in the photos the hatch opening runs to the bulkhead but that is not practical. The opening needs to be set back from the bulkhead by at least 3½ inches.

Once you decide on the size of the hatch opening find and mark the centerline on top of bulk-

Figure 16-1

Figure 16-2

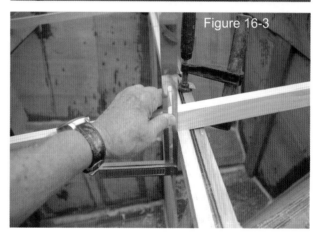

Figure 16-3

heads #2 and #3. You will use these marks to center and place the framework for the hatch.

The first pieces that frame-in the hatch will be fore and aft or parallel to the centerline. In **Figures 16-3** and **16-4** the first fore and aft piece sits on top of bulkhead #2 and a straight edge is used to carry the line of the bulkhead up. **Figure 16-5** shows bulkhead #3 and that the line of the bulkhead has been carried up to the ¾ X 1½ fir brace.

Both the port and starboard pieces were cut, dropped in place to be sure they fit, and then I cut

Figure 16-4

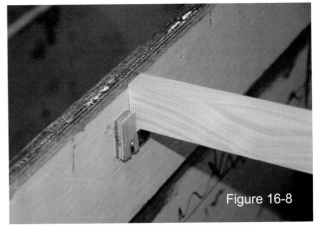

Figure 16-8

Figure 16-5

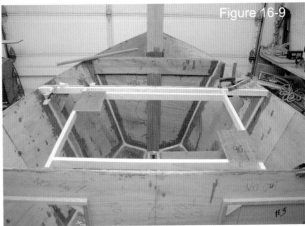

Figure 16-9

Figure 16-6

Figure 16-10

Figure 16-7

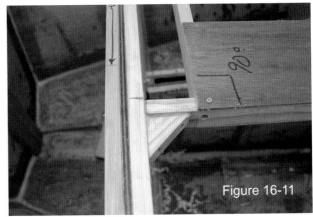

Figure 16-11

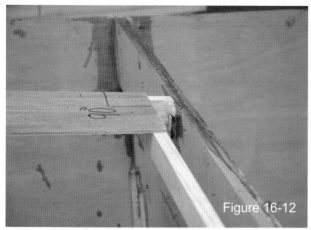

Figure 16-12

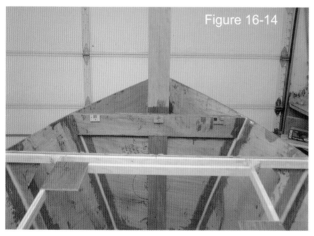

Hatch this side

Figure 16-13

Figure 16-14

Figure 16-15

Figure 16-16

two 33½-inch pieces. These were screwed to the fore and aft pieces to create the framework for the hatch. In my case the interior dimension of the frame was 23 X 33½.

This frame was then dropped back in place. A temporary rest held the forward section on bulkhead #2 (**Figures 16-6** and **16-7**) and a permanent plywood bracket captured the aft end on bulkhead #3 (**Figure 16-8**).

In **Figure 16-9** 90 degree angles have been added to the corners after the first trial fitting of the frame. I did this because I found the corners slightly off when I checked them with a square and I wanted the frame to be as square as possible. Using the squares is a good idea and will insure that the interior frame for the hatch stays square.

Next, I added a small block to outside of both corners on the #2 bulkhead. **Figure 16-10** is a close up of the left hand or port side of the frame with the small block in place. These blocks will secure the frame when the temporary supports are removed.

When the dry fit was complete and I was satisfied that everything thing was as square as possible, I epoxied the frame in place (**Figures 16-11, 16-12,** and **16-13**). I used small fillets and screws on all the joints **except** the four corners of the interior frame. Notice in **Figure 16-13** that there is no fillet in that corner. That's because the plywood for the hatch base must fit on that side (**Figures 16-14, 16-15,** and **16-16**).

As you can see in **Figure 16-16**, I made the first layer from 18mm (¾-inch) plywood 3½ inches

Figure 16-17

Figure 16-21

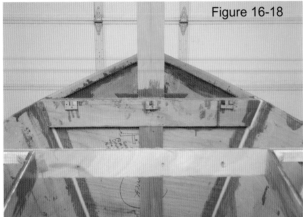

Figure 16-18

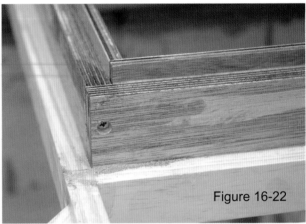

Figure 16-22

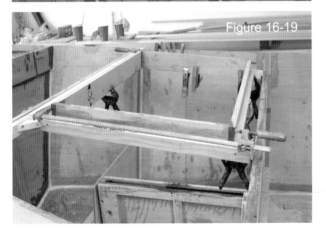

Figure 16-19

Figure 16-23

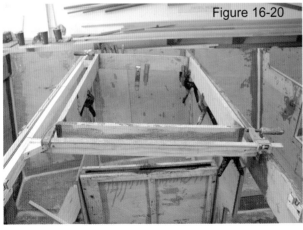

Figure 16-20

Figure 16-24

high. I didn't miter the corners and recommend that you don't either. I think you get a much tighter fit letting one side overlap the other (**Figure 16-17**).

This is one of those areas in which you should take your time and get a very tight fit at the corners. Just imagine green water pouring over the deck trying to find its way below, and you won't be tempted to hurry through the fitting process.

I used epoxy and screws to hold the first layer in place. I wanted to be sure that this joint would stand stress and be a good watertight joint. **Figure 16-18** shows three screws per side and I came back and added three more per side.

Figures 16-19 and **16-20** gives a good clear picture of how I clamped the first layer. The bar clamps pulled the corners together and after the epoxy had set, I used screws to back up the epoxy at the corners. I also cleaned ALL the excess epoxy out of the corners because the next layer needed to fit tight against the first.

With that in mind, be sure to countersink all the screws as well (**Figure 16-21**). Nothing will interfere with a good fit of the next layer of plywood like a screw head standing proud.

I used 9mm plywood 4 inches wide for the next layer and that gave me a ½-inch lip for the hatch to overlap. I staggered the ends of the inter frame as well, to create a strong joint and water proof corner (**Figure 16-22**). I use this type of lap or stagger whenever possible.

Figure 16-23 shows the profile of the hatch cover molding sitting on the hatch base with the 9mm plywood insert in place. This arrangement makes it very difficult for water to make its way below.

I cut a window for a piece of 3/8-inch lexan in the hatch cover (**Figure 16-24**) and I recommend you do so as well. I found the hatch cover without the window too claustrophobic.

The 3/8 lexan sits on a lip (**16-25** and **16-26**) and is bedded in silicone for a watertight seal. We fabricated a bronze lip for the top side, but thin wood would serve the same function (**Figure 16-27**). This created a window that was strong enough to walk on.

Figure 16-25

Figure 16-26

Figure 16-27

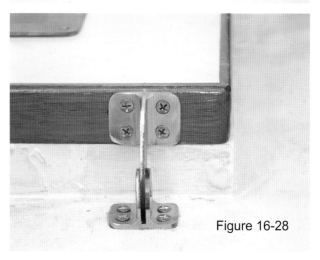

Figure 16-28

I elected to use a special hinge for the hatch cover. I had seen this hinge at some point, but a long search failed to produce a source for the hinge. Its real benefit is allowing a fairly high lip to be used and still lift clear. I felt it was worth the effort to fabricate it from bronze (**Figures 16-28** and **16-29**).

After sailing the boat for a summer I can say, without a doubt, that I'm pleased with the hatch and very happy I didn't build a companionway. I like the way the hatch looks and I like its ability to keep water from getting below decks. That all adds up to a good recommendation for using the hatch.

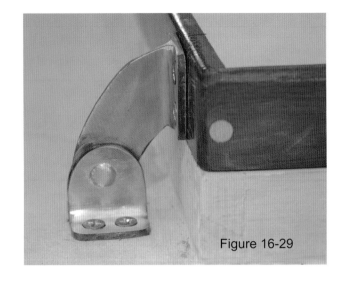

Figure 16-29

17

The Transom and Skeg

I decided to add a skeg to these boats for a couple of reasons. First a rudder that hangs vertically is very easy to build and is much less likely to stall when hard over (dory rudders can suffer from this). Also, a skeg adds some additional keel (lateral resistance) at the very stern of the boat; in the case of the 16.5, the skeg adds 16 inches.

It is a bit more work, perhaps, but I've never been sorry that I added the skeg. The 16.5 responds to the helm in a very positive fashion, even at very slow speeds when the rudder is more likely to stall. This is due, in large part I believe, to the action of the skeg.

Building the skeg and finishing out the transom are, like most of the jobs on this boat, spread out over the building process. While the boat is still upside down you will want to measure for the aft most portion of the skeg (the skeg is put on the boat in two sections—an aft section that attached to the outside of the transom and a forward section that attaches to the bottom of the boat).

In **Figure 17-1** and **17-2** a flat board has been attached to the keel and a tape/plumb bob hung from the end of the board (the tape I used was zeroed at the bottom side of the board which is the line of the keel and baseline). It's important that all the measurements you take are from the underside of the board.

Notice that in **Figure 17-2** the tape/plumb bob rests directly against the top of the transom. You want to be sure that it just touches the transom but still hangs straight down. This will allow you to measure from the true vertical over to the boat (**Figure 17-3**).

Figure 17-4A shows each dimension you will need to take from the tape/plumb bob. Every boat will be slightly different so measure carefully because this will create an accurate picture of the aft most portion of the skeg.

Once I had the drawing of the aft skeg, I lami-

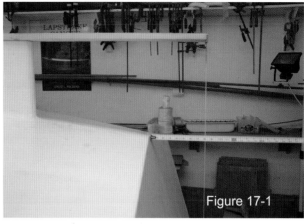

Figure 17-1

Figure 17-2

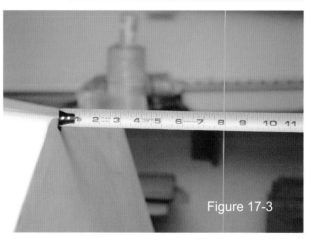

Figure 17-3

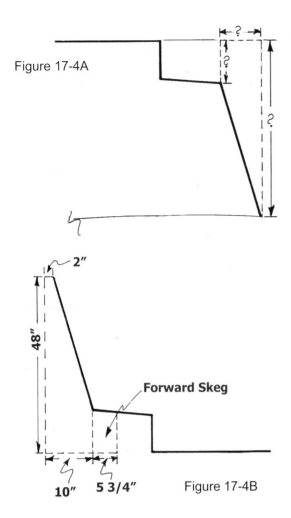

Figure 17-4A

Figure 17-4B

2"

48"

Forward Skeg

10"   5 3/4"

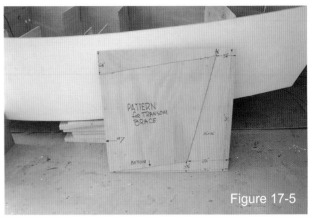

Figure 17-5

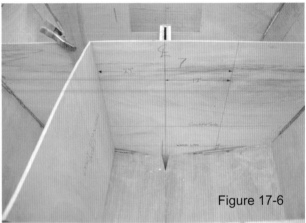

Figure 17-6

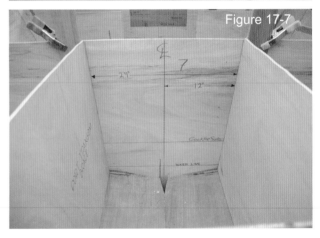

Figure 17-7

nated a blank together that was 48 inches by 10 inches by 1 ¾ inches thick. I added two inches to the width of the aft skeg so hanging the rudder would be easier (**Figure 17-4B**). Remember your numbers will be somewhat different from mine and I added extra to both the height and the width.

The lay-up schedule was a piece of 18mm, a piece of 9mm, and a piece of 18mm. This gave an overall thickness of approximately 1 ¾ inches. Once the epoxy had hardened, I cleaned and squared up the blank and set it aside until I was ready to add it to the boat.

I wasn't ready to continue working on the skeg and transom until the hull was turned over and moved back into the shop. Then it was time to move to the next step, which was adding the transom braces and the internal framing.

Figure 17-5 shows the layout for my transom braces on a 36 inch by 36 inch square. You can use

these numbers as a starting point for your braces. Start with scrap plywood, work until you get a good fit, and then cut each brace from 9mm plywood.

In **Figures 17-6** and **17-7** you can see the dimensions of the motor well and the placement of the braces. Both photos were taken facing forward or facing your bulkhead #6. Remember your #6 is my #7.

It will be best if you get the cleats or framing for the transom braces in place (**Figure 17-8**) before

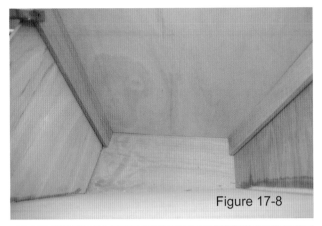

Figure 17-8

Figure 17-12

Figure 17-9

Figure 17-13

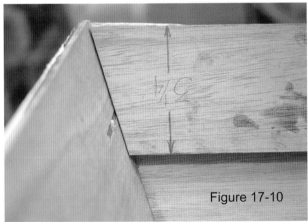

Figure 17-10

Figure 17-14

Figure 17-11

you add the bracing or cleats on the transom (**Figure 17-9**). Please note that the cleats for the transom braces are on the opposite side of the motor well.

The next order of business will be to add the cleats to the sheer (**Figure 17-10**) and to the top of the transom (**Figure 17-11**). When those cleats are epoxied in place, you will want to add heavy fillets to each and every joint and seam. **Figures 17-12** and **17-13** give a view facing forward and aft respectively.

In **Figure 17-14** I'm putting a heavy fillet and tape on the forward side (the side facing the bow)

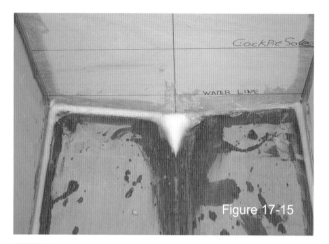

Figure 17-15

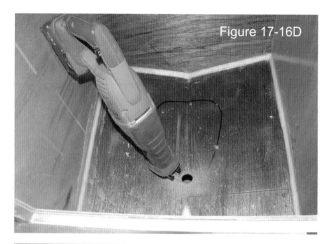

Figure 17-16D

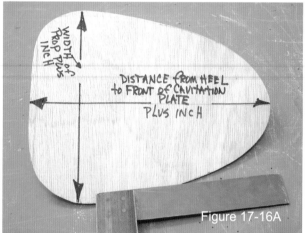

Figure 17-16A

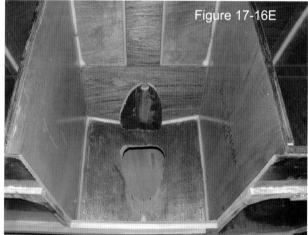

Figure 17-16E

Figure 17-16B

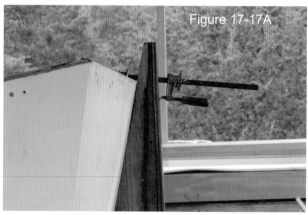

Figure 17-17A

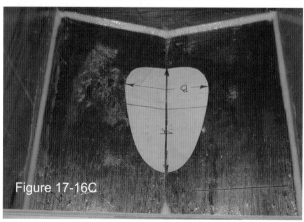

Figure 17-16C

Figure 17-17B

of my bulkhead #7 (your bulkhead #6). The area just behind the centerboard case received a very heavy fillet and extra tape because once the cockpit sole and decking are in place this area will be very difficult to access.

Figure 17-15 is the aft side of my bulkhead #7 (your bulkhead #6) or the aft side of the bulkhead in photo **17-14** and shows heavy fillets being applied to all the joints and seams. This is the inside of the motor well and will have water up to, and above, the waterline marked on the bulkhead whenever the boat is in the water. In other words, this area is the outside of the hull.

Notice the cavity that was in **Figure 17-7** has been filled with thickened epoxy. Actually I poured in the epoxy that had the consistency of thin yogurt. That insured that there was no way water could find a small gap or sit in the cavity and cause problems.

The old ship builders used a similar technique with hot pitch. They would pour hot pitch into those areas that might collect water (particularly fresh water). When the pitch hardened it kept water out of the crevice and increased the longevity of the ship. I always liked that idea and just substituted epoxy for pitch.

At some point after everything has fillets and the cavities are filled you will want to cut out the hole for the outboard motor. I found this to be a very intimidating step. There is nothing like picking up a Sawzall and chopping a big old hole in the bottom of your boat to make you move slowly and thoughtfully.

The first thing you want to do is to make a pattern for the hole based on measurements taken from the outboard itself (**Figure 17-16A**). This means that you need to have the outboard in your possession at this point. It would be a terrible mistake to proceed without having the actual motor that is going to drop in the motor well.

Every brand of motor is different and the 6 horsepower is different from the 8 horsepower and so on. Get the outboard ahead so you will have it sitting by the boat when you arrive at this point. The margin for error here is very small.

Notice in **Figure 17-16A** I added an inch both ways to the pattern. I felt that an inch gave enough room to drop in the motor and I didn't want the hole to be too big. It is important to note that the heel of the cavitation plate sits against the end of the keel, not the heel of the skeg and prop (**Figure 17-16B**). My thinking was I could always make the hole bigger but it was very difficult to make it smaller. As it turned out, for my motor, an inch was just right (the Goldilocks Principle at work again).

The placement of the pattern in the well was the next step. I wanted the heel of the outboard to sit directly behind the keel so I needed to know exactly where the keel ended. I did this by drilling a pilot hole right at the end of the keel up into the motor well. This is located exactly where the pattern should be (**Figure 17-16C**).

I used a black marker to trace around the pattern and then drilled a large hole right at the edge of the mark and on the centerline (**Figure 17-16D**). Be sure to drill the large hole there rather than randomly inside the pattern. This allows you to save the cut out and use it as a drop in filler (**Figure 17-16E**).

Once the cut out for the motor was set a side in a safe place it was time to attach the aft portion of the skeg. I clamped the skeg to the transom (**Figure 17-17A**) and used plywood wings clamped to the side of the skeg to help line it up exactly behind the keel (**Figure 17-17B**).

If the plywood wings are flush with the bottom of the skeg it will help you line everything up with the bottom of the keel. In the very bottom of the photo **17-17B**, you can just barely make out a box that the skeg is resting on. I used shims and the box to bring the bottom of the skeg even with the bottom of the keel. That is, the bottom of the skeg should be on the same level as the bottom of the keel. It goes with out saying that it should be perfectly vertical as well.

When everything thing is lined up perfectly, drill a series of holes on centerline for ¼-inch stainless steel lag bolts (**Figure 17-18** and **17-19**). After all the bolts are tightened, remove the clamps and

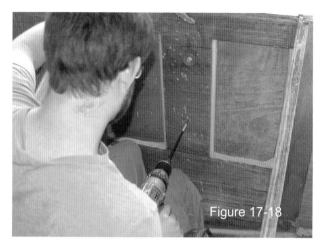

Figure 17-18

Figure 17-19

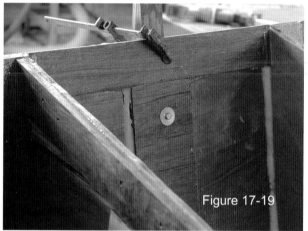

Figure 17-20A

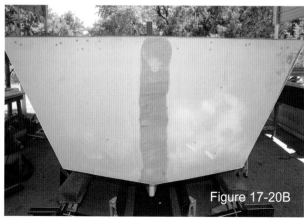

Figure 17-20B

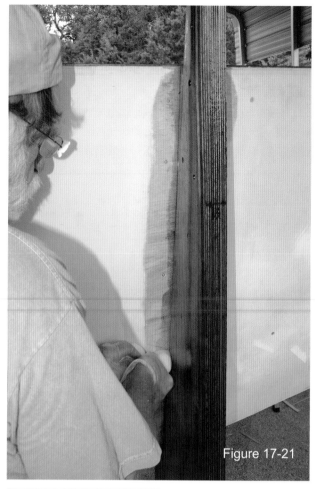

Figure 17-21

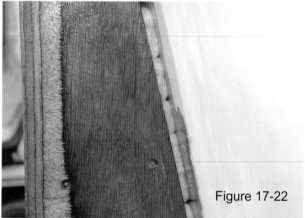

Figure 17-22

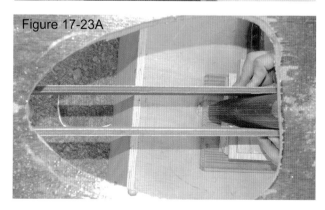

Figure 17-23A

Figure 17-23B

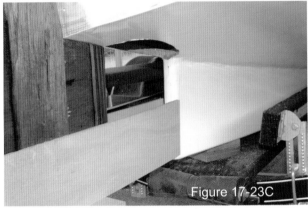

Figure 17-23C

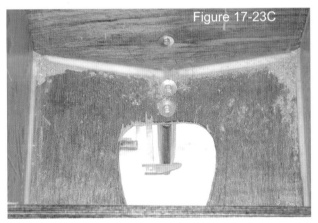

Figure 17-23C

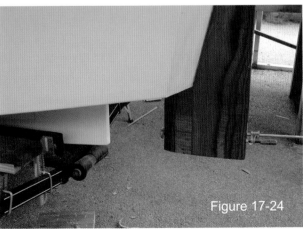

Figure 17-24

strike a line on either side of the skeg. Now remove the skeg, and using a nail set, punch a series of very small holes along the line (**Figure 17-20A**). The purpose of these holes is to assure you that the skeg has returned to its exact position.

Now sand down to bare wood (**Figure 17-20B**) and then return the skeg to the transom. Use the ¼-inch lag bolts as registration pins but don't tighten everything down just yet. Leave a small gap of about a ½-inch and use peanut butter-epoxy to completely fill the space (**Figure 17-21** and **17-22**). Once you have that space loaded with peanut butter-epoxy, tighten the lag bolts down. You want these bolts to be tight, very tight, but it is possible to over tighten and strip out the hole. This will be more likely to happen if you have a great deal of leverage with the wrench.

I used ¼ X 4-inch long lag bolts but towards the top of the skeg you might want to use 3-inchers so you don't run out the other side of the skeg. The long bolts can build up a great deal of friction in a tight hole and it is possible to break one off as you tighten down. So what happens if you twist off a bolt? Not much, just drop down an inch or so and drill a new pilot hole; this time just a tiny bit bigger than before.

What you do want is as much bury as you can get with the lag bolts. This is very important with the forward section of the skeg. By the time you get to the forward skeg you should have a good feel for how tight is too much or not enough.

The alignment of the forward skeg is really critical, so take your time and get it right. The ears on the side of the skeg (**Figure 17-23 A, 17-23B and 17-23C**) will be a big help in getting this alignment exactly centered. The key will be checking and rechecking your dry fit before you set the bolts and do the epoxy (**Figure 17-23D**).

I was satisfied that I had the alignment right but when I pulled the box and all the supports I could see that the skeg would collect pot wraps and other flotsam. Also, an encounter with an underwater obstacle could lead to serious structural issues (**Figure 17-24**).

To keep this from happening I added a bronze

Figure 17-25A

Figure 17-25B

section that spanned the gap and also functioned as an endplate for the skeg. Endplates are well proven to increase the effectiveness of both skegs and rudders (**Figure 17-25A**).

I extended the endplate past the aft face of the skeg so it would serve as a lip for the rudder and its endplate to sit (**Figure 17-25B**). This made installing the gudgeons and pintles really easy.

Stainless steel could be easily substituted for the bronze. See the section in the appendix for the drawing of the skeg endplate and spanner.

18

The Rudder, Tiller, and Gudgeons and Pintles

The rudder and tiller are projects that can be worked on almost from the very start of the boat. Both can be done in odd moments of down time, set aside, and taken back up when time is found to continue work. This will mean that both will be there when they are needed.

Figure 18-1 gives the dimensions you will need to lay out the rudder's shape. Use a scrap piece of plywood (3 or 4mm Luan works very well) and get the final shape before cutting the 12mm plywood.

The lay-up order was the same as the skeg so I cut one 12mm side to the exact shape I wanted and then rough cut the 9mm and the other

12mm. I buttered all the pieces with heavy cream epoxy and clamped them together (**Figure 18-2**). If you look closely at **18-2** you can see where I set screws down the center.

Use stainless screws here because they can be left in place in the upper portion of the rudder. Screws set in the lower half will have to be removed because that will be shaped into a foil section.

A close-up of the end of the rudder (**Figure 18-3**) shows how the 9mm and 12mm hang over the 12mm that was cut to the final shape. This allows

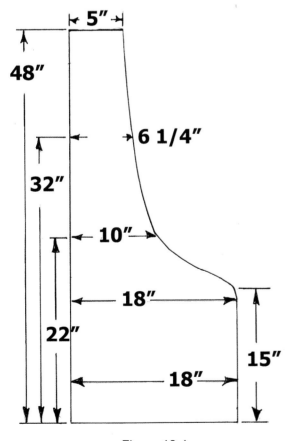
Figure 18-1

Figure 18-2

Figure 18-3

a router with a flush trim bit to bring all the layers to the final shape (**Figure 18-4**). I think you'll find this is a very fast and effective method. If the overhang is greater than about a ¼-inch you may want trim the overhang back with a saber saw first then use the router.

When I had the rudder trimmed up I put it on the boat to be sure everything fit (**Figure 18-5**). This will be a good time to mark the waterline on the rudder as well. You might want to step back a bit and take a look at the rudder on the boat just to be sure you are happy with the aesthetics.

If you decide to make some changes now is the time. You don't want to change the wetted area of the rudder but the shape above the waterline can be adjusted somewhat to your personal taste.

I created the foil shape for the area below the waterline by starting the aft taper 7 inches back from the forward edge (**Figure 18-6A**) and carrying that line back to a point 1/8-inch from the center of the board (**Figure 18-6B**). I didn't taper the end of the rudder more than a ¼-inch even though finer is better. Very thin blades are easily damaged on a "knock-about" beach cruiser like these.

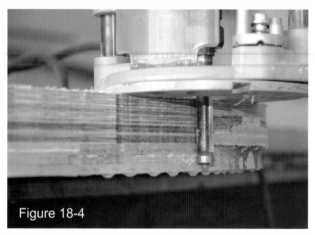

Figure 18-4

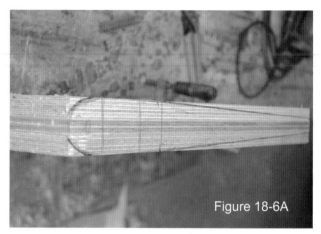

Figure 18-6A

Figure 18-6B

Figure 18-5

Then I placed a mark 3 inches aft of the forward edge and drew the curve on each side. Notice that the forward point ends at the 9mm plywood on both sides making the leading edge 9mm wide (**Figure 18-7**).

Figure 18-8A shows the rudder with half of the foil shape ground away with a belt sander. A belt sander with a 40 grit belt will make removing the material down to the line very fast and easy work.

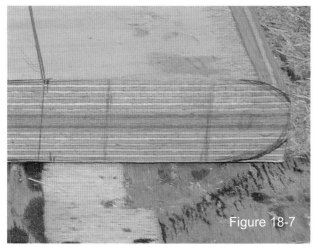

Figure 18-7

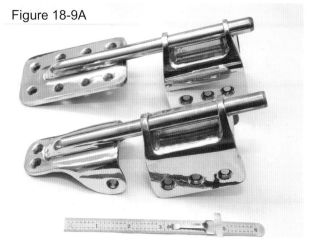

Figure 18-9A

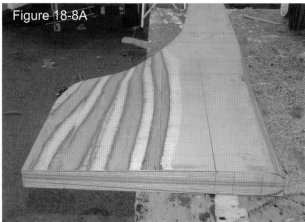

Figure 18-8A

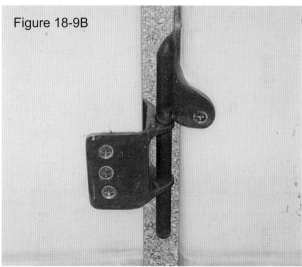

Figure 18-9B

Figure 18-8B

I think it's important to note that I kept the rudder's trailing edge at ¼-inch up to the waterline and then gradually increased the width (**Figure 18-8B**). The waterline ends at the black bottom paint and the blue stripe is 6 inches high.

When you are satisfied with the shape and the taper, coat the rudder with multiple layers of epoxy. I used five coats of epoxy. I wanted to be sure that the laminations were well protected from water

intrusion and the resulting delamination.

The rudder will need to be at this stage of completion in order to work on the gudgeons and pintles. If you are fabricating them yourself, then you can now take the dimensions you need directly from the rudder. If you are having them fabricated, you can take the measurements you need to give to the welder.

Figure 18-9A is a close-up of the bronze gudgeons and pintles. I used ½" rod, 1/8" plate, and 3/16-inch plate to fabricate the pieces. Everything is drilled and countersunk for #10 bronze screws.

The rod allows the rudder to have about 2½ inches of vertical movement. I felt this was important for a beach cruiser that might find itself sitting on uneven ground on a falling tide. The bottom gudgeon and pintle is attached with the rod pointed down (**Figure 18-9B**) and the upper gudgeon and pintle has the rod pointed up

Figure 18-9C

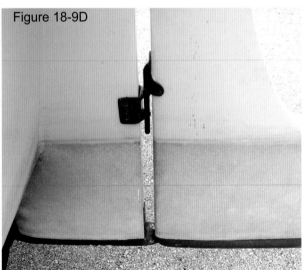

Figure 18-9D

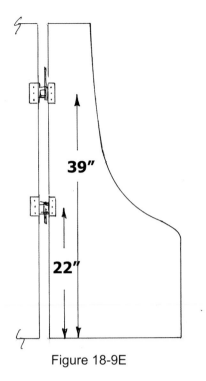

Figure 18-9E

(**Figure 18-9C**). This has the added benefit of locking the rudder on the skeg and unless something is torn loose it will stay in place.

Also, you can see in **Figure 18-9D** that the bottom gudgeon and pintle is above the waterline (the brown line that marks the waterline on the rudder is the result of a summer in the water without any anti-fouling paint) and doesn't interfere

with the flow of water over the rudder. **Figure 18-9E** gives the heights above the base of the rudder for both sets of gudgeons and pintles.

If you don't want to fabricate or have the gudgeon and pintles fabricated I suspect you should be able to find something off the shelf that will do the job. Just like you can buy a tiller ready made if you don't want to make one yourself. I made my tiller and I've had comments ranging from "you made the tiller yourself?" to "Why didn't you just buy a ready made tiller?"

It would have been easy to just buy a tiller, but it was easier to laminate it myself. I wanted a bit of a curve to the tiller so when I set up the laminating jig I put a slight curve in (**Figure 18-10A**). This was purely a personal choice on my part. A straight tiller would certainly work and I've seen many that are straight as an arrow but a slight curve seems more graceful to me. I might add that the amount of curve was completely arbitrary and solely based on what I thought looked good.

I ripped eight ¼-inch X 1 ¾-inch strips, buttered everything with heavy cream epoxy (just like the rudder) and clamped it in the jig. This gave a blank that was 1 ¾ inches X 2 inches (**Figure 18-10B**). Again your dimensions may be slightly different so

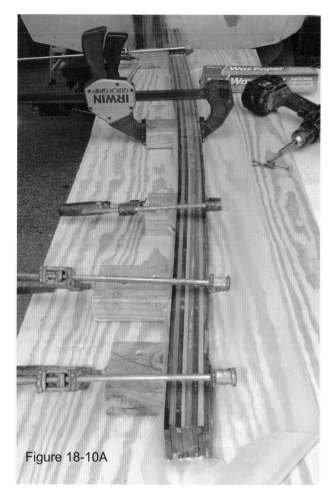

Figure 18-10A

Figure 18-10B

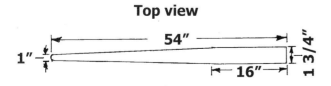

Top view

Figure 18-10C

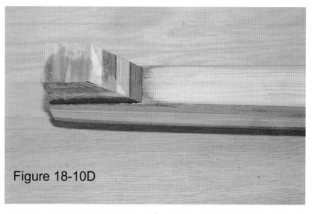

Figure 18-10D

Figure 18-11

be sure the width of your tiller is the same as the rudder so it will fit between the rudder cheeks (**Figure 18-11** and **18-12**).

Figure 18-10C shows the top of the tiller. The taper I used was completely based on what looked good to my eye. You can use these numbers as a rough guide or duplicate my tiller. I suggest looking at a number of tillers to get a feel for what you want. That's exactly what I did.

As you look at tillers you will notice most if not all have some sort of lip or bulge at the very end where you hand fits. I was going to put a Turk's Head knot along with 12 inches or so of service at the end but opted for the more simple

131

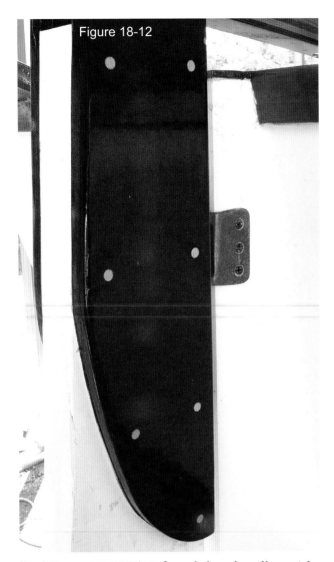

Figure 18-12

Figure 18-13A

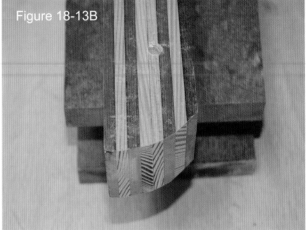

Figure 18-13B

lip (**Figure 18-10D**). I found that the tiller, without anything, felt strange in my hand and it looked incomplete but this is arbitrary.

The shape of the rudder cheeks was just as arbitrary as the shape of the tiller. I'd seen these style cheeks on several rudders and liked the simple clean sweep (**Figure 18-11**). I played with this shape for while and used a lot of scrap plywood before I found the final shape. This will be something that you will live with for a long time so I suggest you do the same.

I used ¾-inch thick African Mahogany for the rudder cheeks and used the plywood pattern cut to a shape I liked. I found a very nice piece with some burl, cut one to the exact shape, rough cut the other, and then used a router to bring them to make them identical.

Both cheeks were put on dry with screws. I put

these on in a pattern and used contrasting dowels on the final fit, so I was very careful with the placement of the screws (**Figure 18-12**). When you're satisfied with the fit, epoxy them in place and leave the screws in place. The rudder cheeks can be subjected to serious stress and the screws are added insurance.

With both cheeks on, you will need to drill for the pin that holds the tiller in place. The best way is to locate the tiller where you want it and then drill all three at the same time (**Figure 18-13A**). This will require that the drill be absolutely vertical and at a 90 degree angle to the face of the rudder cheeks.

Now round the end of the tiller so it will lift vertically in the cheeks (**Figure 18-13B**). This is important and will require a bit of trial and error to get the right curve. Remember it is much easier to take a bit more off than to try and add it back. Work slowly!

I used a bronze pin (**Figure 18-13C**) but stain-

Figure 18-13C

Figure 18-13D

less will work as well. I used thin squares of clear pine to capture the pin on either side of the rudder (**Figure 18-13D**) but I think I'll change them to small bronze plates. The bronze or stainless steel wouldn't be as delicate as the pine.

19

The Main and Mizzen Tabernacles

The Main Tabernacle

The tabernacles are projects that will start almost as soon as you turn over the boat and continue until the boat is almost ready to launch. Unfortunately fabricating the main tabernacle has to take place after the fore deck is down but the good news is the deck is in place early enough so there is plenty of time to have the tabernacle fabricated.

As soon as the boat is turned over and back in the shop you'll want to get the hull level. The hull needs to be level, not only athwart ship, but fore and aft as well.

In **Figure 19-1** I placed a 48 inch level across the bulkhead at station 2 and clamped the main tabernacle compression post to the forward face of bulkhead 1.

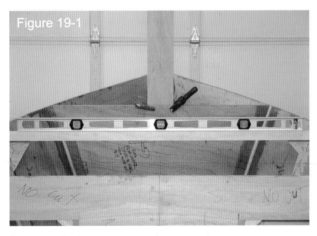
Figure 19-1

This 5-inch wide piece of 18mm (¾-inch) plywood will be permanently epoxied to the face of #1 and extend down to the keel. Its function is to spread the load of the deck mounted tabernacle to the bulkhead and keel.

Because this piece will fit inside the tabernacle it must be perfectly plumb and that means the hull must be perfectly level. **Figure 19-2** is a close up of the bubble. Take your time and get the hull

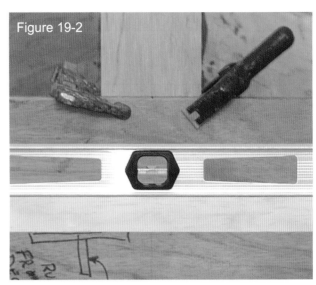
Figure 19-2

Figure 19-3

compression post

perfect. If the bubble is a slight bit off that error will magnify to the very end and the mast will not be plumb.

Once you are satisfied the hull is braced up in a perfectly level position then attach a level to the compression post (**Figure 19-3**). This will need to be as perfectly plumb as you can get the piece. Take your time here as well and center the bubble as best you can (**Figure 19-4**). Remember being off a 1/32-inch here translates to inches at the top of the mast.

Having the centerline of the 5-inch compression post match the centerline of the bulkhead is another area where you don't want any error (**Figure 19-5**). This photo is facing forward and shows the aft side of number 1. The post can drift off as you tap this board plumb so check it frequently. Also notice that another 5-inch wide brace has been added to the top of number 1.

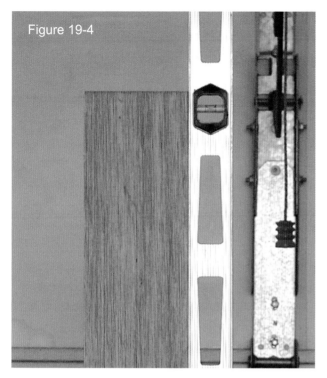

Figure 19-4

Figure 19-5

Figure 19-6A

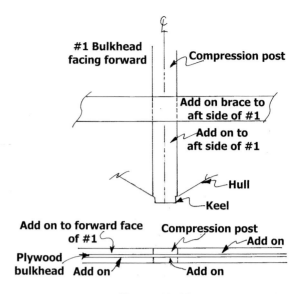

#1 Bulkhead facing forward — Compression post — Add on brace to aft side of #1 — Add on to aft side of #1 — Hull — Keel

Add on to forward face of #1 — Compression post — Add on — Plywood bulkhead — Add on — Add on

Figure 19-6B

Figure 19-7

Figure 19-6A is facing aft and shows the front side of bulkhead 1 and the relationship of the post to number 1. This bulkhead will beefed up considerably as **Figure 19-6B** indicates. I used 5-inch wide by 18mm plywood for all the add-on pieces and you should as well. You may find it simpler to add all the re-enforcement after the compression post is epoxied in place.

The last step for the compression post is to tilt it slightly aft. Use the level to find vertical and then tilt the top of the compression post aft ½ to 5/8-inch (**Figure 19-7**). This kicks the foot out at the keel and leaves a gap between the bulkhead and post (**Figure 19-8**). The best way to fill this gap with thicken epoxy is to load a baggie with very thick peanut butter epoxy and squirt it into the gap from top to bottom (**Figure 19-9**). It will

Figure 19-8

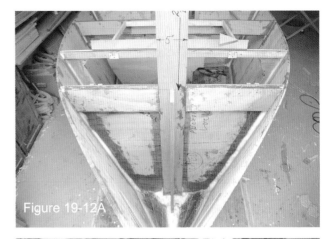

Figure 19-12A

Figure 19-9

Figure 19-12B

Figure 19-10

be important to put a large fillet right in front of the foot of the post as shown in **19-9**. Actually completely bedding it all the way around will be best. Wait until the epoxy has hardened then fasten the post to the bulkhead with #10 X 1½ stainless screws.

I set three right at the top of the bulkhead and then added all the additional bracing (**Figure 19-10**). When I set the vertical piece on the aft side of the bulkhead I used screws that were long enough to reach into the compression post on the other side of the bulkhead. This tied everything together mechanically and with epoxy.

As you can see in **Figure 19-11** I didn't try to match the bevel on the cross pieces and just filled the gaps with epoxy. Would it have been better to have a tighter fit? Maybe, but because these cross-pieces were epoxied and screwed to the bulkhead I doubt if there is any difference.

In addition to the cross bracing I added a piece to the forward side of the compression post (**Figure 19-12A** and **19-12B**). This piece sits directly below the mast with the deck and tabernacle rest-

Figure 19-11

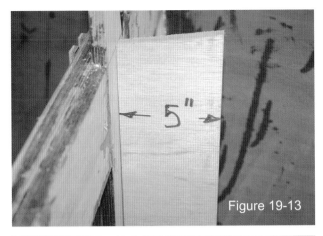
Figure 19-13

Figure 19-14

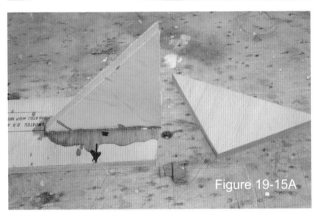
Figure 19-15A

Figure 19-15B

ing on its top. Notice the top of this 5-inch wide piece is cut at a slope to match the deck (**Figure 19-13** and **19-14**).

Then side pieces were added (**Figure 19-15A**) and the entire column was epoxied and taped (fiberglass tape was placed over the large fillets and then soaked with epoxy in place) so when the deck was put in place it carried the load down to the keel (**Figure 19-15B**). The large steel plate, just in front of the post, was cut to help spread the strain of the tabernacle over a much larger area than can be accomplished with large washers.

When the deck is in place then you can turn your attention to either having the steel tabernacle fabricated or fabricate it yourself. If you have it done, I'd recommend using stainless steel rather than steel plate. Aluminum would be a good choice as well because it's lightweight and that makes for less weight at the bow. Certainly wood could be used but I felt it would be too bulky looking.

3/16-inch bronze plate was my first choice until I discovered what that would cost, and then I went with steel plate.

Whatever material you use, the dimensions of the tabernacle will determined by the width of the compression post and the diameter at the foot of the mast. You need to have these before you can build the tabernacle.

In **Figure 19-16** the "A" dimension is the exact width of the compression post. In my case it was 5 inches, so that made the ID of "A" exactly 5 inches. I had to plane a bit off the compression post but this was preferable to a fit that was too loose. This is an area where exact fit is important.

It is important that the diameter of the foot of the mast NOT exceed the width of the compression post for obvious reasons. I had a little over a 1/16-inch clearance on both sides.

The "B" dimension is determined by the diameter at the foot of the mast but this dimension is not an exact one. In fact you want this to be about ¾-inch more than the diameter. This gives you the ability to adjust the center of effort of the mainsail a small amount by moving the foot of

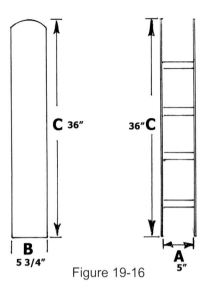

C 36" 36"C

B
5 3/4"

A
5"

Figure 19-16

Figure 19-17

Figure 19-18

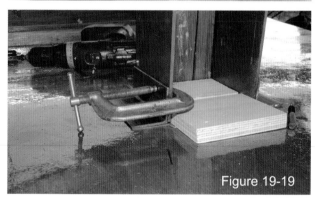

Figure 19-19

Figure 19-20

the mast in or out. A small amount of movement at the foot translates into a much larger movement at the top of the mast.

While the "B" dimension is not an exact dimension it will be better to have the mast already built and shaped. I have found that sometimes, despite our best efforts, a mast can be bigger than expected or smaller than expected.

The "C" dimension in **Figure 19-16** is 35 to 36 inches. This is the amount of bury the mast will have or how much support. Don't be tempted to make the tabernacle less than 35 inches high because the unstayed mast will need that support.

Once you have the A, B, and C dimensions you will need to establish the angle the tabernacle sits on the deck. Because I was fabricating the tabernacle myself, I put it on the boat (**Figure 19-17**), clamped the outside piece to the main body (**Figure 19-18, 19-19, 19-20**), removed it, and then welded everything in place.

If you are having someone else do the fabricating then the best way to establish that angle is with a plywood pattern of the side and a separate bottom piece. Clamp the side to the compression post and then screw the second piece to the side. I found that each side was slightly different so it will be safest to make a pattern for both sides.

When both sides are joined together and all the appropriate holes drilled the tabernacle should look like **Figure 19-21** and **19-22**. The cross-

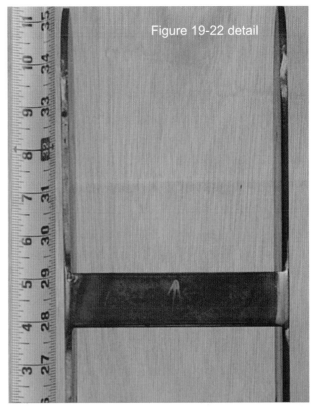

Figure 19-22 detail

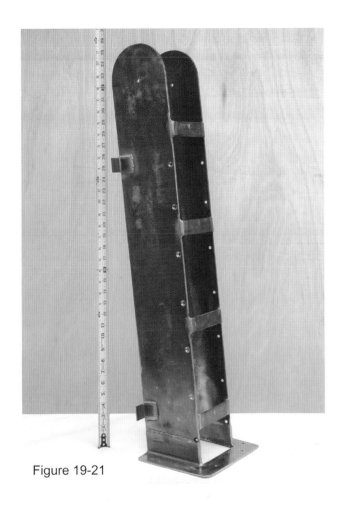

Figure 19-21

Figure 19-23A

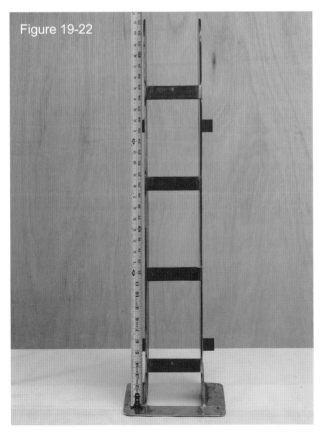

Figure 19-22

pieces are about 7½ inches apart but the top crosspiece should not be above 29 inches (**Figure 19-22 detail**). If the crosspiece is higher than 29 inches it will interfere with the lowering of the mast.

Figures 19-23A and **B** show a close up of the bars used to capture the mast in the tabernacle. There is one at the foot and one at the top. These bars serve an additional function of creating a box and keeping the sides from spreading under side pressure.

I added some other multifunctional braces shown in **Figures 19-24** and **19-25A**. Each brace

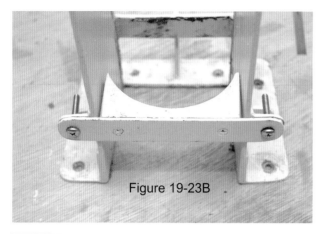

Figure 19-23B

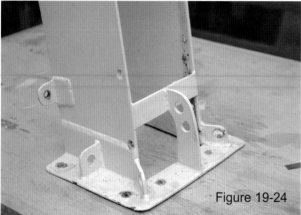

Figure 19-24

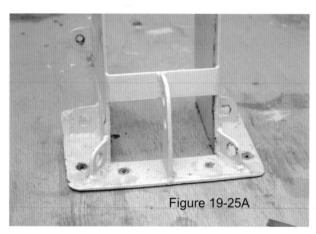

Figure 19-25A

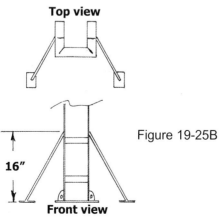

Top view

Figure 19-25B

16"

Front view

is also a location for a block for halyards, down hauls, and other lines. I found these little braces indispensable for attaching blocks and recommend you not leave them off.

After sailing *Pandion* for a summer I felt like I wanted to add some wider braces **Figures 19-25B**. I never saw any indication that the tabernacle was overstressed or signs of cracking on the deck but I added these and you should as well.

The Mizzen Tabernacle

Unlike the main tabernacle, which is steel plate, I choose to build the mizzen tabernacle out of 18mm plywood. Also, the mizzen tabernacle isn't tied to a bulkhead but secured between the two bench seats and stepped right at the front of the aft centerboard case.

In order to accomplish this you'll need to attach two cleats to the face of the bench seat 31 inches from bulkhead 6 (my number 7) as shown in **Figures 19-26** and **19-27**. You will want to set

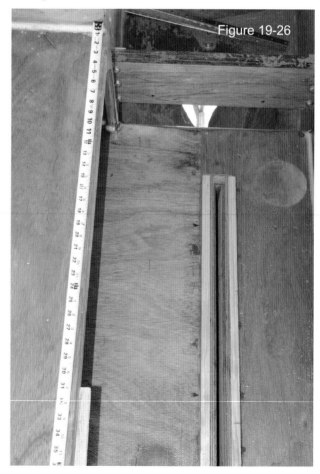

Figure 19-26

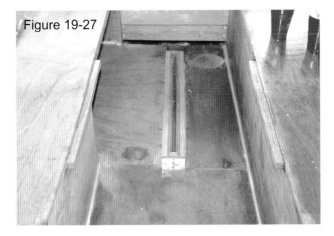
Figure 19-27

Figure 19-28

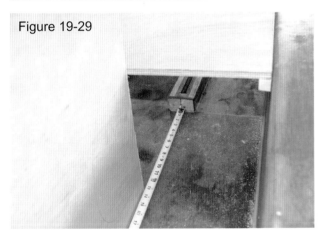
Figure 19-29

Figure 19-30

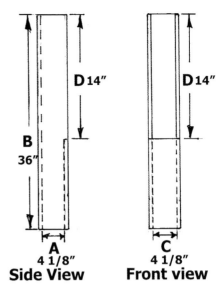
Figure 19-31

these so they are 9mm below the top of the bench seat. I made the cleats 20 inches long (**Figure 19-28**) and I think this is about the ideal length.

That means the board that fits over the cleats will be 20 inches by the distance between the bench seats, which is 21½ inches in my case. So that meant my piece of 9mm plywood was 20 inches by 21½ inches.

Once you have your 9mm piece cut to size, drop it on top of the cleats, and using a square or square piece of plywood, measure the distance to the face of the centerboard case from the forward edge of the board (**Figure 19-29**). This distance was 13½ inches on my boat but will be slightly different for yours.

The next dimension you'll need is the diameter of the base of the mizzen mast (**Figure 19-30**) because this will establish the A dimension and C dimension or the depth and width of the mizzen tabernacle (**Figure 19-31**). Notice I added an 1/8-inch to A and C dimensions. The B dimension or height of the tabernacle is 35 to 36 inches; the same as the main tabernacle. The D dimension is 14 inches but this, like the height, is somewhat flexible.

When I first built the mizzen tabernacle it was a 36 inch high box. That meant the mizzen mast had to be raised well off the deck to drop down inside the tabernacle. I found this to be a dangerous ballet because the balance point of the mast

141

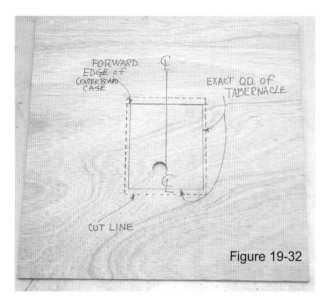

Figure 19-32

Figure 19-35

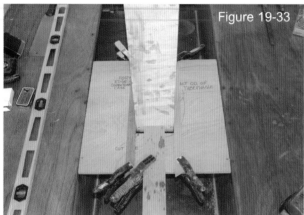

Figure 19-33

Figure 19-36

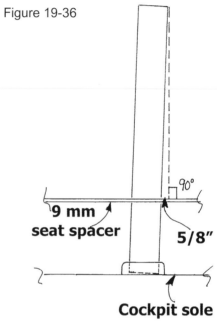

9 mm seat spacer

90°

5/8"

Cockpit sole

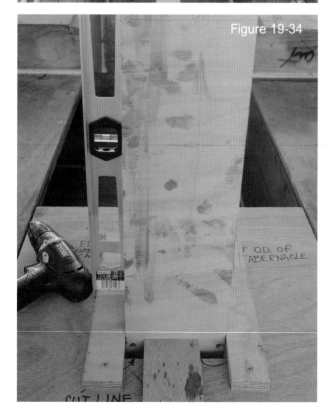

Figure 19-34

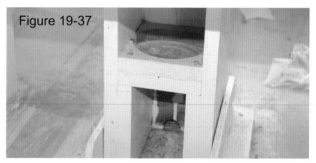

Figure 19-37

Figure 19-38

Figure 19-39

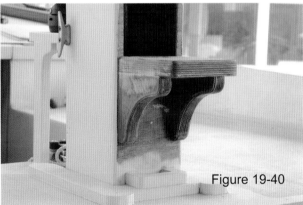

Figure 19-40

had to be so high. I solved this problem by opening the face of the tabernacle 14 inches (Dimension D). The mast is captured in the tabernacle with the same method used on the main mast (**see Figure 19-23B**).

At this point I suggest you build the mizzen tabernacle because you will need the exact OD in order to proceed. **Figure 19-32** shows the layout of the 20 X 21½ piece (your dimensions will be slightly different). I first drew the centerline, then established where the forward edge of the centerboard case would be and then laid out the exact OD of the tabernacle. The dotted cut line has ¼-

inch added to each side at the width and ½-inch added to the fore and aft dimension or depth. The hole is for the saber saw blade.

In **Figure 19-33** the plywood piece has been screwed down and the tabernacle dropped in for a test fit. I centered everything carefully, clamped the capture strips down, checked that the tabernacle was plumb, and marked the location of the capture strips. The permanent capture strips were added, plumb was checked, and then the base capture strips were marked and screwed down (**Figure 19-34** and **19-35**).

Once the base capture strips are in place, drop the tabernacle back in and check for plumb. It is very important that the tabernacle be as close to plumb as you can make it.

The next step will be to tilt the tabernacle slightly aft. Use the same system you used with the main tabernacle. I found 5/8-inch worked very well (**Figure 19-36**). **Figure 19-37** shows the base of the tabernacle fastened between the two capture strips. Notice the limber hole at the back of the tabernacle.

This system is designed to be able to shift the tabernacle slightly aft or forward as needed, and I didn't lock everything down permanently until I had sailed the boat for a while. I might add, I didn't find it necessary to change the amount of tilt but you want that option open to you.

I did several things that are purely cosmetic in nature but important. I rounded the ends of the capture strips and filled the gap between the plywood surrounding the tabernacle (**Figure 19-38**). As I recall, I rounded the ends of the capture strips after they were epoxied down but you will have to the foresight to round them before you epoxy them.

Figure 19-39 is the forward face of the mizzen tabernacle **after** I opened it up, and **Figures 19-40** and **19-41** are details of the small 1-inch thick shelf (18mm and 9mm laminated together). Notice that the shelf was notched into the tabernacle and two screws were set mechanically, fastening the shelf to the forward face of the tabernacle.

This shelf will have holes for belaying pins. It may be used as a sheeting point for the mainsail,

Figure 19-41

Figure 19-43

Figure 19-42

Figure 19-44

and perhaps a platform for mainsail blocks. The square hole in the shelf is for the boom and mast crutch (**Figure 19-42**). The small shelf that the compass sits on serves as additional structural support (**Figures 19-43** and **19-44**). It provides a good solid brace, but it shouldn't be put in place until you are ready to permanently fix the tabernacle.

20

Finishing Out the Cuddy

Like almost everything about the interior of the hull, finishing out the cuddy takes place in stages. You'll want to fit all the floors and the cuddy sole, then paint the entire area before anything is closed in. I didn't do this and skipped ahead so the boat could be put in the water for the summer. I really didn't have a choice or I would have never enclosed the cuddy before it was finished out.

Back when you were working on the cockpit and cutting all the bulkheads you put down the floors for the cuddy sole (**Figures 20-1, 20-2, 20-3**). These photos are of the area in front of bulkhead 2 and will serve as a storage area for gear and the portable head.

You'll want to use 9mm plywood over the top of the floors for the sole of this area. I found doing this section in two pieces was far easier than trying to fit a single piece. I used story sticks off of a centerline to lay out the curved side and on the centerline allowed for a 1-inch spacer of oiled fir. The spacer will simplify fitting the two sides together and it adds a nice visual touch (**Figure 20-4**).

The openings just visible at the bottom of the photo allow for a quick inspection in the bilge for water (it should always be dry) and make it easy to lift out the panel. These panels should be screwed down securely so they don't shift or come loose while you are under way. Remember, gear and the portable toilet will be lashed or bungeed down to these panels and having a portable head banging around below decks should be high on your list of things to avoid.

The openings just visible at the top of the photo are the access ports through the number 1 bulkhead. These ports allow the bolts on the bow eye

Figure 20-1

Figure 20-2

Figure 20-3

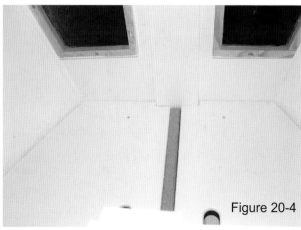

Figure 20-4

and tabernacle to be reached easily. **Figure 20-5** shows the ports with the plywood panels screwed in place and will give you a good idea about the shape of the panels for the sole.

Figure 20-6 is a photograph of the two access ports with the pop out clear plates. The clear plates allow the forward compartment to be checked visually and popped open for air circulation. If more access is needed, the plywood panels may be unscrewed and removed. I bedded the panels in silicone sealant to keep them watertight. That way, if the interior should ever flood the area in front of bulkhead, number 1 will provide flotation.

The size of the panels is arbitrary and after a season of sailing I increased the size to the dimensions in the photo. I wanted to be able to get my head, a shoulder, and my arm through the opening. The smaller size made it difficult to work on the bolts for the tabernacle.

I also found that I needed the sole of the quarter berth level. During the first summer, I spent enough time below to know that was important. I used a combination of oiled fir slats and plywood for the sole in this area. **Figure 20-7** shows the wedges for the slats to rest on, and **Figure 20-8** details the oiled ½ X 1½ fir slats looking down into the quarter berth. Both the port and starboard quarter berths are the same.

The left hand side of the photo shows the forward centerboard case and the plywood panel covering the keel area. The oblong hole allows the bilge

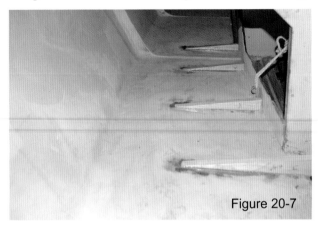

Figure 20-7

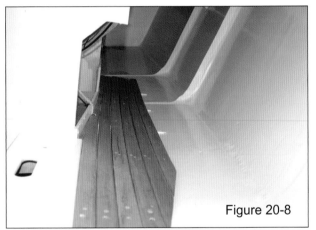

Figure 20-8

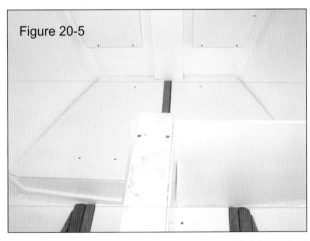

Figure 20-5

Figure 20-6

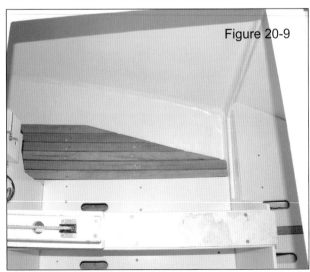

Figure 20-9

to be checked for water (this area should always be dry as well) and makes lifting out the panel easy. These panels and slats, like the others, should be screwed down.

Figure 20-9 is looking straight down through the hatch and both sides of the centerboard case can be seen. You can also see how bulkhead 2 is attached to the forward end of the centerboard case. **Figure 20-10** is from an early stage of working on the cockpit and details the cut of that bulkhead. I didn't cut the starboard side down like the port side because the portable head sits just forward of the bulkhead. Leaving this partial bulkhead separates the two areas and provides a more secure storage for the head.

The slats taper back with the slope of the hull on the port and starboard sides. This layout seems to work well and the port quarter berth is very comfortable. I will say the starboard quarter berth can be a bit cramped because of the partial bulkhead at number 2, particularly if you are tall.

When all the panels and slats have been cut and fitted you'll want to take them out and paint the inside of the hull. You may be tempted to leave the natural wood and just varnish over that, but let me suggest that you paint everything below white, not off-white, but very white. If you don't, the interior will be very dark and very coffin like. It will be a very unpleasant place to be unless, of course, you are a vampire.

Quickly leaving that thought behind, let's jump ahead to a point where the decking is installed and how I covered the ceiling area. In **Figure 20-11** and **20-12** the cleats for the plywood panels have been installed. I broke up the ceiling area into small units rather than trying to fit one large piece. This was much simpler and faster. **Figure 20-13** shows the cleats for the bulkhead 3 and this covered wiring and general clutter. The seams were covered with ¾ X 1/8-inch oiled fir strips (**Figures 20-14** and **20-15**).

You could use fir slats painted white and that would have a nice feel. Slats would be easy to fit as

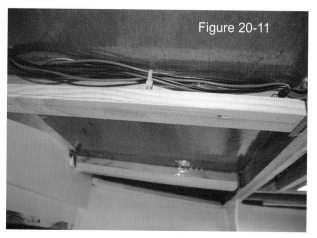
Figure 20-11

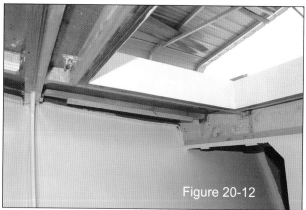
Figure 20-12

Figure 20-10

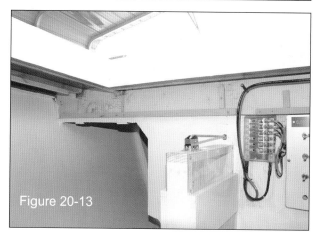
Figure 20-13

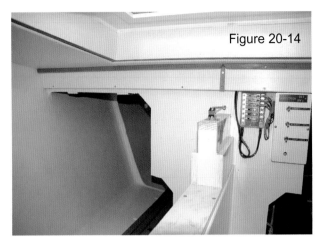

Figure 20-14

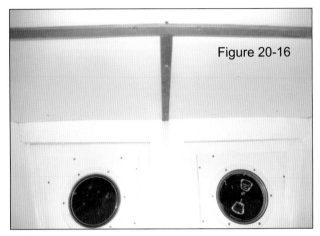

Figure 20-16

Figure 20-15

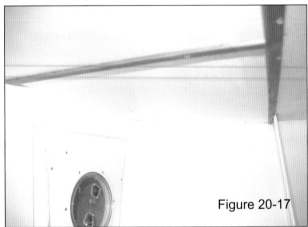

Figure 20-17

they go on one at a time. I mention this as an alternative to point out that there are a number of ways to finish out the cuddy.

You may want to devote some thought to how you want to lay out the interior of the hull. I have found this configuration to be a very good one and it will serve you well. Should you deviate from this layout, make the changes with a great deal of forethought.

21

Decking the Boat

Once you have the interior of the hull painted with the slats and panels cut and fitted, you are then ready to deck the boat. I would suggest that you cover the interior as best you can because with all the heavy fillets of epoxy required to set the decks, some will find its way to your pant job. You should expect to do a certain amount of touch up inside, but you'll want to keep it to a minimum.

You may also find that it's easier to do the decking in sections. Actually I enclosed the cockpit first (see chapter 14) then decked the front of the boat, the area around the motor well, and finished with the combing and side decks. This was an efficient way to do things and I have written the chapters in that order. But remember that all this took place in a nonlinear fashion and decking was halted to finish the motor well or other jobs. With that reminder in the front of your consciousness, let's start decking the boat.

The first job will be to plane down the hull so the top edge at the sheer presents a flat surface for the deck to sit on (**Figure 21-1**). A power planer will make fast work of the job but with a hand plane there is less danger of over cutting (**Figure 21-2**). I like to do the rough work with the power plane and then finish with a hand plane.

Once I had all the surfaces flattened, I installed the deck beams (**Figure 21-3**). These go in just like the deck beams under the cockpit seat. The spac-

ing of these beams was somewhat arbitrary. I felt that one beam on centerline and a beam 14½ inches on either side of centerline provided adequate support under the 9mm plywood in this section of the deck.

I did add additional support under the forward section of deck because the anchor roller and bow cleat would be bolted through this part of the deck. **Figure 21-4** shows the approximate size of the 18mm backing. I used 18mm backing because the area under the roller and cleat can be subjected to very heavy stress.

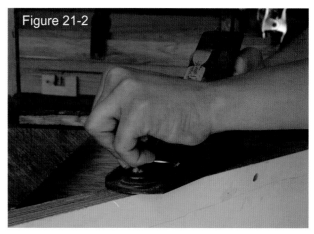

Figure 21-2

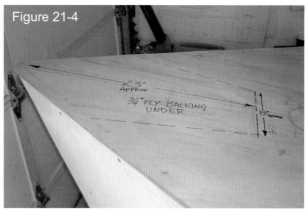

Figure 21-3

Figure 21-4

Figure 21-1

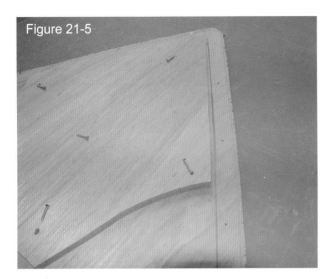

Figure 21-5

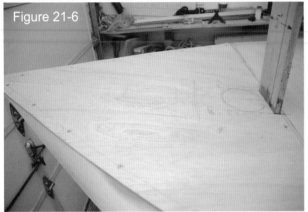

Figure 21-6

Figure 21-7

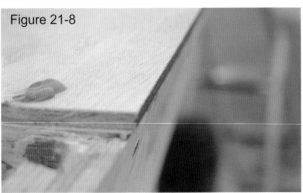

Figure 21-8

This piece will take a bit of hand fitting and you want to have the 18mm backing as close to the hull as possible. I simply drew a line around the outside of the hull and moved the backing in 12mm (the thickness of the hull). I did a dry fit to make sure it all worked (**Figure 21-5**), epoxied the backing in place, and then quickly checked with another dry fit to be sure nothing had shifted.

I did a check to be sure I had finished up the forward compartment before I put this section down with epoxy. I was glad that I took the time to check because I hadn't added the backing for the bow eye. It was much easier to put this in place with the deck off. It's easy to overlook this kind of detail particularly if it's been several weeks since you worked on the boat.

When all the work in the forward compartment was done, that section of the deck was epoxied down and screwed in place (**Figure 21-6**). Notice the line on the deck. That line represents the center of the hull so I could place the screws and not miss the edge of the hull. Let the edge of the deck run wild (**Figure 21-7**) and trim it after the epoxy has set (**Figure 21-8**). Note that the decking has been trimmed to the same face as the hull.

The forward section of the deck was really the most complex with the backing and fitting around the main mast compression post. The rest of the decking is more like fitting a simple puzzle together. First the section between bulkheads 1 and 2 is put in place (**Figure 21-9**). Do a dry fit, leave about ¾-inch overlap and epoxy and screw it down. Follow that piece with one of the side sections. Using a baggie, carry the heavy amounts of peanut butter-epoxy to the tops of the beams, bulkheads, and hull side (**Figure 21-10**).

With both side sections down I turned my attention to the open rectangle in front of the hatch (**Figure 21-11**). Don't assume that space is a true rectangle because I found that none of the angles were exactly 90 degrees. Some quick hand fitting and this little part of the puzzle (**Figure 21-12**) will drop into place with a good tight fit, leaving the little rectangle at the back of the hatch (**Figure 21-13**). Do some fast fitting, let it run wild over the

Figure 21-9

Figure 21-10

Figure 21-11

Figure 21-12

Figure 21-13

Figure 21-14

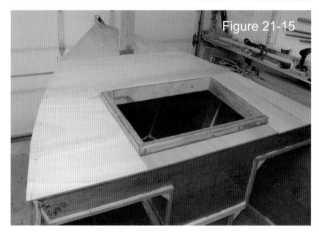

Figure 21-15

cockpit bulkhead, butter everything, screw it down, and you are done (**Figure 21-14** and **21-15**).

As you speed along let me caution you to not forget the three rules of epoxy work—clean up, clean up, and clean up. A failure to clean up after each board goes into place can make for considerable touch up on the great paint job below.

Now that the bow section of the decking is down, step back and check where each section joins over the bulkheads. I found the break kind of sharp and filled and floated the area with fairing compound (**Figure 21-16** and **21-17**). This area was later sanded to give the whole deck the seamless look of a solid piece.

At this point the decking was interrupted and the motor well was finished before the aft sections of decking were added (See Chapter 21 on the motor well).

The aft sections of the deck are very simple and quick, but always dry fit and screw the pieces down before you epoxy. I did the side decks and then the small middle section (**Figure 21-18**). That small mid section is supported by two beams that are attached to the side of the motor well from the inside of the compartments. The beams were needed so that section wouldn't flex.

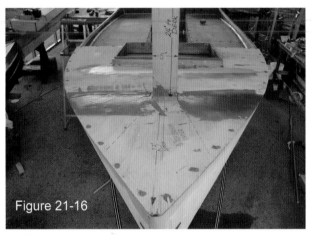
Figure 21-16

Figure 21-17

Figure 21-18

Figure 21-19 gives you a good idea about how much epoxy to put down for the decks and how stiff it should be. This is not an area where you want to be skimpy with the epoxy and you want it to stay put as well.

I put down these decks and then put in the hatches, but you should fit the hatches first and then put down the decks. I had ordered the hatches but they had not arrived when it was time to set these decks. I misjudged the time it would take to get the hatches I wanted and had to press on. I think the lesson here is to order your parts well in advance whenever possible. Nothing is more frustrating than having to stop work until a part arrives.

The aft decks are fast and easy but the combings will take more time. In **Figure 21-20** the backrest section is in place and the section behind it is ready for the decking. The best way to hand fit this part is to use scrap to get the curve and then transfer the curve to the final piece.

The curve of the backrest should match the curve of the hull so I marked the hull curve on the scrap and checked it against the backrest. Once I had that curve I used the scrap pattern to transfer the curve to a rectangular piece of 9mm.

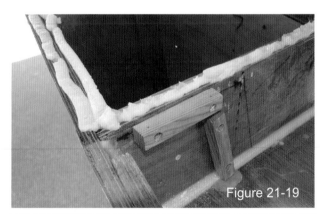
Figure 21-19

Figure 21-20

The rectangle was slightly longer than the distance between the end of the forward decking and the end of the aft decking. It was wide enough to allow for about ¾-inch overhang at the midpoint of the curve.

I cut the curve, pushed it against the back rest to check the fit and then trimmed the length so the piece would drop in between the aft deck and fore deck. When I got a good tight fit I was ready to put it in place with epoxy.

There are several tasks you'll need to do before that is set in epoxy. The area behind the backrest is really an air tight space and that's not good for several reasons. You don't want air and moisture to be trapped, so you'll need to drill one-inch holes (the size of the holes in the braces) into the aft compartment and the cuddy cabin. This allows air to flow through the space and moisture to escape.

If the space is just sealed up, it traps the air and moisture, but more importantly, it doesn't allow heated air to expand. That means every time the boat heats up, the trapped air expands and tries to push apart that space. Eventually the expansion and contraction cycles will cause a joint to fail and compromise the area. Drill the holes. It's important.

You'll also want to coat the inside of this space with several coats of epoxy to protect it from the constant exposure to damp. This will add to the longevity of the boat.

In **Figure 21-21** and **21-22** all the surfaces have been loaded with peanut butter epoxy and in **Figure 21-23** the deck section has been put in place, screwed down, and trimmed flush with the face of the hull.

Because the boat is now completely decked in, you can add the outwales. The outwales cover the edge of the deck and help seal that joint, so this job had to wait until the decking was complete.

I was very fortunate and found some 18 foot long genuine mahogany, so I didn't have to scarf the

Figure 21-23

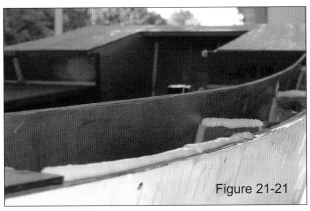

Figure 21-21

Figure 21-22

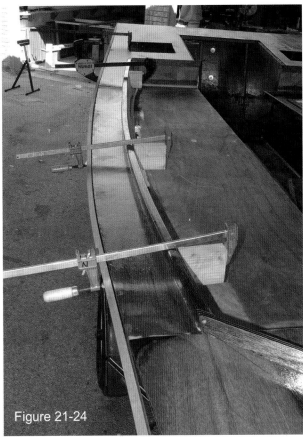

Figure 21-24

153

Figure 21-25

Figure 21-26

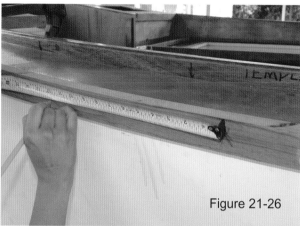
Figure 21-27

Figure 21-28

outwales from two pieces. But if you have to scarf the outwales use at least a 12 to 1 scarf and let it sit for a few weeks before you put it on the boat. You can start with a ¾ X 1½ outwale and if that proves too stiff you can cut it down to 9/16 X 1½.

There is a lot of twist to the sheer and a thick piece may be unable to make the bend without breaking. You can ease this by using the natural bend of the wood to your advantage and by putting a bow in the scarf.

I use a particular technique, if you want to call it that, to put on the outwales. I found it works for me on all types of boats and it certainly worked here.

The first step is to clamp the outwale on the boat (**Figure 21-24**). Notice the blocks between the backrest and the clamp; these blocks allow the clamp to tighten without sliding up the slope of the backrest (**Figure 21-25**). The bow section can be tricky to clamp and I found it easier to use another pair of hands **and** clamps on this section. I screwed a wooden bar down to the deck and used that as a lip for one side of the clamp.

The hard part is getting it clamped in place and keeping it there. Be careful with the outwale. I got a nasty bruise when it popped out of a clamp but if you screw it in place as you go this will help capture it.

I spaced the screws every 12 inches (**Figure 21-26**) and centered them on the outwale. If it doesn't come exactly even at the ends don't worry and just make it visually even. I used #8X 1½ stainless for this job. I have used stainless drywalls as a temporary screw just to get everything to pull up tight and then replaced it with a counter sunk # 8 after the epoxy has set.

When I have the outwale temporarily screwed in place I undo half the outwale, generally just passed station 5 or the midpoint and coat and butter it with peanut butter epoxy (**Figure 21-27**). I always mix wood flour in with the thickener to add a natural wood color to the epoxy.

Then, starting in the middle and working towards the end, I screw everything back in place. I can use the existing screws as registration pins and the outwale will go right back where it was. Then it's clean up, clean up, clean up and do the other half the same way.

I've always liked this method because once I get the outwale up on the boat it doesn't come off again. It makes working by yourself or with just another person much easier and less stressful.

Do clean up **all** the epoxy under the outwale. I use denatured alcohol or another solvent and a rag to wipe up all traces of the epoxy. Remember the hull has the finished paint job and you want to do as little touch up as possible. Masking off the sides of the hull would be a good idea.

Give the outwales at least 24 hours (a little more if it's cold) before you start pulling the screws and countersinking them. That board is under a lot of stress and still wants to go back to its original shape.

At this point there's not much left to do on the outwales. I trimmed the outwales at the bow (**Figure 21-28**) with a Japanese saw and then added a cap of mahogany. I had planned to just taper each side and bring them together but the bow was too wide and round. So I added the cap across the outwales and shaped that (**Figure 21-29**).

I like to round over the outwales on both the top edge and bottom edge. You can use a router with a round-over bit and have the job done in a hurry or use a block plane to put a bevel on each side and sand it round (**Figure 21-30**). The block plane poses far less risk to the outwale than the router. Generally, when something goes wrong with the router, it goes really, really wrong and it's never pretty.

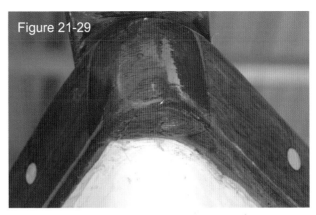

Figure 21-29

Figure 21-30

22

The Motor Well and Bracket

There are a couple of parts you will need to make before you can finish the motor well and set the engine. For the first one, take a 12-inch section of 2-inch X 2-inch stainless steel angle iron and cut it in half. I drilled three 3/8-inch holes on each side. It will be best if these are centered.

You will also need to laminate a 2-inch thick by 6-inch wide by 25-inch long (one inch longer than the width of the motor well) piece of plywood. I used 4 pieces of 12mm plywood 6½ X 25½ and trimmed and squared up the laminated board to 6 X 25. It will be a good idea to measure the bracket on the outboard before you glue everything up. Two inches thick may be too much for some outboards, so be sure to check.

Also, these parts can be made well in advance of when you'll need them. This can even be done before you have the outboard in your possession, as long as you have a model of the outboard you'll order to measure directly from (like in the show room).

I think it's important to mention how important it is NOT to assume that outboard motor dimensions are somehow standard. The motor I used is listed as a short shaft. I would think that indicates a 15-inch shaft, but when I measured the distance between the top of the cavitation plate and the top of the transom bracket, that distance was 18 inches. Had the size of the well been very small I would have had to modify the well. This wouldn't have been impossible but it would not have been easy or fun.

You must have the outboard in your possession to place the bracket in the well, so order the motor enough in advance to have it on site by this point in the construction.

I found it very easy to set the motor in place by clamping the motor to the plywood bracket and sliding it into the well (**Figure 22-1**). If the plywood laminate and stainless steel angle iron are **exactly** the width of the motor well, actually a 1/32-inch wider will be best (*experiment with scrap 9mm to find to exact dimension and then cut the laminate*), there is enough friction to hold the motor in place while you check the fit. This was critical in getting the motor in precisely the right position. It allowed me to shift the motor in fractions rather than gross movements and guessing.

Figure 22-1

There were a number of factors that determined the position of the motor. I wanted, and you will as well, the heel of the motor to sit right against the end of the keel and be parallel to the end of the keel (**Figure 22-2A**). The water intake absolutely had to stay below the waterline, even in very rough water. In my motor the intake is on the underside of the cavitation plate rather than on the foot (**Figure 22-2B**). Also I want the prop as deep as I could have it, but I want about a half an inch clearance above the bronze skeg bar (**Figure 22-2C**) so that hitting a submerged something would be less likely to drive the bar up into the prop.

You also want to make sure there is enough room in front of the motor for drop boards and that the engine isn't so high it would interfere with a top to the well. My goal was to completely enclose the motor yet be able to open the compartment up.

When I determined that all these criteria had been met, I carefully lifted the motor of the bracket so it could be bolted in place (**Figure 22-3**). It's

Figure 22-2A

Figure 22-3

Figure 22-2B

Figure 22-2C

probably a good idea to mark the location of the bracket and bolt holes before you lift out the engine in case it should shift while you are lifting the motor out.

With the motor out of the way it was easy to drill the holes through the side of the motor well (**Figure 22-3**). This allowed me to place a 9mm backing board on the inside of the compartment to beef up the bracket assembly and distribute the load. I also used large stainless washers and nylon locking nuts to spread stress and secure the bolts.

This is a good time to remind you, I suppose, that holes in the wood must be sealed. To not seal these holes is to invite rot onto your boat. So drill them slightly oversize, seal them with epoxy and when you put in the bolts use a good marine silicone sealant. Be extremely vigilant about this because it affects the life of your boat.

I did put the motor back on the bracket and rechecked that everything still worked. Over the years I've learned, the hard way, I'm afraid, to check and re-check my work. Things shift and I have been known to overlook details until it's too late. Getting in the habit of re-checking your work can save you lots of grief.

Secure in the knowledge that everything fit, I pressed on finishing out the motor well. I placed a sheet of 9mm plywood against the lip of the well with a spring clamp (**Figure 22-4**) and struck a line on the back side of the board (**Figure 22-5**). This established where the back cleat needed to be in order to capture the drop boards (**Figure 22-6**).

It was important that the drop boards not come all the way to the cockpit sole because that would

Figure 22-4

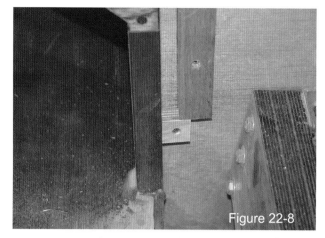

Figure 22-8

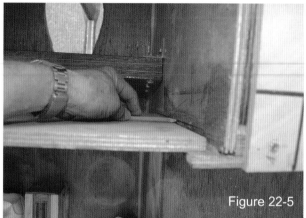

Figure 22-5

Figure 22-9

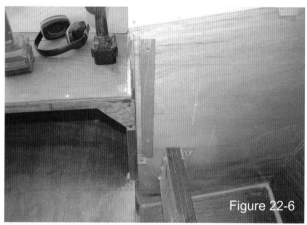

Figure 22-6

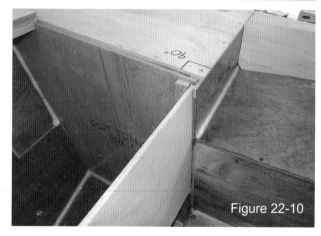

Figure 22-10

Figure 22-7

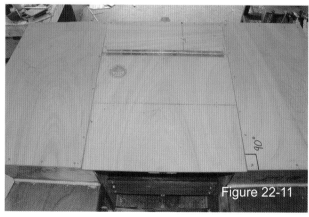

Figure 22-11

Figure 22-12

Figure 22-13

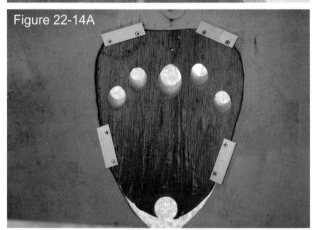

Figure 22-14A

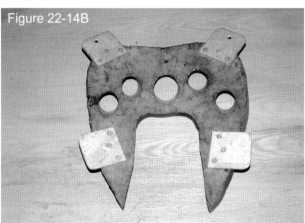

Figure 22-14B

slow the ability of the cockpit to drain (**Figure 22-7**). I raised the bottom of the first drop board 4 inches up from the cockpit sole. This was an arbitrary amount, but I don't think I'd have a smaller space. I accomplished this with a small stop at the bottom of the channel (**Figure 22-8**).

This made the distance from the stop to the top of the channel about 16 inches. I just divided this in half as two 8-inch drop boards would be easier to store than one 16-inch drop boards (**Figure 22-9** and **22-10**). The dimensions of your boards will probably be a bit different but just take all the measure from the boat.

I not only wanted to be able to close off the face of the motor well with drop boards but I wanted to close off the top also (**Figure 22-11**). I decided that two panels and stainless piano hinges would work. They would fold back out of the way and still be readily accessible (**Figure 22-12**).

The width of the two folding pieces was determined by the width of the aft fixed piece, which was 9 inches in my case. This small fixed section was braced with deck beams (like under the cockpit and deck) and was secured with epoxy and screws driven from the inside of the enclosed compartments on either side (**Figure 22-13**).

There was one more area I wanted to enclose—the area around the foot of the motor. I saved the cutout and now with the motor hanging on the bracket I could cut away enough for the piece to drop in around the motor (**Figure 22-14A** and **22-14B**). With the cutout in place around the foot of the motor the flow of water was deflected and didn't build up at the back edge of the well. Left open, the well would act like a scoop, trapping water and slowing down the boat. I drilled large holes in the cutout that were angled to allow water to drain away but also not act as a scoop.

I've been very happy with this arrangement and because the motor always stays down, the cut out is left in place. When and if the motor needs to come out, I just undo the two small screws and lift the piece out. The screws are necessary to hold it in place.

23

The Masts, Spars, and Boomkin

Masts

There are a number of ways to build hollow masts and I used the "birdsmouth" technique to build my masts. I had known about this method for a long time but was always put off by how complicated it seemed. But a conversation with Chuck Leinweber at *Duckworks Magazine* convinced me to give this technique a try. Now it's the only way I'll build a hollow mast.

At one point you had to do some serious computations to get the stave width for a given diameter of mast. But then Gaetan Jette wrote an article and designed a calculator for *Duckworks Magazine,* and birdsmouth masts became plug and play. You just plug in your information, hit calculate, and it gives you the needed stave width. Actually, you don't even have to do that because in **Figure 23-1** I've done that work for you.

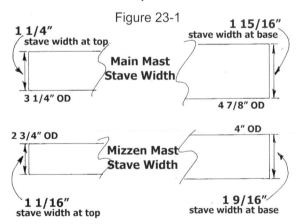

Figure 23-1

1 1/4"
stave width at top

1 15/16"
stave width at base

Main Mast Stave Width

3 1/4" OD

4 7/8" OD

2 3/4" OD

4" OD

Mizzen Mast Stave Width

1 1/16"
stave width at top

1 9/16"
stave width at base

I ripped my staves for the main mast 2 inches wide and for the mizzen mast 1 5/8 inches wide and used ¾-inch thick material. I also bought 1X4's to save a great deal of milling.

I built my mast and spars from fir. I tried to find vertical grain or at least very tight grained fir but that's not really necessary. Even a small knot should-

n't disqualify the board. You don't even need long boards because unless you can find eighteen foot long fir you'll have to scarf anyway. That means a mix of six and eight footers will do the job nicely and allow you to stagger the scarfs.

You'll want to cut a scarf that is at least seven to eight inches long. The best would be nine inches or a 12 to 1 scarf. **Figures 23-2** and **23-3** are of the scarfing jig I use. Notice there is a bolt at the front end of the upright that allows the angle to change. This is easily made and will do a good job.

Glue up the scarfs with unthickened epoxy sandwiched between some heavy cream epoxy. I just use spring clamps to hold everything together while the epoxy cures. Do keep the scarfed staves as straight as possible, that's important. It's difficult to cut an accurate taper on a crooked stave.

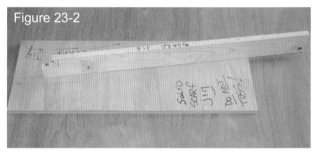

Figure 23-2

Figure 23-3

When I first moved into my shop I built a dedicated mast-making table along a 22-foot wall. I used laser levels and spent a great deal of time getting it very level across the width and entire length. You don't have to build a dedicated mast-making table but you will need some kind of long, level surface to glue up your masts and spars. A series of sawhorses work well for many boatbuilders.

To cut the taper on my scarfed staves I lined them up with the straight edge of my table and held them in place with spring clamps (**Figure 23-4**). Then I measured over the correct amount at both ends (**Figure 23-5**), made a cut with a Japanese saw, set a snap line (**Figure 23-6**), and made a series of marks under the string (**Figure 23-7**). These marks were connected with a long straight edge (**Figure

Figure 23-4

Figure 23-7

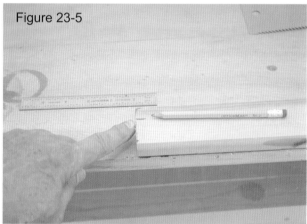

Figure 23-5

Figure 23-8

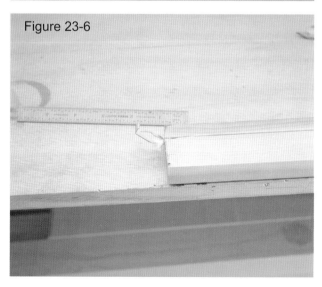

Figure 23-6

Figure 23-9

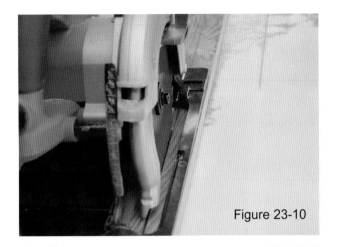

Figure 23-10

Figure 23-11

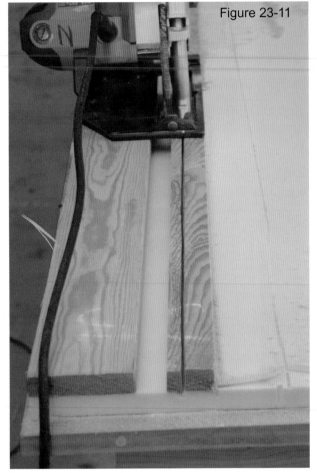

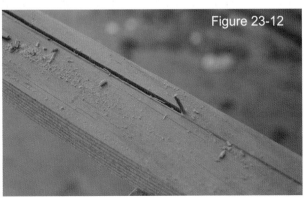

Figure 23-12

Figure 23-13

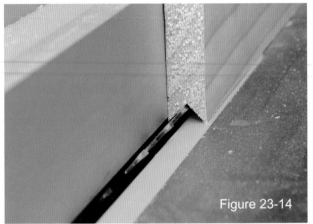

Figure 23-14

Figure 23-15

23-8) and then the stave was cut with a six-inch circular saw (**Figure 23-9, 23-10,** and **23-11**). I only cut the taper on one side and left the other side straight, in case that wasn't clear.

Notice one side of the saw rests on a 1X4 while the blade side sits on the stave. Both pieces are on top of hard foam insulation with the blade depth set at 1/16-inch below the stave. This let me cut the full length of the stave while it was completely supported by the foam. This works on a concrete floor

Figure 23-16

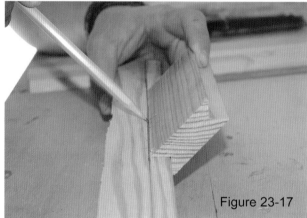

Figure 23-17

Figure 23-18

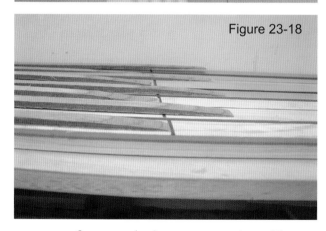

or any surface you don't want to cut into, like my good work tables. I learned this really great technique from my friend Pat Mohan, the head instructor at Great Lakes Boat Building School in Cedarville, Michigan, when I was teaching there in the summers.

Having the saw fully supported makes it easy to cut just proud of the line (**Figure 23-12**). I then turned the stave up and planed down to the line with a hand plane (**Figure 23-13**).

Now the stave was ready to have the birdsmouth

cut on the straight side. You can use a table saw with the blade set at 45 degrees (**Figure 23-14**) or, if you have a table mounted router, you can use a bit to cut the 45 degree angle (**Figure 23-15**).

I've used both methods and if your table saw will cut a good 45 then that will be the most cost effective way. I can't say I have any preference one way or the other and would let your table saw make the determination.

Once all the birds mouth's are cut you'll find it much easier to assemble the mast with at least three cradles (**Figure 23-16**). I would recommend you do about three or four dry runs to get a feel for how the staves fit together and to be able to anticipate potential problems. It took me about three tries to get the process down. The mast really does want to go together, but you don't want to be learning the fitting process when the staves are coated with epoxy.

The next step is to add some additional support where the mast strikes the tabernacle. All masts have some sort of additional support at the partner, deck, or tabernacle. Solid masts swell at that area and hollow masts have an internal support.

The question was what kind of internal support wouldn't interfere with the way the mast assembled. I decided on using strips of 6mm plywood epoxied to the inside of the mast.

I needed to establish where each stave fit on its neighbor so I took a short section of stave and lined off the point of contact (**Figure 23-17**). This gave me the shape of the 6mm piece and exactly where it could and couldn't be on each stave.

Because the tabernacle was 36 inches high, I drew a line at 48 inches on the inside of the mast. I made four 6mm strips 48 inches long and four at 52 inches long (**Figure 23-18**). By staggering the ends and tapering all eight pieces there was no hard line where the support ended. **Figure 23-19** shows half the mast assembled and the way the 6mm fit inside.

Figures 23-20 and **23-21** show the 6mm strips fastened to the staves. I found I had to put a slight bevel on the 6mm strip for the best fit. These strips were epoxied in place, allowed to cure, and then a

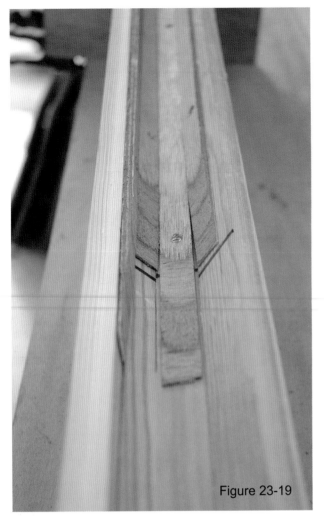

Figure 23-19

Figure 23-20

Figure 23-21

Figure 23-22

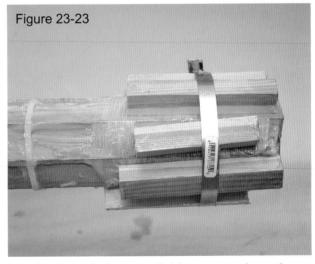

Figure 23-23

last test fit was done before final glue-up.

During the glue-up stage another pair of hands will be very welcome. This is a job best done by two people, but it can be done single handed. Rehearse, rehearse, rehearse is the name of the game. Do a dry run. That is, go through the motions of putting the epoxy on each stave and then assemble the mast as if it was loaded with epoxy.

If you think this sounds like too much work just think about how much time you have invested in each stave. You really don't want anything to go wrong once you have each stave full of peanut butter epoxy. Carefully coat the inside of the mast because this is the time you'll have access to that side. **It goes without saying you want the longest pot life for the epoxy you can get.**

164

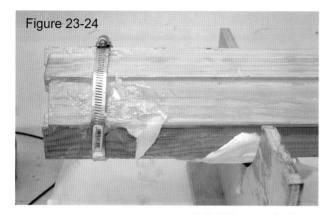

Figure 23-24

Figure 23-25

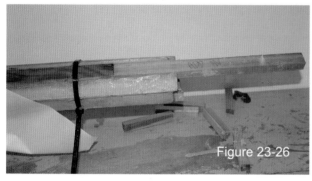

Figure 23-26

Figure 23-27

In all our rehearsals, we came up with a system that worked well. All eight staves were turned V side up on a table (close to the assembly area) and one person mixed epoxy while the other loaded the Vs with a baggie full of peanut butter epoxy (**Figure 23-22**).

Working together we were able to get all the staves filled in fairly short order. We did find that the light baggies weren't strong enough to stand up under the stress so we used freezer grade baggies. Also we were in such a rush that we forgot to add wood flour to the thickened epoxy for color. Try not to make that mistake.

Once they were all full (more is better here) we assembled the staves as fast as we could. We had plenty of hose clamps and large zip locks at hand so that once we had it together we could keep it together. We also used stretch wrap but I liked the large zips better (**Figures 23-23, 23-24,** and **23-25**). In **Figure 23-26** I found one stave a few inches short so I added a short section.

After the mast was assembled and all the hose clamps were tightened we pulled a swab down through the inside to clear all the excess squeeze-out. There are a number of ways to do this but we used a rag on a long piece of wire. Be sure the wire is strong enough to take the pull because it gets tight at the end. You'll be amazed at how much epoxy you'll pull out.

With the swab-out, do a bit of clean-up and then reach for a carbonated beverage of your choice before you and your helper collapse into a chair. You've both earned a rest. I know we certainly did.

After all the work of assembly, rounding over the mast will seem like a vacation. There's nothing to do really but plane away the lip (**Figure 23-27** and **23-28**) for a round shape and then sand everything smooth (**Figure 23-29**).

The next job will be to square the ends of the mast. I found a simple way to do this was to block up the mast so the centerline was parallel to the table and then use a guide for the Japanese saw (**Figure 23-30**). I would suggest you use an old saw because all those screws you set to hold the 6mm strips can play havoc with a new saw blade (**Figure 23-31**).

Figure 23-28

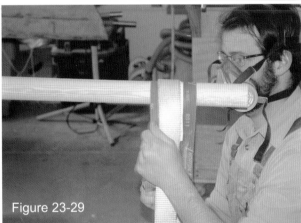

Figure 23-29

Figure 23-30

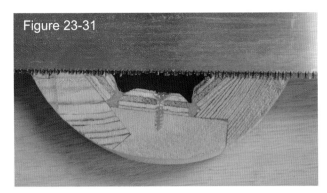

Figure 23-31

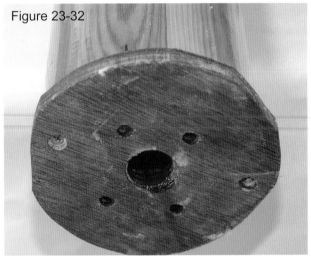

Figure 23-32

Figure 23-33

You'll want to add a cap to both the heel and the top of both masts (**Figures 23-32** and **23-33**). These caps were sanded flush with the face of the mast. I put large holes in the bottom cap to allow for air movement and to keep moisture from being trapped in the sealed mast. Remember the expanding and contracting air?

For the next step, the tabernacle will need to be fixed in place on the boat. You will need another person for this job. I'm sure it can be done with just one person but it was easier to grab another pair of hands.

We stood the mast up in the tabernacle and drilled the hole for the mast pin. Using some guides to keep the drill bit level and at 90 degrees to the face of the tabernacle will be very helpful. Be sure the mast is well captured in the tabernacle so everyone's full attention can be turned to drilling

Figure 23-34

Figure 23-35

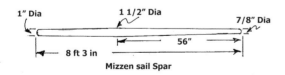

Mizzen sail Spar

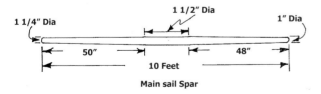

Main sail Spar

Figure 23-36

an accurate hole.

Because the mast is hollow I drilled the ½" hole from each side rather than all the way through the mast. I used a drill bit that was slightly larger than the tubing's outside diameter using the first hole as a pilot.

I set copper tubing with an inside diameter of ½-inch so my ½ bronze rod would slide through. I roughed up the surface of the copper tube with 80 grit sandpaper and then epoxied it in place (**Figure 23-34**). The excess was trimmed off, the mast put back in the tabernacle, and the bronze rod run through the mast for a test fit (**Figure 23-35**).

I did find that we had to grind off some wood on the heel for the mast to fit perfectly. You want the base of the mast to just touch the deck area in the upright position so the pin doesn't carry the entire load.

Solid Spars

Solid spars are just as easy to make as the hollow ones and in some ways simpler. There are fewer parts to make and the only glue-up is laminating the solid stock together.

In **Figure 23-36**, I give the dimensions for the spars for both the main and mizzen standing lug sails. You need to have straight clear fir for these as well. I like to make the blanks about ½-inch over-size then trim and square them. Just like the mast, you want the glue-up to be a straight as possible (**Figure 23-37**).

Once squared up, cut the taper and then they are ready to eight side. Eight siding is the traditional method of taking a square block of wood and making it round. If you are going to eight side the spars you'll need a jig to line off the square piece. I've used several marking jigs and methods for arriving at the spacing for the jig but the best I've found is one used by Pat Mohan. **Figure 23-38** is a crude version of Pat's lining jig.

Actually, what's important is the spacing and Pat's jig uses a 7-10-7 pin spacing. That is, for 3-inch spars or less you would use 8 as the denominator, so the spacing would be **7/8 - 10/8 - 7/8**. This was the pin spacing used for the jig in **Figure**

Figure 23-37

Figure 23-40

Figure 23-38

7/8   10/8   7/8

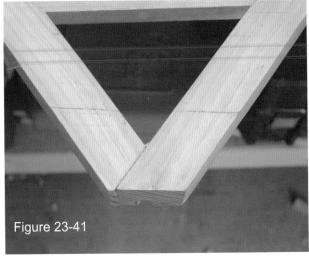

Figure 23-41

Figure 23-39

Figure 23-42

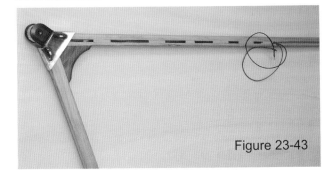

Figure 23-43

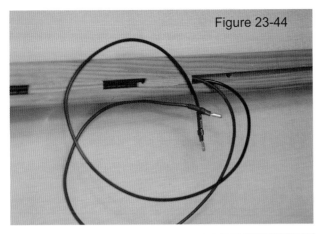

Figure 23-44

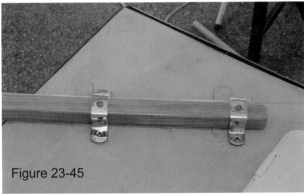

Figure 23-45

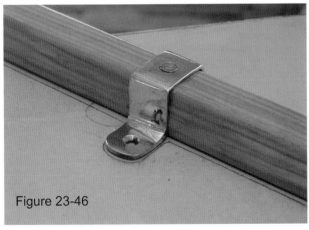

Figure 23-46

23-38. There are other more complicated methods for arriving at the pin spacing, but Pat's **7-10-7** is easier for me to remember. Should you want to build a solid 5-inch mast (that would be very heavy) you would use 4 as the denominator. That pin spacing would be **7/4 - 10/4 - 7/4**, and that will take you up 6-inch diameter spar.

So when you get the square lined off, you turn it up and plane down between the lines (**Figure 23-39**) so you have eight sides instead of four. Then take those corners down so you have sixteen sides. Generally I'll just round everything from eight sides

(**Figure 23-40**).

Use the same sanding method that you used on the birdsmouth and you have the spars ready to coat with epoxy. At this point you'll need the sails to go any farther.

Boomkin

I used a boomkin on the Sea Eagle 16.5 because I needed the sheeting point to be aft of the stern. The only way I know to do this is with a boomkin. I also needed a place for the stern navigation light and the boomkin seemed a good choice for that too.

You can make this a very simple utilitarian boomkin or it can be decorative and functional. I picked the latter route.

Like the mast and spars, I used fir for the boomkin but instead of laminating the sections I used solid wood. You can certainly laminate the boomkin but it's much faster to cut them from a fir 2X4. You can get both 1½ X 1½ sections from an 8 foot long 2X4.

It's square, so there's nothing to do but rip the 4 foot long pieces and round the corners slightly. The real work will be getting the angle where the two pieces join. This will depend on where you place them on the deck and that will depend on where you have placed hatches and deck hardware like cleats.

In **Figure 23-41** the two pieces have been temporarily clamped in the position I wanted them, the angle marked, cut, and the two pieces screwed together. Notice the channel cut in the bottom of the right section. This channel is for the wiring from the stern navigation light.

I didn't think the joint in **Figure 23-41** would be strong enough so I added a mahogany wedge as support and backing (**Figure 23-42**). This was epoxied and screwed in place. Measurements for the bronze piece were taken after the wedge was in place.

Figure 23-43 shows the small spacers used to hold the navigation light wiring in place. **Figure 23-44** is a detail of the quick disconnect leads I put on the navigation light wiring. That way, should the boomkin need to come off, I don't have to re-wire. I did the same thing on the main mast steaming light, allowing the mast to be removed without cutting wires.

Figure 23-45 is a shot of the boomkin hold downs and the general location on the stern. I used large washers and a strip of backing under the deck. The boomkin can be subjected to lots of stress so beef up the under side of the deck. **Figures 23-46** and **23-47** are close up details of the hold downs.

The hold downs and the other bronze work on the boomkin represents an attempt on my part to add some artistic touches to the boat without drifting over into showy and flashy. This is an area I am not comfortable in and council others to avoid as well.

The hold downs could be easily made from wood and have the boat look just as good. Feel free to be creative with these details. This is what makes your boat truly yours.

Figure 23-47

24

The Sails

Sails are the engine of your boat. The sails move the boat through the water and without them it is a short voyage. They act in an almost mystical manner as they respond to the invisible forces of the wind.

There is beauty in a nicely set sail that is as sculptural as the boat. In the not-too-distant past sailmakers were considered masters of an art. They were people who could take pieces of canvas and sculpt those pieces into a wing.

But sailmaking and boatbuilding always seemed to be two totally separate art forms. Sailmakers, in general, didn't understand boatbuilding and boatbuilders, in general, were mystified by sailmaking. The truth is they have a lot in common.

I came to sailmaking from boatbuilding because I wanted to make the sails for the boats that I had built. I think there is a completeness or immense satisfaction that comes with moving through the water in a boat that you built and made the sails for. Your hand connects with both the water and the wind in a very personal way. It's a very Zen experience.

That's why I have included this chapter on building the sails for the Sea Eagles. The goal of this chapter is to give you enough knowledge to build the sails for your boat; not turn you into a sailmaker.

A long detailed discussion of why and how sails work is way beyond the scope of this small chapter. A number of books have been written that cover that subject and I think *Aero-Hydrodynamics of Sailing* by C. A. Marchaj and *Sail Power* by Wallace Ross are among the best. Just these two highly technical volumes will tell you more than you ever wanted to know about sails.

What you will need to know, if you don't already, is some vocabulary. **Figure 24-1** shows a four-sided sail with its parts labeled. Both Sea Eagles use four-sided sails, standing and balanced lug sails to be

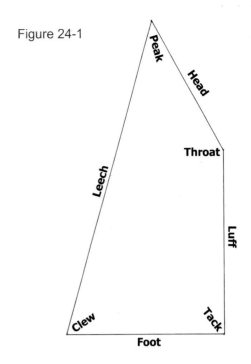

Figure 24-1

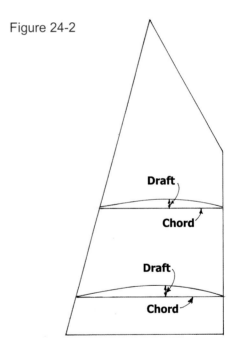

Figure 24-2

exact, so that is the sail type that will be discussed here.

Those terms let us discuss the parts of the flat sail but sails aren't flat so we need to be able to describe the curve of the sail. In **Figure 24-2** the curve of the sail is the draft and the flat side of the draft is the chord. The amount of draft built into a sail is expressed as a ratio. That ratio is 1 foot of draft for X chord length like 1:10 (1 foot of draft for a 10 foot long chord) or 1:13 (1 foot of draft for a 13 foot long chord).

Sails with a ratios of 1:13, 1:12, or 1:10 have an average amount of draft. The extreme ends of the spectrum are ratios of 1:20 (very flat or very little draft) and 1:7 (Very full or a great deal of draft). As with most things in life the extreme ends of the spectrum should be avoided.

There are basically two ways to build draft into a sail. Cloth can be added at the luff, foot, or head so when that edge is pulled straight it forces the extra material back into the body of the sail. For the most part this process is done to the luff of the sail and there are set formulas for how much cloth is added and where.

The other method is done by putting darts or gores in the panels so the panels form a rounded shape rather than a straight line. This process is called broadseaming and it can be accomplished by cutting a wedge from one panel and sewing that panel to a straight panel or by overlapping the set amount and sewing that. Is it better to cut a wedge or overlap? It's strictly a matter of preference and I prefer to cut the wedge.

So in a very small nut shell, that covers the minimum you need to know, and now that we share a bit of vocabulary, I can describe how I designed the sails for the Sea Eagles. I suppose it will be easiest if I discuss the process in two parts; designing the sail on paper and building the sail out of cloth. I'll go through the process for the mainsail on the Sea Eagle 16.5 and then give all the information you need to build the sails for each boat at the end of this chapter.

The mainsail for the 16.5 has a foot of 8 feet, a luff of 11 feet, a head of 9 feet, and leech of 19 feet 6 inches. The diagonal is 19 feet 3 inches (**Figure 24-3**). I like to use a scale of ½-inch to a foot when I design sails on paper. This gives me enough detail to scale the measurements I need from the drawing.

I suppose the first decision I made, even before I drew out the sail, was how much draft to give the sail. I wanted a sail that was just on the full side of average for the main so I used a 1:10 ratio in figur-

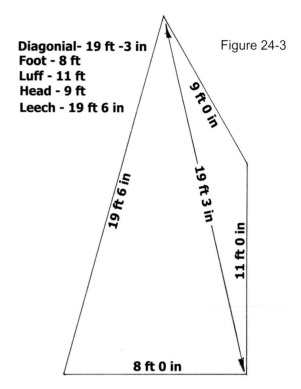

Figure 24-3

Diagonial- 19 ft -3 in
Foot - 8 ft
Luff - 11 ft
Head - 9 ft
Leech - 19 ft 6 in

9 ft 0 in

19 ft 3 in

19 ft 6 in

11 ft 0 in

8 ft 0 in

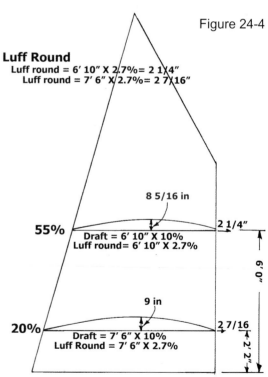

Figure 24-4

Luff Round
Luff round = 6' 10" X 2.7%= 2 1/4"
Luff round = 7' 6" X 2.7%= 2 7/16"

8 5/16 in

2 1/4"

55%
Draft = 6' 10" X 10%
Luff round= 6' 10" X 2.7%

6' 0"

9 in

2 7/16"

20%
Draft = 7' 6" X 10%
Luff Round = 7' 6" X 2.7%

2' 2"

ing the draft.

In **Figure 24-4** I've drawn two chords. The first chord is drawn 20 % up the luff which is 2 feet 2½ inches and has a chord length 7 feet 6 inches. The second chord is 55% up the luff and located at 6 feet. I multiplied both chord lengths by 10% and got a draft height of 9 inches and 8 5/16 inches respectively.

Now I had what I needed to calculate the luff round (remember luff round is adding extra cloth to the luff so when the edge is pulled straight the cloth moves back into the body of the sail and creates draft). I just multiplied the chord length by 2.7% to get the amount of round at that point. For example the first chord, 2 feet 2½ inches up from the foot, is 7 feet 6 inches long and that chord length is multiplied 2.7% to give 2 7/16 inches of round. That means on the luff I come up 2 feet 2½ inches and out 2 7/16 inches. The other chord is 55 % up the luff which is 6 feet up. At that point the chord is 6 feet 10 inches and this is multiplied by 2.7% to give a luff round of 2¼ inches. That means I go up 6 feet on the luff and out 2¼ inches.

The number 2.7% is from the set of formulas mentioned a few paragraphs above. How that number is arrived at is not important here, only the number.

Actually on the top chord I have rounded up the numbers. If you multiply the chord length by 2.7% you get 2 7/32 inches and this is slightly less than 2¼. I took that number and rounded it up to 2¼ inches of luff round. I've found rounding up is always better in sailmaking.

With calculating the luff material there is always a bit of rounding up but with broadseaming there is not only rounding up but also fudge factors, and "Maybe a bit more is needed." "Maybe a bit more is needed" is a little known sail making term that allows the sailmaker to intuitively add additional (or subtract) amounts where needed. I mention this to point out that broadseaming and sail making, in general, can be very flexible.

Broadseaming and draft placement are "hand in glove" and it's broadseaming that allows the sailmaker to position the draft. In **Figure 24-5A** I've drawn the draft at 41% to 44% aft of the luff. Also note that I have added 36 inch wide panels to the drawing. 36 inch wide sail cloth is a standard width and gives enough opportunities to put in draft with broadseaming.

I use two formulas to determine the width of the broadseams; ½-inch of width for every 3 feet of

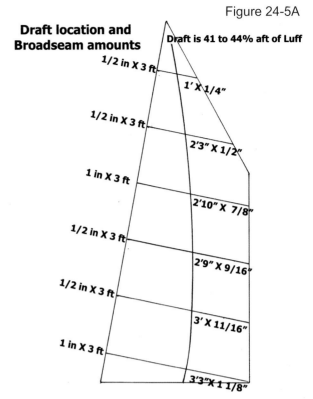

Figure 24-5A

Draft location and Broadseam amounts

Draft is 41 to 44% aft of Luff

1/2 in X 3 ft
1' X 1/4"
1/2 in X 3 ft
2'3" X 1/2"
1 in X 3 ft
2'10" X 7/8"
1/2 in X 3 ft
2'9" X 9/16"
1/2 in X 3 ft
3' X 11/16"
1 in X 3 ft
3'3" X 1 1/8"

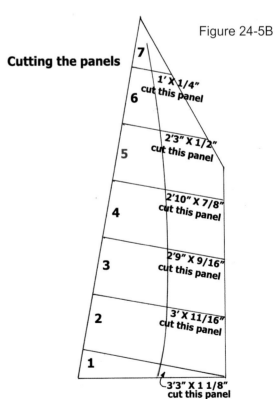

Figure 24-5B

Cutting the panels

7
1' X 1/4"
cut this panel
6
2'3" X 1/2"
cut this panel
5
2'10" X 7/8"
cut this panel
4
2'9" X 9/16"
cut this panel
3
3' X 11/16"
cut this panel
2
3'3" X 1 1/8"
cut this panel
1

length and 1 inch for every 3 feet of length. The ½-inch for every 3 feet breaks down to 3/16-inch for every foot of length and 1/64 for every inch of length. The other formula, 1 inch of width for every

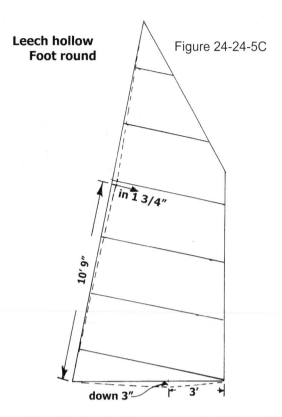

Leech hollow
Foot round

Figure 24-24-5C

in 1 3/4"

10' 9"

down 3"

3'

3 feet of length, breaks down to 3/8-inch for each foot and 1/32 for each inch of length. *These numbers were arrived at by some rounding up and because of that give slightly increased figures.*

Using that information let's look at the first seam or joint between the two panels of sail cloth. Notice that seam is at a right angle to the leech and ends directly at the tack. The draft line I drew crosses that seam 3 feet 3 inches back from the luff.

This first seam is one where I use 1 inch of width for every 3 feet of length so that means the width of the broadseam at the luff is 1 inch (1 inch for every 3 feet of length) plus 3 X 1/32 (1/32 for every inch of length) or 1 3/32. I rounded that up to 1 4/32 or 1 1/8. More simply said the broadseam wedge at that seam is 1 1/8 inches wide at the luff.

The next seam, I use ½-inch of width for every 3 feet of length. That section is 3 feet long so that's very straightforward and means the width of the wedge is ½ plus a fudge factor of 3/16 to make a total width of 11/16. *Experience suggested that I add a fudge factor at the seam and whispered 3/16-inch.*

The third seam up I also use the ½-inch for every 3 feet of length formula. That section is 2 feet 9 inches where the drawn draft line crosses the

seam. The width of that broadseam at the luff is calculated by multiplying 2 X 3/16 (3/16-inch for every foot of length) = 3/8 that is added to 9 X 1/64 (1/64-inch for every inch) = 9/64 which is 3/8 + 9/64 = 33/64 and that is rounded up to 9/16-inch. That means that the broadseam wedge at the luff for the third seam is 9/16-inch.

With the fourth seam up I go back to 1 inch for every 3 feet of length. This seam is close to the throat and experience has shown sailmakers that seams in the throat area need to be treated like the seam at the tack, made a bit fuller. In this case the section was 2 feet 10 inches long where the drawn draft line crossed the seam. I multiplied 2 X 3/8 = ¾ plus 10 X 1/32 = 10/32 or 5/16 and totals 1 1/16.

This is more than 1 foot for every 3 feet of length (this sometimes occurs because with the breakdown I always round up) so in this case I used a negative fudge factor of 3/16 so the wedge becomes 14/16 or 7/8 at the luff.

In next seam up, the section was 2 feet 3 inches long. I did all the multiplication using the ½-inch per 3 feet of length ratio and added a fudge of 1/16 which gave a wedge of ½-inch at the head of the sail. In this case the head of the sail is treated like the luff.

The top most seam has a section of 1 foot and I added a fudge factor of 1/16 for a total wedge at the head of the sail of ¼ inch. I used the ½-inch ratio here as well. This was the last seam and now the sail was completely laid out.

In **Figure 24-5B** you can see that the wedge for the first seam is cut from panel #1, the wedge for the second seam is cut from the **top** edge of panel #2, the third seam wedge is cut from the **top** edge of panel #3 and so on. Look at this carefully when the time comes to cut the wedges so you don't cut the wedge from the wrong panel.

Laying out the wedges is the biggest job, certainly the most calculations, but there are two small jobs left to do. I always put a bit of leech hollow in this kind of sail and a small amount of foot round. **Figure 24-5C** shows the location of the leech hollow (this stops the leech from fluttering) and foot round (this ads a bit of shape right at the foot).

Figure 24-6

Figure 24-7

Figure 24-8

Figure 24-9

Figure 24-10

Now I had the luff round amounts and where they went, the location of the leech hollow, the placement of the foot roach or round, and I had the broadseam wedges with the lengths of the sections. At this point I could start building the sail with cloth.

Really, this process is just to duplicate the drawing of the sail on paper. The first thing is to loft the sail on the floor. I always lay out the luff first as a vertical line (**Figure 24-6**).

Then I lay out the foot (**Figure 24-7**), then using two tapes I lay down the leech. One tape has the leech (19 feet 6 inches) and the other tape the diagonal (19 feet 0 inches) (**Figure 24-8**). In **Figure 24-9** I'm checking that the leech and head dimensions work on the loft room floor. All these dimensions were scaled from a small drawing so it's a good idea to check that everything works. If it's off a bit, juggle the tapes until it comes very close.

Figure 24-10 shows the sail lofted and awls driven into the four corners.

It would unusual for you to build this sail where you can drive awls in the floor, but all is not lost if you can't use awls. It's just as easy to use masking tape to outline the sail (**as in Figure 24-10**) and then use duct tape in place of the awls for the next step.

Now take string (I like day-glo pink because it's so easy to see under the sail) and tape it to all four corners. The string should be tight enough so you get a straight line between the corners and a sharp bend at each corner. You want to try and duplicate what you would get using pins (**Figure 24-11**).

Figure 24-11

Figure 24-14

Figure 24-12

Figure 24-15

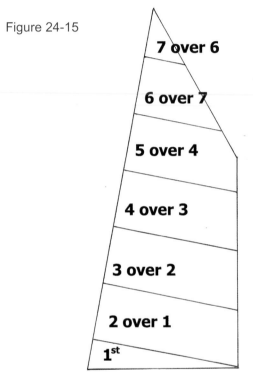

7 over 6

6 over 7

5 over 4

4 over 3

3 over 2

2 over 1

1st

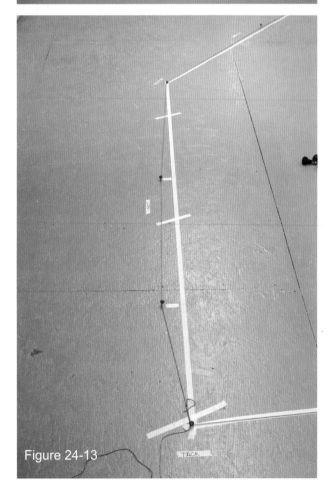

Figure 24-13

TACK

The purpose of the string is to outline the shape of the sail with the luff and foot round as well as the leech hollow. In **Figure 24-12** you can see the pins (you would use duct tape instead of pins) located out from the luff the indicated amounts. **Figure 24-13** is another angle of the luff round.

The next step is to roll out the cloth over the string and tape (**Figure 24-14**). But you don't just roll it out you roll it out in a specific order (**Figure 24-15**). Notice that panel #1 is 90 degrees to the leech and splits the tack point. The #2 panel is placed **over** #1 panel, the #3 panel is placed **over** #2 panel, #4 **over** #3 and so on up to the top of the sail.

You want each panel to overlap the panel under

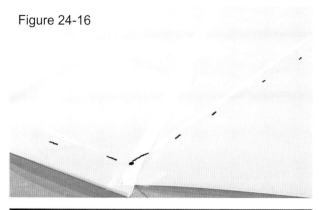

Figure 24-16

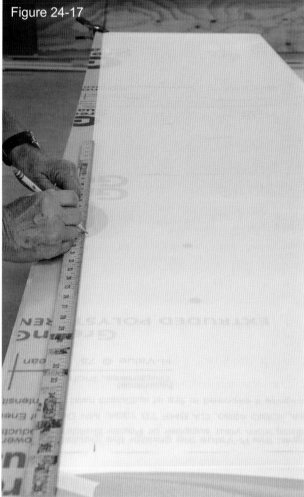

Figure 24-17

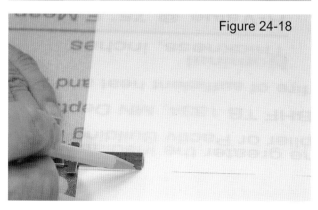

Figure 24-18

it by 1 inch. This doesn't have to be exact but needs to be close. I have also found that taping each panel to the floor helps keep the panels from shifting.

I rough cut each panel from the main roll of cloth. I like to let the cloth extend beyond the string by 4 to 6 inches on each end. Don't leave too much over the string or you could run short of cloth. As I recall, I came up a yard short on a sail once because I got carried away with leaving too much extra.

Using a **pencil**, put strike-off marks (about 12 inches apart) where the string lies under the sail (**Figure 24-16**). You'll want to be sure a strike off line crosses the panel seams. This is done on all sides of the sail. It is also important to clearly mark the tack, clew, throat, and peak points on the sail cloth. Once the sides of the sail are clearly outlined with strike-off marks and the four corners are marked you want to clearly label each panel. You should not only label each panel you will need to indicate what panel shares the edge. For example; the #2 panel shares an edge with #1 **and** #3 so you will need to clearly mark which is the #1 edge and the #3 edge. I also label the luff and leech strike off marks and clearly mark where the leech crosses each seam. These lines will be registration marks when the sail is assembled with tape.

It's also important to mark where the **true luff** line falls (the masking tape line). The luff round line is where the pink string falls. The measurements for the broadseaming are taken from the **true luff** line and a strike-off mark over the masking tape is critical. I put a two-inch-long strike-off right at each seam and label it **true luff**.

All the labeling helps when the panels are picked and you start to work on the sail. Think of the panels of the sail as pieces to a puzzle that you must take apart and then reassemble exactly the same way. The designing of the sail may be loose and not very exact but the assembly is.

I like to label each panel as I pick it up as well. I start at the top, roll the panel up from leech to luff, rubber band it and put the panel number on the outside. I do this with each one, always rolling from leech to luff and stacking them in order from top to

Figure 24-19

Figure 24-20

bottom or from peak to foot. It will help eliminate mistakes if you keep everything in order and very organized.

I start with panel #1 and roll it out on the table. Because I rolled it up from the leech to the luff I now have the luff end on the table and that's the end I want to work on. I set the work table up so the foot of the sail is on the opposite side of the table with the luff to **my right**.

That is the orientation in **Figure 24-17**. I'm facing the foot of the sail and the luff is on **my right**. Why is this so important? Remember in **Figure 24 -5 B** where it indicates the edge of the panel that is cut? And where I said it's very important to not get the edges mixed up and cut the wrong edge? Well, carefully organizing everything and keeping it consistent helps minimize those mistakes.

So on panel #1 the draft hits the seam at 3 feet 3 inches from the luff. That means I measured up from the **true luff** 3 feet 3 inches and put a mark on the edge of the panel (**Figure 24-17**). Then I marked the exact half way point which is 1 foot 7 ½ inches from the **true luff**.

Then checking the work sheet (**Figure 24-41A at the end of the chapter**) I found the width of the wedge for panel #1 or the first broadseam, which is 1 1/8 inches wide at the **true luff**. I measured up from the edge of the panel 1 1/8 inches and put a mark (**Figure 24-18**).

For the halfway mark you multiply the width of the wedge (1 1/8) by 25% which is 9/32. I rounded up to 5/16. That means at 1 foot 7½ inches I made a mark 5/16-inch up from the edge of the panel (**Figure 24-19**).

In **Figure 24-20** I've placed a batten at the three points on the edge of the sail and checked to see if it was a fair curve. I let the batten run out past the luff round strike off mark (remember this will be the finished shape of the sail).

Notice the batten is about ¼-inch square and I'm using stick pins on top of foam insulation. The foam makes it easy to use the push pins on a table top. I found it much easier on my back to work at table height rather than on the floor.

All that was left to do now was draw a line along

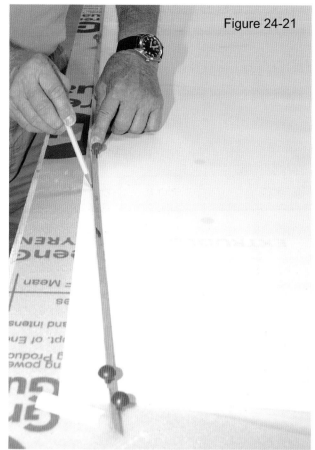

Figure 24-21

Figure 24-23A

Figure 24-22

Figure 24-23B

the batten (**Figure 24-21**) and the cut the wedge (**Figure 24-22**) with the sharpest scissors I could find. Great care should be taken at this point to follow the line exactly.

The woman that taught me to make sails, Robin Lincoln, insisted that I split the line with the scissors. In the beginning I thought that was a bit

overkill, and not really necessary. But as my experience grew I could see I had a beautifully fair panel cut when I took the time to split the line. The lesson then is to invest in a very sharp pair of scissors and split the line. Robin was right.

When I finished splitting the line on #1, I carefully rolled it up from leech to luff, labeled it #1 and

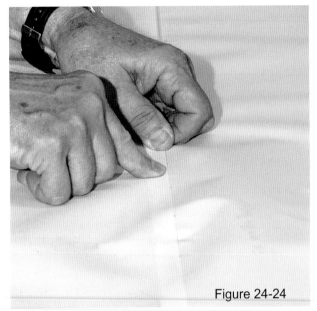

Figure 24-24

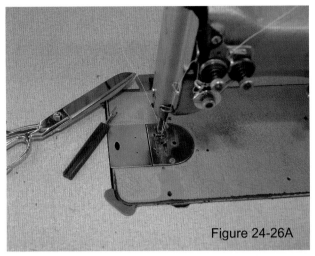

Figure 24-26A

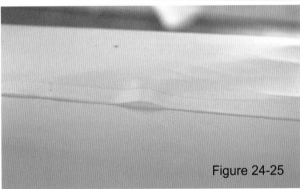

Figure 24-25

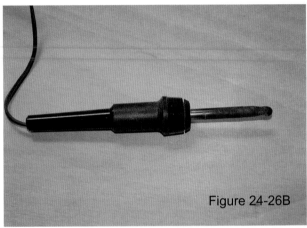

Figure 24-26B

set it back in order. Obviously, the next panel I picked up was #2. From here on, until all the panels are done, the process is the same. Roll the panel out so you have the luff on **your right** and you are facing the foot of the sail. Check to be sure the edge that is closest to you is the edge that joins #2 and #3. This should be clearly marked on the sail.

A check of **Figure 24-41A the work sheet** gives the wedge as 3 feet X 11/16-inch. Measure from the **true luff** along the edge of the panel (the edge shared by #2 and #3) and place marks at 3 feet and 18 inches (one half of 3 feet). Now go back to the luff and measure 11/16 up from the edge of the panel right at the **true luff** like in **Figure 24-18**. Then move to the 18-inch mark and measure up 25% of the 11/16 dimension or 3/32-inch. Normally I just round a number like this up to a 1/8 but in this case I try to get as close as I can. I think this makes a much truer curve. Just like before spring the batten, let it run beyond the luff round strike

off, mark it and then split the line.

Roll it up leech to luff, label it, and pick up the next panel and do the same thing. Move slowly checking and rechecking as you go and this will keep mistakes to a minimum. Continue this until all the panels have the wedges cut.

The next step is putting the panels together, and the first step in that process is marking a ½" wide band along the cut edge of each panel. In **Figure 24-23A** I'm putting a series a tick marks ½" up from the cut edge. The purpose of these marks is to give a reference as I put on the double stick tape and when I'm sticking to two panels together.

On a sail this size I use a ½" seam. This allows enough room for two rows of stitching, which gives more than adequate strength to the seam. Also, the panels need to be put together with a constant ½-inch seam because if the seam varies in width then the broadseaming won't function as intended.

I suppose there are any number of ways to put the panels together. But I have found that putting the tape on the cut edge of the panel and then sticking the straight edge of the other panel to it works best for me.

I start with panel #1, roll it out just like before with the luff on the right and the cut edge nearest me. Generally I clamp the panel to the table so it doesn't shift around. It can be a pain if the panel is constantly sliding off the table. Then I put the tick marks on, clearly establishing the ½" band for the seam (**Figure 24-23A**), and then starting at the luff, put on the double stick tape. If your tape is ½" wide then it will be very easy, but most of the double stick tape is 3/8 wide so you want to put the top edge of the tape on the tick marks (**Figure 24-23B**).

When the #1 panel is taped then pick up panel #2 and roll it out like before with the luff on the right. Be sure the edge facing #1 panel is the edge that shares a seam and is not the cut edge. I like to start at the leech, lining up the strike-off marks on the two panels and work my way to the luff. This is not a process you want to rush, so take your time and maintain a constant ½" seam (**Figure 24-24**).

The tricky part will be when you get to the broadseam because then you're putting a curved edge on a straight edge. I find it's not unusual to have to pull up sections and take out bumps and bubbles (**Figure 24-25**). The cloth itself won't lie smooth because you've just put a curve in it but you want the seam to be smooth. Maintaining the constant ½" seam is very important.

Once you have the complete seam stuck together, slide the panels off the table so the cut edge of #2 is now centered on the table. Clamp it in place, put the ½" band of tick marks on, add the double stick tape, and pick up panel #3. Roll #3 out so the straight edge is facing #2's cut and taped edge and check to be sure the luff is on the **right hand side**. Start at the leech, line up the strike-off marks, and put the #3 panel on the #2 panel always maintaining the ½" seam. Take your time and don't hesitate to pull apart a seam that isn't smooth. When you have #3 completely attached to #2, center up the cut edge of #3 and repeat the process until the whole sail is stuck together.

The sail can now be carried over to the lofting on the floor for a check up. You'll want to handle the sail gently so a seam doesn't come unstuck, but the double stick tape does hold fairly well.

Put the sail tack on the lofting tack and then center up all the other corners. Each corner should be close. If it's way off, don't go to the next step until that is corrected. If you put everything together the correct way and you were very careful to line up the strike off marks so the sail lies directly over the lofting, you can start to sew the sail together.

Figure 24-26A and **B** are photos of your new best friends. The scissors you are acquainted with, but unless you have done some sewing before you won't recognize the small little tool with the brown handle. That little tool is a seam ripper; it's the sail maker's eraser. That wonderful little tool allows you or me take out a mistake very quickly. This chapter is too small for me to list all the reasons you'll need a seam ripper. What's really great is that little tool isn't expensive so there's absolutely no reason not to have one. Get two, then you won't have to spend a lot of time looking for it.

The tool in **Figure 24-26B** is a hot knife and it's used to seal the cut edges of the sail cloth. All the edges where you cut a wedge, the edges on all four sides of the sail that you cut and any other edge you have cut with scissors should be sealed with a hot knife. Will your sail crumble into dust if you fail to seal the cut edges? No, but it might start looking slightly frayed after three or four seasons.

I think it's important that you know how dangerous this hot knife is. There is no off switch so if you forget to turn it off it can start a fire and burn down your house and shop. If you get this type of hot knife (any type of hot knife really) **be very careful and never, absolutely never leave it on.** I also suggest you spend some time sealing the edges of scrap sail cloth before you start on the sail it self.

That leaves the sewing machine. The machine in the picture is a heavy-duty professional zigzag machine that I bought used from an upholstery company. The heavy-duty professional machine is best, and this is followed by a good heavy-duty machine, and lastly the home sewing machine. My experience has been that the home machines are too

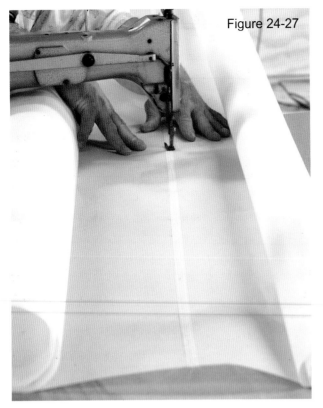

Figure 24-27

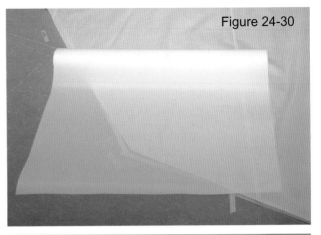

Figure 24-30

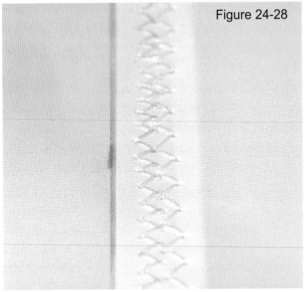

Figure 24-28

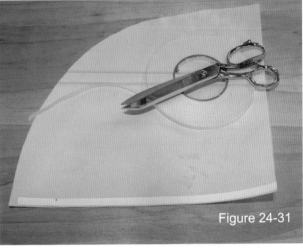

Figure 24-31

Figure 24-29

light weight to do the job. I think it's a mistake to try and use one to make these sails.

Let me just say that it's possible to buy a sewing machine that will do the job nicely for less than you'd pay to have a sail maker build the two sails for these boats. You may have to look some but the machines are there. Also, Sailrite Kits, a supplier listed in the appendix, sells new machines that fall into a reasonable price range. Sailrite and their products have a good reputation.

Once you get your machine, use it before you start on the sail. Practice on scrap sail cloth and practice on multiple layers of sail cloth. Practice enough so you can sew a nice straight row in a ½" band. In other words, teach yourself to use this tool just like you would any other tool in your shop. If you had a machine then you have already done this.

Each person will set up their work differently but I like to use an in-feed table and an out-feed table. The tables I use are narrow and long. I roll the sail up on both sides of the seam I'm working on (**Fig-**

ure 24-27) and I find this method the best. I've sewn sails with material loose on each side of the seam and while that works I find the other method better.

You probably will find it easier to start at the top of the sail first just because the seams are shorter, but wherever you start, remember you are not in a race so take your time. Try and keep the rows of stitching as straight as possible and evenly spaced. The stitching in **Figure 24-28** is a bit bunched to the center and each row should be more to the edge of the ½" seam.

Sailmakers pride themselves on the stitching. They insist that the rows are straight and evenly placed on the seam. So what happens if your rows wander along the seam like a drunken cat? Nothing, the sail will still work and the seam will be just as strong. But I would encourage you to keep the rows as straight as possible.

If you are not happy with a row, you have a seam ripper and that can correct the problem in a hurry. If you start at the top of the sail, the shorter seams are faster to rip out. Also they are up above every one's head on the boat so rows that aren't exactly straight can't be easily seen and by the time you get to the lower seams the rows will be perfect.

When I finish sewing all the seams I like to suspend the sail at the four corners. This gives an idea about the draft and if I have a problem I want to fix. Even though this will take some extra sets of hands, it's a good idea.

I'm occasionally not happy with what I see and I'll take the sail apart to correct the problem, but that doesn't happen very often. Generally I put the sail on the floor and spring a long batten on the strike off lines and trim the sail to those lines. Just make sure you trim a fair curve.

I always put the trimmed sail back on the lofting to check it against the string and then start to put on the patches (**Figure 24-29**). Corner reinforcement or corner patches seem to vary in size and style almost from sailmaker to sailmaker. Some use a percentage of the edges others use an amount per foot of length of the edge of the sail but in general the patches are within a few inches of each other.

My patches tend to be slightly larger than the average and I use a radius because I like round patches. Is one patch style better than another? I don't think so but there are some who might feel more strongly about it than I do.

The number of patches will also vary somewhat but I used three patches on each corner with 1½-inch space between each patch. See **Figures 24-42 A, B, C,** and **D** at the back of this chapter for the patch radii for this sail and all the others.

Work will progress much faster if you a have a large compass to draw the radii for the patches but a nail, pencil, and string will do the job.

There are a couple of things to remember about making patches but the most important is getting the warp and weave to match the sail cloth. This very easy to do when you are roughing out the patches and you don't even have to know what wrap and weave are. Just take the roll of cloth and lay it over the sail so the roll matches the direction of the panel (**Figure 24-30**). Adjust the roll to maximize cloth use, mark the corner point, and put strike off marks along the edge of the sail. You should be able to see the sail under the cloth but if not just rough cut the piece and then mark where the sail crosses the edge of the patch. You can make three rough patches or make two more using the large patch. Just keep the orientation of the cloth in the same direction. I like to label the sides of the sail, as well, so there is no question how the patch fits.

Labeling will be very important when you lay out the patches for the reef points. The distance up the luff and leech for each sail are noted on the work sheets for each sail, along with the location of the reef nettles. My reef points tend to fall on the deep side of average.

One of the most difficult things about patches is getting them to lay flat and smooth. Double-stick tape will make this job much easier. Tape the sides (**Figure 24-31**) and on the round part use short strips.

I'm sure it's obvious to you that you start with the smallest patch and work out so each patch is protected against chafe by the next patch. I overlay the patch under by 1½ inches. Keeping everything

Figure 24-32

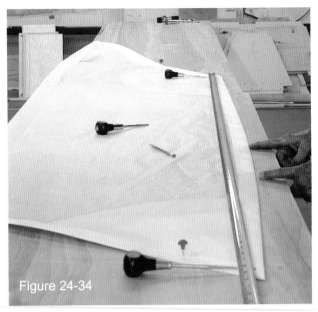

Figure 24-34

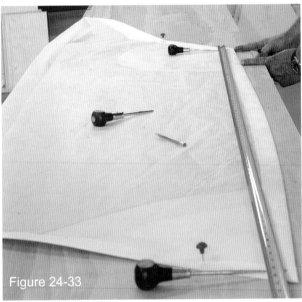

Figure 24-33

Figure 24-35

smooth will be the most difficult.

The edges of the sail will need support and re-inforcement just like the patches reinforced the corners. The two edges needing the most re-enforcing are the luff and head, with the foot and leech in that order.

There are a number of ways to accomplish this but I use layers of tape just like the corners. Many sail lofts make their own tape or it can be ordered. Unless you special order the tape, it will come 3 inches wide. Making your own tape isn't difficult. It's just a matter of slitting the cloth into even, very

even strips.

I used three layers of 3.8 oz tape (the same as the cloth) on the luff and staggered each layer by ½-inch so I started with 3-inch tape and put 4-inch tape over that and covered that with 5-inch wide tape. The tape is folded in half so each side is 1.5, 2, 2.5. I did the same on the head and the foot I used a layer of 3-inch and a layer of 4 inch. The leech got one layer of 3 inch.

Each layer of tape was put down with double stick tape (**Figure 24-32**), sewn in place, and the next layer added. This is almost straight-line work

184

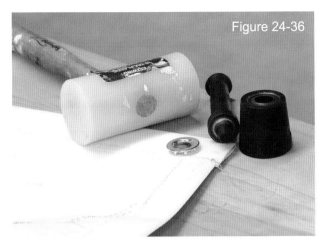

Figure 24-36

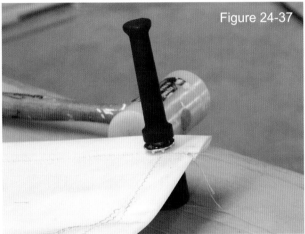

Figure 24-37

Figure 24-38

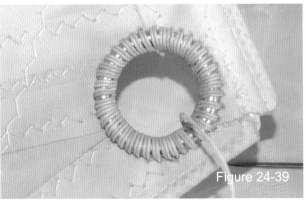

Figure 24-39

for the most part and goes quickly. The most time consuming part will be slitting the tape and then folding it.

With all four edges reinforced there not much left to do. You will need to add grommets at the peak and throat. I also set smaller grommets along the head (**Figure 24-33** and **34**) to lace the head of the sail to the yard.

Spur grommets come in brass (which I use) and nickel. They come in various sizes but I used #2 and #4 grommets for these sails. The #2 grommets were used along the head for lacing and the reef cringles and #4 grommets were used at the peak, throat, and reef points on the luff and leech.

Setting spur grommets is very easy and that's one reason they're so popular. You just cut a hole with the proper sized hole cutter (**Figure 24-35**) and then using the setting tool hit it a few times with a mallet to set it and the job's done (**Figures 24-36, 37,** and **38**).

I suppose the downside of grommets is they take special tools to use them, but that has been overcome by the people at Duckworks Magazine. They will rent you the tools. You buy them from Duckworks and then they will buy them back at a set price. This helps keep the cost of making the sail down.

If you were keeping track of all the points, you've noticed I haven't mentioned the tack and the clew. That's because I used #6 bronze rings and 36 brass liners at those points. I could have used #4 grommets but I felt the 36 rings and liners were better.

The bronze ring is sewn by hand to the sail (**Figure 24-39**) and then a brass liner is placed inside the ring, then rolled over with a setting tool much like the spur grommet tool (**Figure 24-40**). This makes a very strong a chafe-resistant corner.

If you want to do some hand finishing, like sewing the cut ends of the corners, and a few other areas, let me suggest *The Sailmaker's Apprentice* by Emiliano Marino.

At this point you should have a very serviceable sail—one that will give years of service and, more importantly, one that you made.

I hope you will choose to build the sails for your

boat. I have always been glad I did.

Should you elect to not build the sail for your boat—and that's a perfectly fine option—take the information in this book to a good sail maker. Consider the sails an investment.

I have had Duckworks make several sails for me and I find them to be reasonably priced and a good sail. The sails are an excellent value for your money.

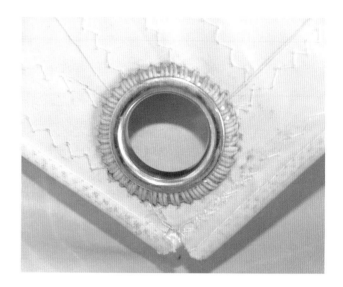

25

Odds and Ends

There are always a few odds and ends; bits and pieces that weren't big enough for a chapter on their own but need to be explained or discussed. So the purpose of this chapter is to sweep what's left into a pile at the very end of the book.

Navigation Lights

I put the red and green running lights on the tabernacle and in **Figure 25-1** the red navigation light (port side) and steaming light can be seen as *Pandion* sails along. I've always liked the idea that all those lights, both red, green, and white steaming, were about 5 feet off the water and very easy to see. After all, the whole idea is to be easily seen.

The steaming light was fairly simple to put on the mast. A block was shaped to fit the curve of the mast and have a flat mounting surface (**Figure 25-2**) and then a hole was drilled all the way through the mast. The wire with disconnects can be seen in **25-1**. The quick disconnects are important so the mast can be easily taken off the tab-

Figure 25-1

TX 2290 AW

ernacle. *Watch how high you put the steaming light because it can interfere with lowering the sail if it's too high.*

There were some downsides to putting the lights where I did and I'm not sure I'd do it again. The biggest downside was the wiring. It would have been much easier to wire the lights through the deck. The other issue was drilling the tabernacle for the lights. It wasn't easy and I had to work hard to get everything lined up correctly. Also, the wiring is exposed slightly on the inside of the tabernacle.

Does the high visibility outweigh the installation issues? Yes, now that all the work is done. But if you are going to mount the lights on the tabernacle, you will need to plan for the wiring and the through-the-deck connection. Maybe a separate bracket for each light that attaches to the outside of the tabernacle.

The stern light also has good visibility sitting on the boomkin (**Figure 25-3**) and I certainly love

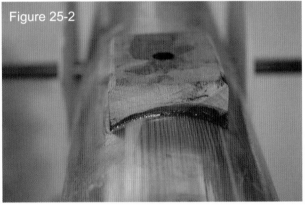
Figure 25-2

Figure 25-4

Figure 25-5

Figure 25-6

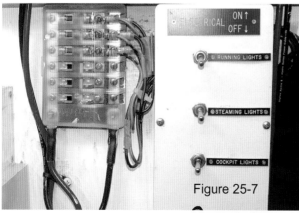

Figure 25-7

the bronze piece we fabricated for the light. In fact, the entire boomkin adds to the overall look of the boat. Was that worth all the work involved? Yes, but I would recommend you use stainless steel or wood instead of bronze because of the cost.

Electrical Wiring

If you are not are not familiar with 12-volt wiring, let me recommend *Sailboat Electrics Simplified* by Don Casey. I had this book close at hand when I wired *Pandion*.

There are too many ways to wire your boat for me to give a detailed description of what I did. I did come up with a nice way to bundle the wires so they stay neat and tidy. I used soft garden hose and hose clips (**Figure 25-4**). It's easy to pull wire through. We had to undo a couple of clamps where the hose went around corners, pull the wire, and redo the clamps. The hose made things very easy going through bulkheads as well. This is always a high chafe area and the hose protects the wire (**Figure 25-5**).

Every time wire passes through a bulkhead, label each wire. You'll always be glad you did.

I decided to make my own switchbox (**Figures 25-6** and **25-7**). I think this is one project that I wouldn't do again. It worked out nicely but I don't think it justified the time spent.

Bilge Pumps

Bilge pumps. Don't leave the dock without them! I have two 1000 GPH auto bilge pumps in the boat, one on either side of the aft centerboard case (**Figure 25-8**). There was just enough room for the pump to fit down in the keel. You'll want to install these before you enclose the interior. **Figure 25-9** shows how I ran the hose. Be sure and put a check valve (*this keeps water from flowing in should the through-the-hull fitting become submerged*) right at the through the hull fitting. Also note I've secured the hose in two places to keep it from flopping around.

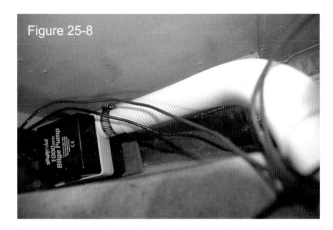

Figure 25-8

Figure 25-9

Figure 25-10

Figure 25-11

Figure 25-12

Topping Off the Centerboard Cases

Chapter 10 covered about everything except how to rig the pennants for the centerboards. You may want to vary this to suit your own personal taste but I found this system works well.

In **Figure 25-10** I have set a block 21 inches back from the forward edge of the aft centerboard case. This block turns the pennant as it comes up out of the case and directs it to a block at the forward end of the case. That block directs the pennant up and through the decking/seating surrounding the aft tabernacle. **Figure 25-11** shows another block that directs the pennant to a jam cleat. *A close look at 25-10 show a red cockpit night light under the seat*

I've been very happy the placement of the pennant. It's within easy reach yet out of the way. The only thing I'm not satisfied with is how exposed the wire and blocks are. I think the best solution would be a false floor or sole that is level with the top of the blocks and has an open slot over the case. This would allow easy access to the centerboard and wire but would protect everything from being trod on.

The forward case is a bit different and only uses one block set at 22 inches from the forward

Figure 25-13

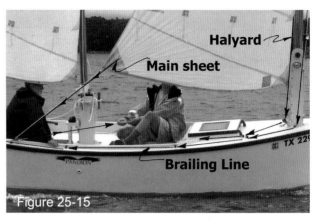

Figure 25-15

Halyard

Main sheet

Brailing Line

Figure 25-14

Figure 25-16

edge and up about 8 inches (**Figure 25-12**) to turn the pennant through the bulkhead (**figure 25-13**). There is a fairlead in the bulkhead and the cleat is above it by a few inches. The filled holes in bulkhead are where I experimented with the placement of the cleat. For me, placing the cleat above the fairlead seemed to be the best solution (**Figure 25-14**).

Rigging the Sails

If you've read my book *The Working Guide to Traditional Small-Boat Sails* you know that there are a huge number of ways to rig a standing lug sail—a good deal to do with personal preference and how simple or complex you want to be.

Here is how I rigged *Pandion*. This will work for both boats and is simple and fast to set up. Both sails are rigged with a single halyard, a brailing line (one of the things I like about boomless sails), and the mainsail has two sheets while the mizzen has one.

In **Figure 25-15** I've labeled the halyard, brail-

ing line, and main sheet. The halyard has a block at the top of the mast and a block at the bottom of the tabernacle. It turns and runs along the deck, passing through a single fairlead and then the combing to a cleat next to the hatch. The brailing line runs from the heel of the yard to a small block at the bottom of the tabernacle and then is fed aft on the outside of the combing, by a series of fairleads, to a cleat by the helm. The main sheet runs to a block outside the combing and then to a hand.

I moved the sheeting point for the main several times before I hit the right spot.

A look at the mizzen tabernacle (**Figure 25-15**) reveals several belaying pins (two on each of three sides) where I have sheeted off the mizzen halyard and mizzen brailing line. The two belaying pins in the front of the tabernacle provide a convenient point to cleat off the main sheet (**Figure 25-16**).

Figure 25-17 shows one of several ways to attach the halyard to the yard. Each sail will be slightly different so experiment with this point. Start at about a third and move back toward one

Figure 25-17

Figure 25-18

half. This is all about luff tension, because without your sail won't be very weatherly. I also use a 2-to-1 down haul on each sail.

Figure 25-18 shows the mainsail being brailed up. The wind was rising and it was time to drop some sail. Brailing lines provide a very fast way to kill a sail.

If you want to use a different sail combination on these boats just place the combined center of effort of the sails about 9 inches in front of station #4. That will give about a 10% lead and that seems to be about right. I would caution you to allow for some adjustment in the center of effort of the sails.

The Trailer

You have two options for a trailer. You can have a custom trailer built, and any good trailer manufacturer can take the information in this book and build you a trailer designed to carry these boats. Remember the ballast lies on either side of #4. It may be the manufacturer will want the finished boat so the trailer can be fitted exactly. Sometimes they do and sometimes not. It is a good investment, and if that is a viable option I suggest you do it.

The other option is to buy a used trailer and convert it to fit the boat. This is what I did and here is how I did it.

Pandion weighs 1990 pounds (I had the boat weighed at certified scales), and the 14.5 will weigh 900 to 1100 pounds. This is important because you don't want the boat to exceed the weight limit of the trailer.

Just because you are fitting the boat to the trailer does not exempt you from staying within the maximum load limits. To exceed the limits, even by a small amount, endangers you, the boat, and everyone who shares the road with you. Ignore those who would tell you that there is "plenty of fudge factor built into trailers and it doesn't matter if you run over a few hundred pounds." It does matter. Don't do it!

Each trailer will have a sticker somewhere around the front that will list the maximum allowable loads (**Figure 25-19**). Please note the message at the very bottom of the label. **Trailer brake laws vary from state to state and you must find out if your boat and trailer requires brakes.**

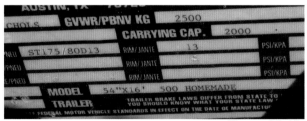

Figure 25-19

Figure 25-20 was a trailer I had custom made several years back for a boat I no longer own. The gross limit was 2000 pounds and *Pandion* was less than that. Just barely, but still less. Also the cross-

Figure 25-20

Figure 25-21

Figure 25-22

Figure 25-23

Figure 25-24

pieces dropped to the center which was another plus (**Figure 25-21**). I knew the length was right, but would the hull fit between the wheel wells? To answer this question we made a pattern of station #4 and placed it where it would fall on the trailer (**Figure 25-22**). Note the scrap labeled bow eye. This gave us enough information that I decided the trailer would work.

We added uprights to capture the keel as the boat went on the trailer (**Figure 25-23**) and adjusted the side bunks using the plywood pattern. A certain amount of adjustment was left until the boat was actually on the trailer.

Figure 25-24 shows the finished trailer waiting for the boat. We did have to make one more adjustment to the height of the winch. The original winch was too low and we had to fabricate a new post for the winch.

There will be one more issue you'll need to deal with once the boat is loaded on the trailer. You must be sure that the tongue weight (the amount of weight applied to the hitch from the trailer) does not exceed the limits of your hitch. My hitch had a 500 pound limit and I made sure (by weighing the tongue weight on a scale) that it was with in that limit. Actually I had to shift the boat back 4 inches to get the tongue weight to 500 pounds.

It goes without saying that your vehicle and hitch should be able to safely tow the boat. The Sea Eagle 16.5 is a substantial boat and shouldn't be at the upper limits of what your vehicle can pull.

When you are shopping for used trailers take the plywood pattern with you and be sure it will work before you buy the trailer. Start looking almost as soon as you lay the keel. That way you can load the hull on the trailer right after you turn it over. It's much easier to load the lightweight hull than a completed very heavy boat. As with most used stuff all sales are final.

The Ladder

The Sea Eagles have a great deal of freeboard. That translates into reserve buoyancy and stability. That also means that they are almost impossible to board from the water. I certainly can't do it without a ladder. There are a number of premade stepladders that fit the transom. These are heavy, and can be expensive.

Whatever solution you choose, it should provide a means to board the boat from the water.

Figures 25-25, 26, and **27** are a rope ladder I made from instructions in *The Marlinspike Sailor* by Hervey Garrett Smith. This ladder stores easily and can be kept attached to a cleat when under way. I trail a light line over the side so I can pull the ladder down should I find myself unexpectedly in the water.

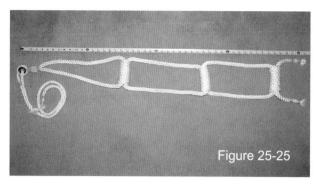

Figure 25-25

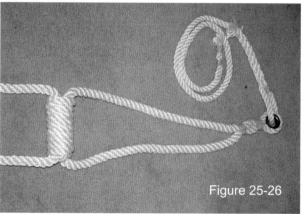

Figure 25-26

Figure 25-27

APPENDIX

Materials list for Sea Eagle 14.5

30 yards 9 oz fiberglass cloth
3-50 yard rolls of 9 oz fiberglass tape
400 6 X ½ stainless steel screws
400 6 X 5/8 stainless steel screws
200 #8X1
200#8X1¼
200 #8X1½
100 #10X2
3 pounds of graphite

Strongback
2 4X8 sheets of cheap plywood minimum 5/8"
thick
4 8' 2X4's

1 4X8 sheet ¼ thick cheap plywood for strongback template

**Plywood is approximate and depends on how
efficiently the builder uses it**
12 sheets 6mm plywood first layer hull skin and
bulkheads 1,3,4,5. You will want to use 4mm on
the hull bottom.
12 sheets 6mm plywood for remainder of laminations on hull. You may want to substitute
4mm for the hull bottom.

5 sheets 9mm for decks, seats, and miscellaneous
parts
15 gals of epoxy resin and appropriate amount of
hardener
10 pound bag of silica thickener (Cab-o-sil)

Scantlings for the Sea Eagle 14.5

Scantlings for the Sea Eagle 14.5

Hull:
    ½-inch hull bottom—layers of 4mm
    ½-inch keel bottom—layers of 6mm
    ½-inch keel sides—layers of 6mm
    ¼-inch hull sides—6mm
    ¼-inch bulkheads—6mm

Same fiberglass cloth and tape schedule used
on the 16.5

Mast and boom

The single mainmast is 15' 6" over all. The base
of the mast is 4" in diameter and tapers to 3".
    The boom is 11' 2" long. It should be 1 ¾
inches at the front, and about 3 feet back swell to
2 1/8 inches and then taper to 1½ at the end.
    The spar is 8' 3" long. It should be 1¼ inches at
the front and about 3 feet back swell to 1 5/8 inches
and then taper to 1 inch.
    Build the mast hollow and the boom and spar
solid.

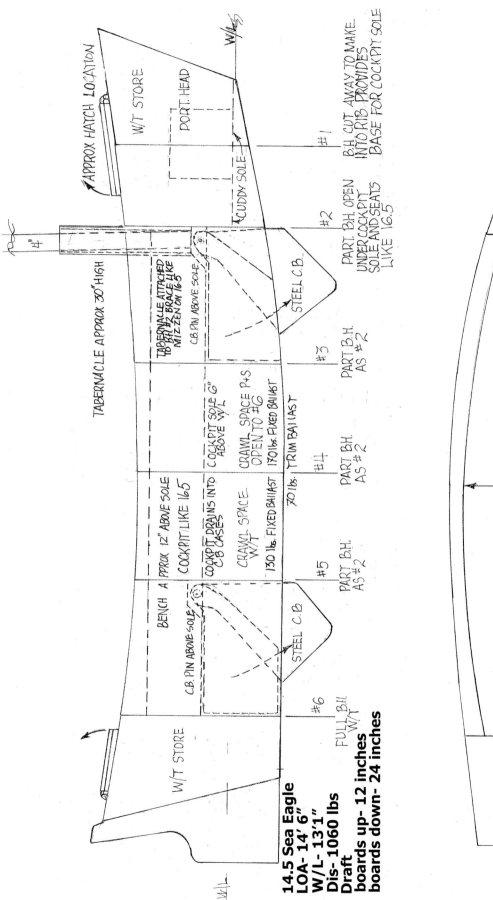

14.5 Sea Eagle
LOA- 14' 6"
W/L- 13'1"
Dis- 1060 lbs
Draft
boards up- 12 inches
boards down- 24 inches

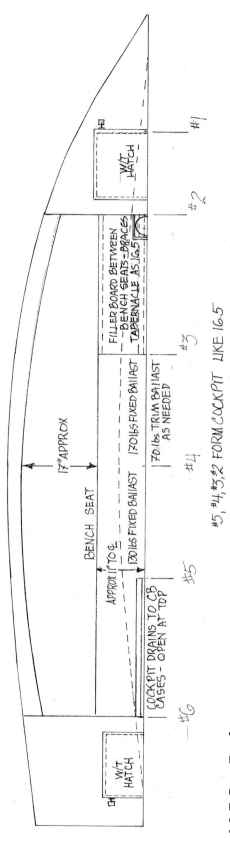

14.5 Sea Eagle

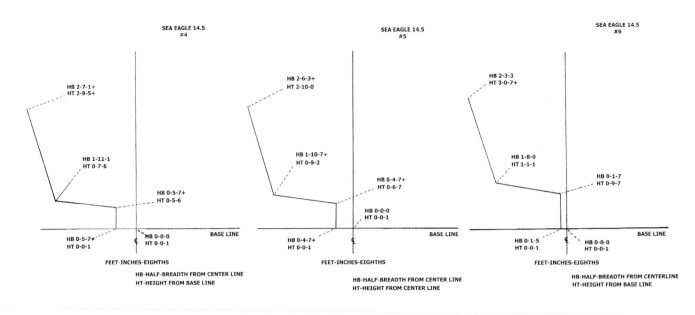

SEA EAGLE 14.5
#4

HB 2-7-1+
HT 2-9-5+

HB 1-11-1
HT 0-7-6

HB 0-5-7+
HT 0-5-6

HB 0-5-7+
HT 0-0-1

HB 0-0-0
HT 0-0-1

BASE LINE

FEET-INCHES-EIGHTHS

HB-HALF-BREADTH FROM CENTER LINE
HT-HEIGHT FROM BASE LINE

SEA EAGLE 14.5
#5

HB 2-6-3+
HT 2-10-0

HB 1-10-7+
HT 0-9-2

HB 0-4-7+
HT 0-6-7

HB 0-0-0
HT 0-0-1

HB 0-4-7+
HT 0-0-1

BASE LINE

FEET-INCHES-EIGHTHS

HB-HALF-BREADTH FROM CENTER LINE
HT-HEIGHT FROM CENTER LINE

SEA EAGLE 14.5
#6

HB 2-3-3
HT 3-0-7+

HB 1-8-0
HT 1-1-1

HB 0-1-7
HT 0-9-7

HB 0-1-5
HT 0-0-1

HB 0-0-0
HT 0-0-1

BASE LINE

FEET-INCHES-EIGHTHS

HB-HALF-BREADTH FROM CENTERLINE
HT-HEIGHT FROM BASE LINE

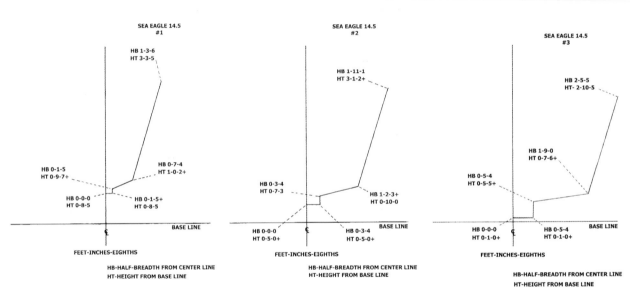

SEA EAGLE 14.5
#1

HB 1-3-6
HT 3-3-5

HB 0-1-5
HT 0-9-7+

HB 0-7-4
HT 1-0-2+

HB 0-0-0
HT 0-8-5

HB 0-1-5+
HT 0-8-5

BASE LINE

FEET-INCHES-EIGHTHS

HB-HALF-BREADTH FROM CENTER LINE
HT-HEIGHT FROM BASE LINE

SEA EAGLE 14.5
#2

HB 1-11-1
HT 3-1-2+

HB 0-3-4
HT 0-7-3

HB 1-2-3+
HT 0-10-0

HB 0-0-0
HT 0-5-0+

HB 0-3-4
HT 0-5-0+

BASE LINE

FEET-INCHES-EIGHTHS

HB-HALF-BREADTH FROM CENTER LINE
HT-HEIGHT FROM BASE LINE

SEA EAGLE 14.5
#3

HB 2-5-5
HT- 2-10-5

HB 1-9-0
HT 0-7-6+

HB 0-5-4
HT 0-5-5+

HB 0-0-0
HT 0-1-0+

HB 0-5-4
HT 0-1-0+

BASE LINE

FEET-INCHES-EIGHTHS

HB-HALF-BREADTH FROM CENTER LINE
HT-HEIGHT FROM BASE LINE

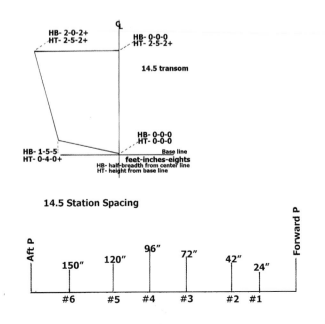

HB- 2-0-2+
HT- 2-5-2+

HB- 0-0-0
HT- 2-5-2+

14.5 transom

HB- 0-0-0
HT- 0-0-0

HB- 1-5-5
HT- 0-4-0+

Base line
feet-inches-eights
HB- half-breadth from center line
HT- height from base line

14.5 Station Spacing

Aft P

150"   120"   96"   72"   42"   24"

Forward P

#6   #5   #4   #3   #2   #1

Station elevations:

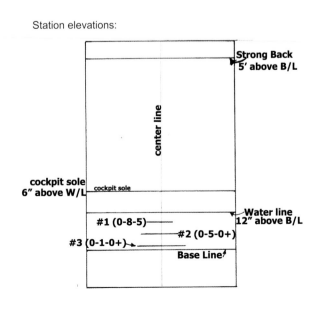

Strong Back
5' above B/L

center line

cockpit sole
6" above W/L

cockpit sole

Water line
12" above B/L

#1 (0-8-5)

#2 (0-5-0+)

#3 (0-1-0+)

Base Line

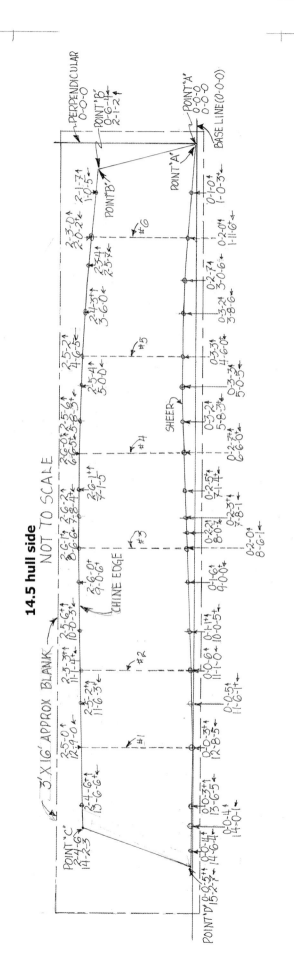

14.5 hull side

NOT TO SCALE

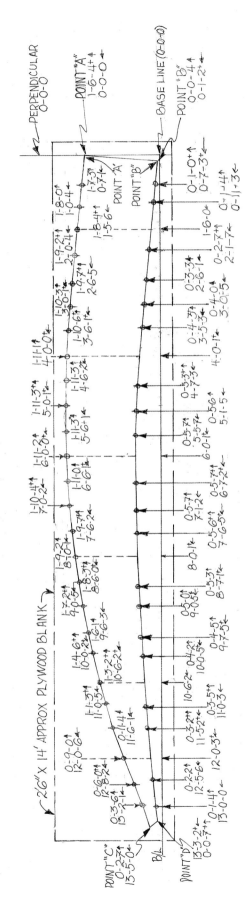

14.5 hull bottom

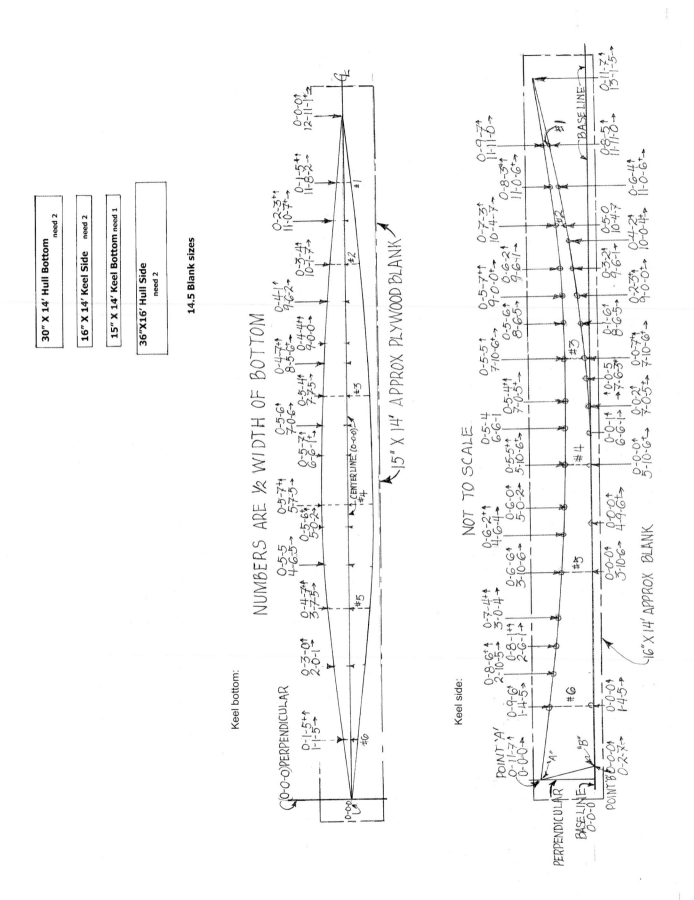

Materials list for the Sea Eagle 16.5

33 yards 9 oz fiberglass cloth
3-50 yard rolls of 9 oz fiberglass tape
400 6 X ½ stainless steel screws
400 6 X 5/8 stainless steel screws
200 #8X1
200#8X1¼
200 #8X1½
100 #10X2
3 pounds of graphite

Strongback
2 4X8 sheets of cheap plywood minimum 5/8 thick
4 8' 2X4's

1 4X8 sheet ¼ thick cheap plywood for strongback template

Plywood is approximate and will depend on how effiecent the builder uses it.
15 sheets 6mm plywood first layer hull skin and bulkheads 1, 3, 4, 5,
3 sheets 9mm #2 bulkhead and #6 bulkhead and transom. You may want to substitute 4mm for the hull bottom.

15 sheets 6mm plywood for remainder of laminations on hull. You may want to substitute 4mm for the hull bottom.

5 sheets 9mm for decks, seats, and miscellaneous parts
15 gals of epoxy resin and appropriate amount of hardener
10 pound bag of silica thickener (Cab-o-sil)

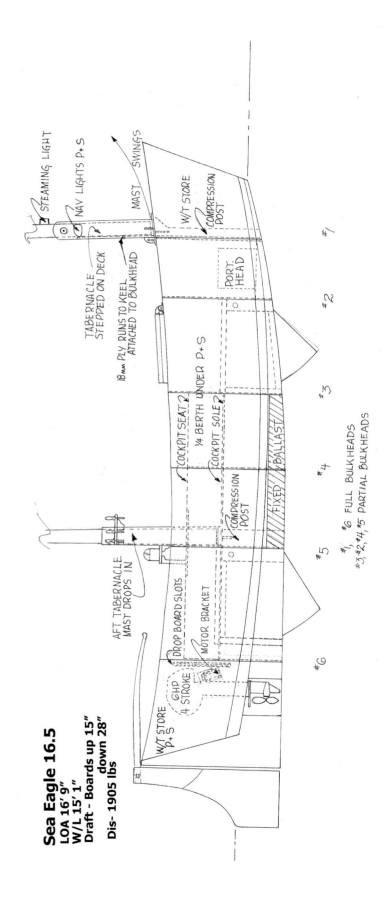

Sea Eagle 16.5
LOA 16' 9"
W/L 15' 1"
Draft - Boards up 15"
down 28"
Dis- 1905 lbs

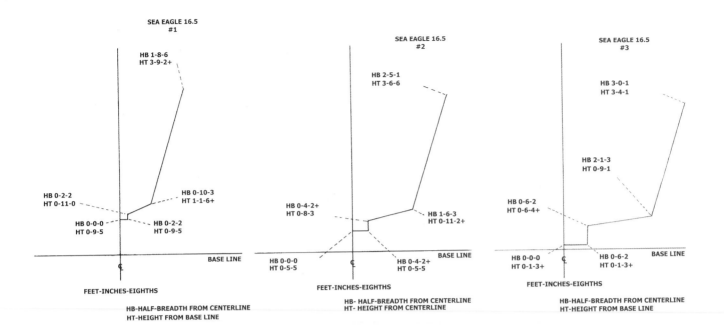

SEA EAGLE 16.5
#1

HB 1-8-6
HT 3-9-2+

HB 0-2-2
HT 0-11-0

HB 0-10-3
HT 1-1-6+

HB 0-0-0
HT 0-9-5

HB 0-2-2
HT 0-9-5

BASE LINE

FEET-INCHES-EIGHTHS

HB-HALF-BREADTH FROM CENTERLINE
HT-HEIGHT FROM BASE LINE

SEA EAGLE 16.5
#2

HB 2-5-1
HT 3-6-6

HB 0-4-2+
HT 0-8-3

HB 1-6-3
HT 0-11-2+

HB 0-0-0
HT 0-5-5

HB 0-4-2+
HT 0-5-5

BASE LINE

FEET-INCHES-EIGHTHS

HB- HALF-BREADTH FROM CENTERLINE
HT- HEIGHT FROM CENTERLINE

SEA EAGLE 16.5
#3

HB 3-0-1
HT 3-4-1

HB 2-1-3
HT 0-9-1

HB 0-6-2
HT 0-6-4+

HB 0-0-0
HT 0-1-3+

HB 0-6-2
HT 0-1-3+

BASE LINE

FEET-INCHES-EIGHTHS

HB-HALF-BREADTH FROM CENTERLINE
HT-HEIGHT FROM BASE LINE

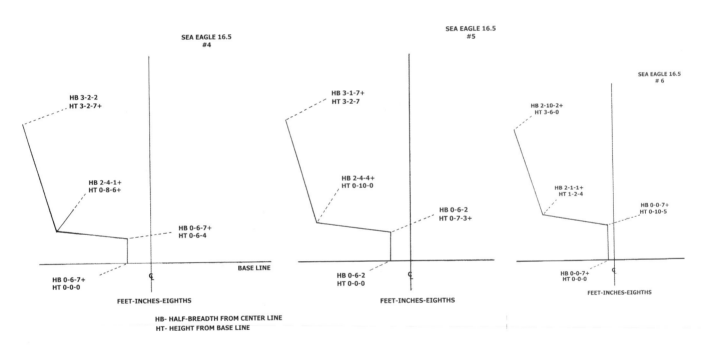

SEA EAGLE 16.5
#4

HB 3-2-2
HT 3-2-7+

HB 2-4-1+
HT 0-8-6+

HB 0-6-7+
HT 0-6-4

HB 0-6-7+
HT 0-0-0

BASE LINE

FEET-INCHES-EIGHTHS

HB- HALF-BREADTH FROM CENTER LINE
HT- HEIGHT FROM BASE LINE

SEA EAGLE 16.5
#5

HB 3-1-7+
HT 3-2-7

HB 2-4-4+
HT 0-10-0

HB 0-6-2
HT 0-7-3+

HB 0-6-2
HT 0-0-0

BASE LINE

FEET-INCHES-EIGHTHS

SEA EAGLE 16.5
6

HB 2-10-2+
HT 3-6-0

HB 2-1-1+
HT 1-2-4

HB 0-0-7+
HT 0-10-5

HB 0-0-7+
HT 0-0-0

FEET-INCHES-EIGHTHS

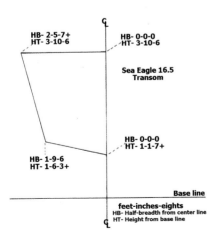

HB- 2-5-7+
HT- 3-10-6

HB- 0-0-0
HT- 3-10-6

Sea Eagle 16.5
Transom

HB- 0-0-0
HT- 1-1-7+

HB- 1-9-6
HT- 1-6-3+

Base line

feet-inches-eights
HB- Half-breadth from center line
HT- Height from base line

16.5 hull side

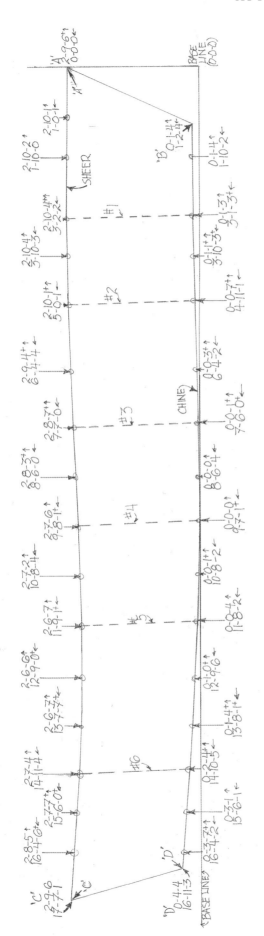

16.5 hull bottom

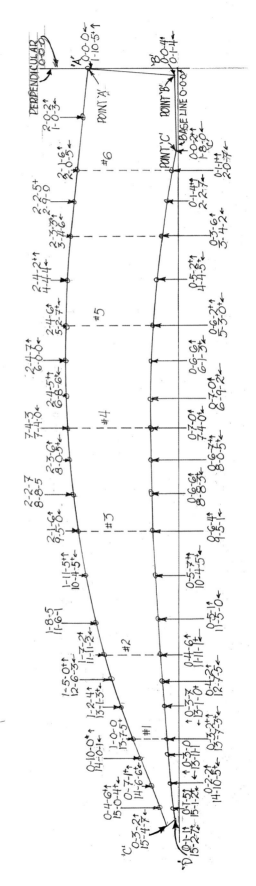

201

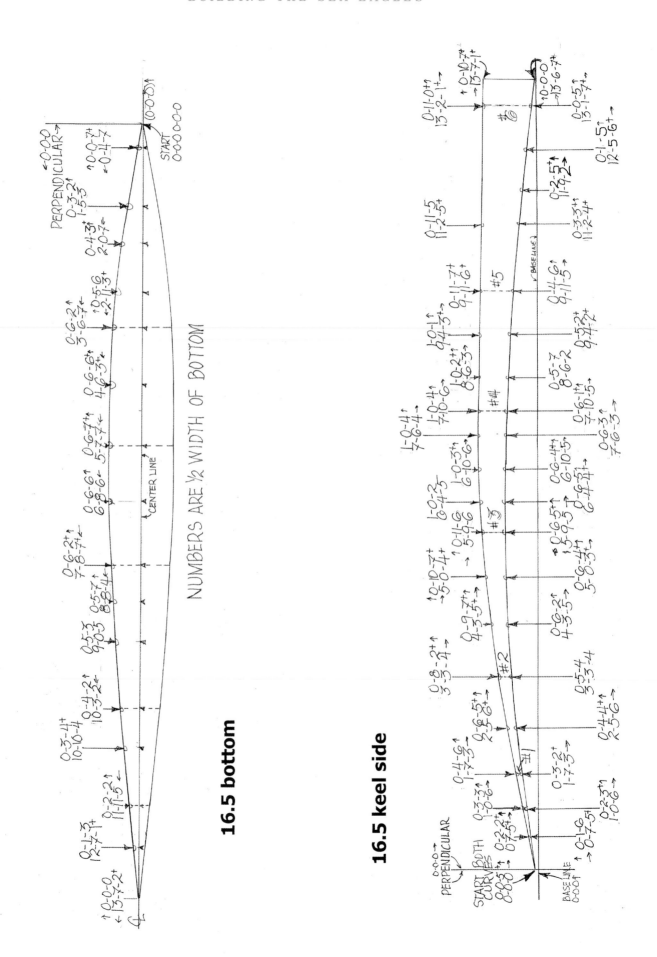

16.5 bottom

16.5 keel side

HARDWARE DRAWINGS

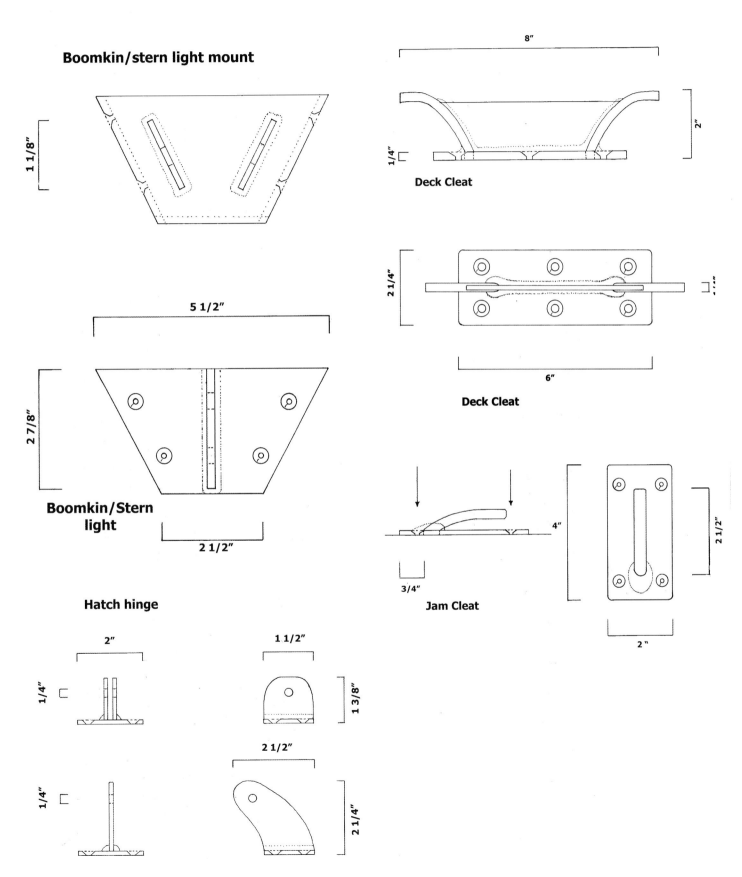

Boomkin/stern light mount

1 1/8"

8"

2"

1/4"

Deck Cleat

2 1/4"

6"

Deck Cleat

5 1/2"

2 7/8"

2 1/2"

Boomkin/Stern light

4"

3/4"

Jam Cleat

2 1/2"

2"

Hatch hinge

2"

1 1/2"

1/4"

1 3/8"

2 1/2"

1/4"

2 1/4"

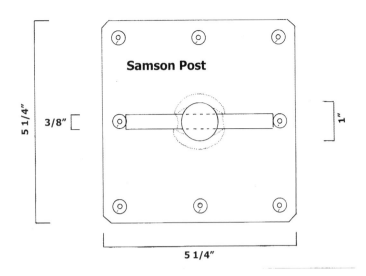

Samson Post

5 1/4"

3/8"

1"

5 1/4"

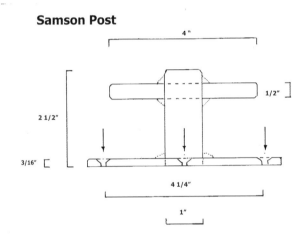

Samson Post

4 "

2 1/2"

1/2"

3/16"

4 1/4"

1"

Suppliers

Here is a list of suppliers I used to build these boats. If they are listed below I was happy with the service and products.

Duckworks Magazine
608 Gammenthaler
Harper, TX 78631
www.duckworksmagazine.com
A wide variety of boatbuilding supplies (many hard to find items) and sails. I ordered a set of sails from Duckworks and found it to be a good value and well made.

System Three Epoxies
3500 West Valley Highway North #105
Auburn, WA 98001
www.systemthree.com
I've used System Three epoxy for almost 20 years. They have great products.

Jamestown Distributors
www.jamestowndistributors.com
Stainless steel and bronze fasteners, tools, and boat-building supplies

Fine Lumber and Plywood
9407 Brown Lane
Austin, TX 78754
www.finelumber.com
Good selection of marine plywood and hardwoods, great staff, and Fine lumber's CNC staff cut all my boats and kits.

New Wave Systems
79 Narragansett Ave.,
Jamestown, Rhode Island 02835 USA
www.newavesys.com
The boats in this book were designed with New Wave System software. It is excellent software but the tech support is exceptional. Steve Hollister at New Wave System never fails to answer my questions and provide assistance. I highly recommend the software and I don't believe there is any better tech support.

Sailrite Kits
4506 S. State Rd. 9
Churubusco, IN 46723
www.sailrite.com

More Designs by David L. Nichols

A 17-foot-6-inch powerboat and a 16-foot drift boat are just a few of the well-tested designs you will find on David's web site at **www.arrowheadboats.com**. You'll also find easy-to-assemble kits for the Sea Eagles, a sailing canoe, and other sea-kindly craft. In addition, the site has photos of some custom boats designed and built by David—like the sit-on-top kayak with outriggers that store in the forward watertight compartment.